AN INTRODUCTION TO EARLY IRISH LITERATURE

FROM SOME REVIEWS

'A thorough, engaging, comprehensive introduction to early Irish literature and the society that produced it ... an invaluable resource to those interested in Irish studies and/or myth ... Highly recommended'
  V.A. Murrenus Pilmaier, University of Wisconsin–Sheboygan, *Choice*.

'*An introduction to early Irish literature* is a guide to the literature of the Old and Middle Irish period, 600–1200, and has been written as a textbook for students and the general reader. The author's style is a story-telling technique in its own right, which makes the book all the more enjoyable ... a very readable book, and readers will find much to interest them'

Tom Condit, *Archaeology Ireland*

'The book is a marvel of condensation – of the tales themselves, their original context and the current issues surrounding them ... If your shelves groan with books about Ireland, you still need this one; if they don't, you need it more'
  Ciaran Murray, Chuo University, *Journal of Irish Studies*

'It is quite clear throughout the book that here is an author who, in addition to being an academic of twenty-five years standing, is also someone who stands within the tradition, knows and loves the Irish language in all its stages of development and possesses the breadth and depth of knowledge necessary to present such a comprehensive and readable overview ... This book, while building on past studies ... makes a significant and distinguished contribution to the field'
  W. Ann Trindade, University of Melbourne,
  Australasian Journal of Irish Studies

An Introduction to

Early Irish Literature

MUIREANN NÍ BHROLCHÁIN

FOUR COURTS PRESS

Typeset in 10pt on 13.5pt Sabon for
FOUR COURTS PRESS LTD
7 Malpas Street, Dublin 8, Ireland
www.fourcourtspress.ie
and in North America for
FOUR COURTS PRESS
c/o ISBS, 920 NE 58th Avenue, Suite 300, Portland, OR 97213.

First published 2009, reprinted 2011

A catalogue record for this title is available
from the British Library.

ISBN 978–1–84682–176–9 hbk
978–1–84682–177–6 pbk

Printed in England by
Antony Rowe Ltd, Chippenham, Wilts.

Contents

Illustrations

appear between pages 118 and 119

Acknowledgments

I and white Pangur
Practice each of us his special art:
His mind is set on hunting,
My mind on my special craft.

This book would never have been completed without the encouragement and badgering of many people. It was Dr Edel Bhreathnach who first suggested to me that I should write a book for students. Thank you to those who offered and read the typescript or parts of it: Terri and Niall, Caroline, Lisa, Bea, Hanna-Mette and Dee. I want to thank Seamus Mac Gabhann for his careful reading of the manuscript, the late Michael Adams of Four Courts Press for his forensic examination and Martin Fanning for taking over stewardship of the work and for his patience. I'd like to thank Mary and Leonie for their unstinting support and their helpful comments. Thanks to the friends in Caleta de Fuste, Fuerteventura, for their hospitality as I read drafts of the manuscript on that island. I'd like to thank all my students in NUIM for their questions, insights and interpretations. Thank you also to Don Foley for his support while I worked on this project. I would like to thank Mary Leenane and Raymond Cormier for their help with some changes and corrections to this edition.

I would like to acknowledge the help of the staff of the Royal Irish Academy, Trinity College Library and the National Museum, for their help and permission to reproduce the pages from manuscripts and exhibits in the museum. I would also like to acknowledge the help of the National University of Ireland, Galway and Marcus Casey (aerial photograph of Rathcroghan), and Eamon O'Donaghue (aerial photograph of Tara). Thank you to Conor Newman, Joe Fenwick and Professor John Waddell for their help with these images as well. A special thanks is due to Jim Fitzpatrick for the use of his image, 'Oisín at Royal Tara', for the cover as well as a second image within the text.

I dedicate this book to my mother who, along with my deceased father, instilled in me a love of these stories when I was a very young child.

Because of the nature of this material, the stories may be discussed in different chapters: for example The *Battle of Moytura* appears in the chapter on the Mythological Cycle and also in the chapter on Sovereignty. There is a great variation in the original spellings of titles, personal names and place names. Consistency is aimed at throughout but quotes within the text may use different spellings. For example, Cruachu is used in the text but quotes from other books may use other spellings, including Cruachan and Cruachain. The same applies to personal names: for example the goddess is found as Morrigu, Morrigan, Mórrígan etc. The titles of the stories are given in the original Irish with an English translation when they are mentioned for the first time but usually only the English translation is used afterwards. Sometimes, if the occurrences are far apart, both Irish and English forms may be used again.

Introduction

> Perhaps ... we should never assume too serious a purpose in this litera-
> ture, even if it was written by clerics ... Perhaps we should stop wasting
> our time asking what it's for and just enjoy the stories as literature. If you
> let the words wash over you like warm waves, rather than sully the sea by
> setting nets to snare symbols or deep meanings or any meanings at all,
> you may be enjoying the stories as they were meant to be enjoyed.[1]

This book aims to give an overview of the saga and poetic literature of early
Ireland, mainly the pre-Norman period of 600–1200, described as the Dark
Ages elsewhere. When Christianity came to Ireland, in the person of St Patrick
in the middle of the fifth century, it brought about a quiet revolution. Not only
did a new religion arrive in the country but, for the first time, the Bible and
Latin literature brought the ability to read and write and access to a new world
of written sources. The complicated relationship between the two traditions,
pre-Christian and Christian, resulted in what now survives of the early material.
In common with other European countries, this new written tradition was pre-
ceded by an oral tradition of unknown length that continued long after writing
began. Because oral tradition is of its very nature transient, there is no way of
finding out what it was like, and we are entirely dependent on the written
sources that have come down to us today. But the two cultures existed side by
side and must have been in constant contact; as a result, the written material
probably came from a combination of the native, oral tradition and the new
Christian writings.

From the beginning, the Christian Irish were interested in their own pagan
past, so much so that by the seventh century they were writing down tales of the
Otherworld. The early Irish Church grew up around monastic centres rather
than dioceses as such (it had bishops, of course) and the resulting monasteries
became large, rich centres of learning that developed into towns such as Armagh,
Kells and Trim. Many of the clergy were married, and church offices could be
hereditary. By the eighth century some of the monks considered the Church to be
too secular, and this led to a reforming movement known as the Culdees (from
the Irish words *Céili Dé*, the servants of God). Their main leader was Mael

Ruain (†792), whose monastery was situated around the modern-day Tallaght. They wanted to return to a more ascetic way of life with strict rules that prohibited meat, drinking and even music in some cases. The Vikings arrived at the end of the eighth century and the Church became more secularized during the following centuries until the twelfth-century reform that organized the Church in dioceses and parishes under the control of bishops. In 1142 the Cistercian monks established a monastery at Mellifont near Drogheda and other orders began to arrive from the Continent. This marked the closure of the native monasteries and the end of the writing of secular (as opposed to religious) manuscripts by clerical scribes. There is a visible break in the manuscript tradition at this point, and after some time secular writing is taken up by hereditary families of scribes, some of whom continued writing in unbroken line to the early twentieth century.

The manuscripts that contain the literature date from the seventh century; about 4,000 of them survive in Ireland and abroad but it is impossible to judge how many have disappeared or been destroyed and what texts have been lost as a result. Despite this, a vast amount of material has come down to us in comparison with material in other European vernacular languages of the same period.

Unusually, both prose and poetry are used to record material where prose would be used and expected today. Some texts survive in prose only, many are in a mixture of both prose and poetry, called 'prosimetrum', and, although some few sagas are found as poems, unlike Latin and Greek literature there is no epic poetry. The distinctions of modern literature between the novel, short story, play and poetry do not exist in dealing with traditional literature.

General Features

A number of general features, most of which are specific to Ireland, occur throughout the literature. There is an understanding that there are four provinces, Munster, Leinster, Ulster and Connacht as there are today, and the stories often mention the people and kings of these geographical areas. But the Irish word for a province is *cúige* (fifth) and the five are said to come together at Uisnech. There are different theories about the elusive fifth province; Munster may have been divided into two different provinces or perhaps Meath (*Mide* 'middle') was a separate province. The fifth could also be the centre, where one is standing and the remaining four are north, south, east and west.

The stories mention four different festivals: the first of November or Samain (Hallowe'en) the first of February or Imbolc (St Brigit's day), the first of May, Beltaine (Mayday), and finally the first of August, Lugnasad, that has no English equivalent.

Some motifs also occur throughout the stories themselves – for example the concept of taboo (*geis*) that prohibits the hero or king from carrying out certain actions; the breaking of these taboos will lead to disaster or death. Noblemen and kings are frequently said to play chess as entertainment but also as a demonstration of their status in society. On certain occasions kings compete for a woman by playing chess. The name given the game in the texts is *fidchell* (literally 'wisdom of wood'); and there was another less-mentioned game *brandub* (coming from the adjectives 'dark', 'black'). Upper-class women are frequently said to pass the time in embroidery, and this marks their status in society. The early Irish law on fosterage mentions both chess and embroidery as part of the training that should be given to the son and daughter of a king respectively. Music, musicians and particularly harpers appear in many of the stories, and different types of music are used to trigger certain plot lines.

The language in which the texts are written is referred to Old Irish (AD 600–900), and Middle Irish (900–1200). Old Irish is the linguistic link between Greek and Latin and the later vernacular languages of Europe, and it was used in manuscripts far earlier than other languages such as English, French, German, Spanish etc. and, therefore, there is far more material extant in the Irish language from early times than is the case with these languages.

Some Reading Material

On the Celts see B. Cunliffe, *The ancient Celts* (London, 1997) and J.J. Tierney, 'The Celtic ethnography of Posidonius', *Proceedings of the Royal Irish Academy* 60 C, 5 (1960) 189–275. For a short history of the early historical period see D. Ó Corráin, 'Prehistoric and early Christian Ireland' in R.F. Foster (ed.), *Oxford illustrated history of Ireland* (Oxford, 1989). The most comprehensive is D. Ó Cróinín, *A new history of Ireland; i, Prehistoric and early Ireland* (Oxford, 2005) with surveys of every aspect of history, archaeology, society and literature. General books include N. Chadwick, *The Celts* (London, 1970, repr. 1972), M. Dillon (ed.), *Irish sagas*, Thomas Davis Lectures (Cork, 1968, 1970), M. Dillon and N. Chadwick, *The Celtic realms* (London, 1967, 1973), M. Dillon, *Early Irish literature* (Chicago, 1948, repr. Dublin, 1995), J. MacKillop, *Myths and legends of the Celts* (London, 2005) and the very useful J.T. Koch, *Celtic culture: a historical encyclopedia* (Santa Barbara, CA, 2005).

The most comprehensive collection of translations can be found in T.P. Cross and C.H. Slover, *Ancient Irish tales* (New York, 1936, repr. 1996) but this is out of print. Another good collection is J. Gantz, *Early Irish myths and sagas* (London, 1981) and there are modern Irish versions in P. Mac Cana and T. Ó Floinn, *Scéalaíocht na Ríthe* (Baile Átha Cliath, 1956). Some of the stories appear in S.H. O'Grady (ed.), *Silva Gadelica: a collection of tales in Irish with extracts illustrating persons and places*, 2 vols (London, 1892), but the editions and translations are old and not very good.

The *Táin* and other stories are found in T. Kinsella, *The Táin* (Oxford, 1969). A wide-ranging collection in J.T. Koch and J. Carey, *The Celtic heroic age, 3rd ed.* (Andover, MA, and Aberystwyth, 2000). Two tales in M. Tymoczko, *Two death tales from the Ulster Cycle: the death of Cú Roi and the death of Cú Chulainn* (Dublin, 1981). J. Carey, *King of mysteries: early Irish religious writings* (Dublin, 1998) also contains some translations. Fenian material is to be found in A. Dooley and H. Roe, *Tales of the elders of Ireland* (Oxford, 1999) and particularly in K. Meyer, *Fianaigecht: being a collection of hitherto unedited Irish poems and tales relating to Finn and his Fiana with an English translation*, Todd Lecture Series 16 (Dublin, 1910, repr. 1993).

For some Irish language books, see J.E. Caerwyn Williams and M. Ní Mhuiríosa, *Traidisiún Liteartha na nGael* (Baile Átha Cliath, 1979), P.L. Henry, *Saoithiúlacht na Sean-Ghaeilge* (Dublin, 1976) and M. Nic Eoin, *B'ait leo bean: gnéithe den ide-éolaíocht inscne i dtraidisiún liteartha na Gaeilge* (Baile Átha Cliath, 1998).

CHAPTER I

The Background

The Irish vernacular literature ... came into being about AD 600. Its very coming into being, in face of the dominant Latin culture, was something of a miracle; its continuation for nearly fourteen centuries no less so. No vernacular literature in Europe has had such a lengthy run and this very fact places Irish literature in a special position.[1]

Stories and Storytelling

The early Irish sagas are the most popular area of study and interest to the general public. Sagas and poetry are 'the substance of literature' and the main focus of this book.[2] Both prose and poetry are used to record most of the material regardless of its content, and many sagas are a combination of both prose and poetry, with prose being the main medium and the poetry inserted at suitable intervals.

One Irish text says: 'The four things to be asked of every composition must be asked of this composition, viz., place, and person, and time, and cause of invention.'[3] Although quite different from modern literature, there are similarities to the modern list of the four elements that are necessary – the work itself, the creator, the world that is described (such as the people, actions, ideas, feeling, material things and events), and finally the audience who are the readers or listeners.[4] This traditional literature differs from the modern novel that aims to create realism and give an authentic account of the actual experiences of an individual.[5] The plots are traditional and timeless, characters are usually presented as stereotypes, the names are traditional, and new ones are seldom introduced; generally speaking, time is unimportant unless it is an integral part of the plot such as 'time out of joint'. Usually, the environment of traditional stories is unimportant, but the Irish tales describe the beautiful or frightening landscapes of the Otherworld in detail and often place the events in the real landscape of Ireland. Generally, the plots cannot be subverted: for example, if a new story were written Cú Chulainn and Finn Mac Cumaill could not meet.

The strands of this traditional learning (*senchas*) are not separate; different elements can and do combine in the written sources as they probably did in the pre-existing oral culture. Therefore, sagas can appear in genealogy, and the stories can be used as a vehicle to give a political, historical or even a legal message.[6]

There are lists of the story titles available from about the tenth century; in these the sagas are organized by the contents of the story, and there are approximately 185 titles mentioned.[7] The main titles are: destructions, cattle raids, wooings, battles, terrors, voyages, deaths, feasts, sieges, adventures, elopements, plunderings as well as eruptions (of lakes), visions, love stories, hostings and migrations; there are only two Christian titles.[8] There are many poems about the battles and deaths of famous heroes, and the tale lists may have been modelled on them. The lists seem to be written in prose, but it has been shown that some sections are in verse; the lines alliterate so the list was probably meant to be memorized. For example:

> *Togla 7 Tána 7 Tochmarca*, Destructions and Cattle Raids and Wooings,
> *Catha 7 Uatha 7 Imrama*. Battles and Terrors and Voyages.
> *Oitte 7 Fessa 7 Forbassa*, Deaths and Feasts and Sieges.
> *Echtraí 7 Aithid 7 Airgne*. Adventures and Elopments and Plunderings. [9]

There are titles that appear in these lists for which we have no story today – for example *Serc Caillige Bérre do Fhothud Chanainne* (The Love of the Caillech Bérre for Fothad Canainne) and *Cath Aichli* (The Battle of Achall). Many of the existing stories are absent from the lists, or the titles are slightly different from the original. An eleventh-century poem about the fair of Carmun, held at Lugnasad, also contains a list of the type of lore that would be recited – a good indication of what was current at the time: 'Tales of Finn and the Fianna, a matter inexhaustible, sacks, forays, wooings (*togla, tána, tochmorca*).' It also includes: 'Satires, keen riddles, proverbs ... and truthful teachings of Fithal, the *Dinnshenchas* ... Instructions of Cairpre and Cormac ... the tale of the household of Tara ... the *Banshenchas*, tales of armies, conflicts, hostels, tabus, captures ... tales of death and slaughter.'[10]

In his book, *Early Irish literature*, M. Dillon divided the stories into four cycles: Ulster Cycle, Fenian Cycle, Mythological Cycle and the Historical Cycle as well three groups about visits to the Otherworld – *Echtra* (Voyage), *Immram* (Journey) and *Fís* (Vision). This arranges the stories according to the characters – the Ulaid in the Ulster Cycle, the Fianna in the Fenian Cycle, gods and goddesses in the Mythological cycle – rather than by the content of the story. In the mid-twelfth century, when the poet Gilla Mo-Dutu Ó Caiside was compiling the *Banshenchas* (The Lore of Women), he is using a similar chronology – first the Book of Invasion material followed by the Mythological Cycle, the Ulster Cycle and the Fenian Cycles before moving onto the lists of kings.[11]

Some of the characters in the stories of the kings in particular are bordering on history – such as Niall Naígiallach (of the Nine Hostages) and Cormac mac Airt. But the 'real' Cormac and Niall are the characters who appear in the stories as there is no historical information about them. The line between pre-history and history is notoriously difficult to define; as F.J. Byrne said, 'In the absence of contemporary documents the political scene of the fifth century and *a fortiori* of the preceding centuries is lost to history.'[12]

The storyteller (*scélaige*) is mentioned in the sagas themselves, and they usually told stories during the winter months, from Samain (Hallowe'en) to Beltaine (May), and this period for storytelling is still used today.[13] Feidlimid Dall (the blind) was the storyteller to king Conchobar of Ulster and Donn Bó is said to be a great entertainer and storyteller. The different types of tales may have been told at a suitable event – birth tales at births, etc. This is borne out elsewhere: the Luapala people of central Africa only recite certain traditions when they are passing the places mentioned in them, and this is also true of the Bahaya of northern Tanzania.[14]

People are warned against telling stories in daytime, and the collector of folklore, Jeremiah Curtain, says that old people will only tell stories during the night and that it was bad luck by day and he mentions a Munsterwoman who became ill and on being taken to hospital said that her illness was due to telling stories in daytime.[15] A proverb also warns: 'Two things that are unlucky; whistling at night or telling stories of the Fianna by day.' P. Mac Cana has pointed out that the Ashanti only told stories at night and among the Yuki of California the myths are called 'night stories' and even to think about telling them during the day could result in becoming a hump-back.

In Irish tradition, stories are not just about events; they are also about the sites where the events take place, and the story may unfold in the real physical contours of the countryside; story and place are inextricably linked. The reference to God as *Rí na nDúl* (King of the Elements) shows their respect for the environment and physical surroundings. Throughout the literature important events such as the deaths of gods, goddesses, people and animals, combats and battles are commemorated in the landscape. It was seen as a living thing with a name for every feature.

Among the Western Apaches, place names anchor their stories in the landscape and describe such places as *Green Rocks Side by Side Jut down into Water* (A Group of Mossy Boulders on the Bank of a Stream), *Trail Extends across Scorched Rocks* (A Crossing at the Bottom of a Canyon) and *Whiteness Spreads out Descending to Water* (A Sandstone Cliff next to a Spring). They have four types of stories: myths that happened in the beginning and are intended to instruct; historical tales that happened long ago and are used to warn or criticize; sagas that are modern and designed to entertain; and gossip that informs or maligns. K. Basso says that the concept of place-making may be among the most basic human tools of all. For the Western Apaches, the story cannot exist without the place: 'Placeless events are an impossibility; everything that happens must happen somewhere. The location of an event is an integral aspect of the event itself, and identifying the event's location is therefore essential to properly depicting – and effectively picturing – the event's occurrence. For these reasons, placeless stories simply do not get told.'[16] A lost place is accompanied by loss of the wisdom associated with it.

Many writers and philosophers, including Aristotle, have written about storytelling. C. Booker maintains that there are only seven basic plots: overcoming the monster, rags to riches, the quest, voyage and return, comedy, tragedy, rebirth. He concentrates on the plots of modern novels and films and points out that much of our modern lives are still spent reading, listening to or watching stories in novels and on stage, film and television. Even the news is presented in the form of stories.[17] In Irish the word for story (*scél*) in the plural becomes news (*scéla*), and the person who turns news into a story is the *scélaige* (storyteller).[18] Storytelling is a ubiquitous activity and the plots are similar regardless of the location and there is a deep-seated need to explain how the world came to be the way it is.

The scribes/authors are concerned with the nature of storytelling and how the craft of written learning came about in a society that had only practised oral tradition until then. They had their own 'creation myth' to explain how the two traditions came together; a man called Cenn Faelad (†AD 679) was injured in the battle of Mag Ráith (AD 637) and he lost his 'brain of forgetfulness'. He was taken to recover at a centre of learning at Tuaim Drecain (Tomreegan, Co. Cavan). Bricín ran the three schools there: one for Latin learning, one for native law and one for poets (*scol léiginn 7 scol fénechais 7 scol filed*). Cenn Faelad is said to have learnt by day and then he wrote what he had learned by night; and this explains how material was first recorded. It does not matter whether the story is true or not; the intention is clear – to explain the reality of how the two traditions came together.[19]

There are texts where conversations or dialogues take place between old men from the past and younger men from the present; important information is passed from one to the other and then written down. There is a tradition that the story of *Táin Bó Cuailnge* (The Cattle Raid of Cooley) had been forgotten and that it was evoked and remembered when two poets visit the grave of Fergus mac Róich and he recites the story to them. In some of the earliest stories to survive, St Colm Cille is involved in meeting ancients from the past and hearing secret information about the Otherworld in particular. This happens most dramatically in the long Fenian text *Acallam na Senórach* (The Interviewing of the Old Men), where the ancient Fianna pass their stories to St Patrick, and his scribe, Brocán, writes them down, thus the tradition is carried into the future. These 'dialogue texts' may be one of the basic patterns used to explain where the literature came from.[20]

In the same text, the author tries to explain and deal with the nature of storytelling itself; Patrick describes an episode as complicated (*gablánach* from the word *gabul*, branch, fork). This implies that one story is piled upon and conjured up by another and that they are all inter-connected. It is also difficult to move the stories into a Christian, literary form, and the text seems to refuses to act normally and unfolds 'a gigantic series of variations on a limited number of themes'. This defies the usual structure of a story that has a beginning, a middle and an end.[21]

The poet and the storyteller are said to have memorized hundreds of stories and other material and probably used mnemonic devices such as alliterating poetry as a memory aid. If a story is told very often, then it will be remembered more easily than if it is told very seldom. P. Mac Cana mentions the Peruvian *quipu*, 'a tangle of knots and strings and colours that could keep a narrator going for days with letter-perfect renditions of myths, genealogies, poetry, and legends in the same way that a rosary is used to tally the 180 prayers in that garland of Catholic devotion.'[22]

Studies have taken place elsewhere on the abilities of storytellers to remember; in his well-known book, *The singer of tales*, A.B. Lord examines the oral epic traditions of Yugoslavia and gives the following example of testing a singer of the tales: he arranged to have the singer listen to a song unknown to him without telling him that he would have to sing it afterwards. When the singer was asked to sing the tale, he added 4,000 lines to it, developing the version that he had heard with a feeling and ornamentation that was not found in the first version. The second rendition was much better than the first, according to Lord.[23]

Linda Dégh, who worked on the tales of Hungarian singers, tells of a different experience with the storyteller Peter Pandur, showing that motifs in the stories do not live unchanged in the memory. While giving a lecture, she asked Pandur to tell a story; the title had been agreed between them and it was a story that he had told to her before. But while the title was the same, the story he told was completely different; its content had been transformed in the course of the years. When he was challenged about the form of the tale, he said that 'our memory was faulty and that he had told it the same, then and now, word for word'.[24] He maintained this although there was a recording of the original story to prove that the content was not the same.

Druids, Poets and Bards

Before the arrival of Christianity it was the native learned classes, mainly those called the poet (*file*) and the bard (*bard*) who passed on the oral learning to future generation; along with the druid (*draí*), they were members of the people of arts (*aes dána*), who were very highly regarded by this society. There were many other entertainers including the harpist (*cruit*), piper (*cuislennach*), horn player (*cornaire*), juggler (*clesamnach*), jester (*fuirsire*), acrobat (*monach*), raconteur (*creccaire*), the professional farter (*braigetóir*) as well as the satirist, female satirist and the jester (*drúth*).

The first references to the three learned classes of druid, poet and bard are from the descriptions of the so-called 'Celts' by the classical writers on the Continent. The use of the name 'Celt' is relatively modern and causes some problems today. Although Greeks used the word 'Keltoí', and Caesar used the word 'Celtae' to refer to the Gaulish people in the place that we now call France, there is little evidence that these people are related to the inhabitants of modern Ireland. Many descriptions are attributed to a writer called Posidonius, and although his writings are lost he is quoted by surviving writers. There are accounts from Aristotle, Plato and Julius Caesar, to mention the more famous classical authors.[25] But they were all outsiders, the language and customs of the Celts were unfamiliar to them, and their accounts should be read with some scepticism.

The writers mention the three categories of learned men, calling them *druides*, *vates* and *bardos*. The Irish druid (*draí*) and bard (*bard*) are recognizable, and the word *vates* is probably the equivalent of the Irish word for prophet (*fáith*). Many of the accounts mention the druids, but the line between them and the poets is blurred, and in Irish sources 'the druids remain obscure.'[26]

Caesar (about 45 BC) says that the druids originated in Britain and that they often return there to train, sometimes for a total of twenty years. They offered sacrifices, and their knowledge was stored orally in verse because they wanted to keep it a secret from ordinary people.[27] Other writers such as Strabo and Diodorus Siculus (about 50 BC) say that they were honoured philosophers and theologians who believed in the immortality of the soul and, unwilling to share their knowledge, they used riddles to hide the true meaning from the listeners. Riddles and mysterious messages are also a feature of the early stories. Druids were responsible for sacrifices and made prophecies based on the death-spasm of the victim. There are references to human sacrifices in huge figures of straw (the wickerman).

Pliny (AD 23–79) says that druids considered oak trees and the mistletoe (Modern Irish *drualus*) to be sacred, and that they named themselves from the Greek word for oak (*drus*). They thought the mistletoe to be 'the healer of all' and that when taken as a drink it cured all poisons and made barren animals fertile. He also mentions that white bulls were sacrificed to ensure prosperity. In early Ireland, bulls were considered sacred, and they are used in sacrifice in the stories and appear on statues and in personal names.

By the time the Irish are writing down their stories themselves, druids are not often given a high profile, and it presumably means that their powers had waned; but the Christian monks would have been wary of druids, and they may have intentionally diminished their status. The most famous druid in the literature is Cathbad the father of king Conchobar of Ulster and the foster father of Cú Chulainn, the most famous martial hero. They were considered dangerous to Christians, connected with love potions and on a level with satirists and thieves. Druids are said to practise heron or crane killing (*corrguinecht*), reciting spells and satires while standing on one leg, one arm lifted up and one eye closed. The killing of the bird may have been ritualistic, as happens when a cock is killed in voodoo cults. The Gaulish god Esus is sometimes depicted with crane-like birds.

The poet is associated with what appears to be a druid-like activity – extempore satire or black magic called *glám dícenn*. He could kill a king who offended him by sticking thorned sticks in a clay effigy while chanting satirical verse. It is said that the seven grades of poet should go to the top of a hill before sunrise with their backs to a whitethorn, the wind from the north, and a thorn from the whitethorn in each one's hand to chant the satire.[28]

Diodorus Siculus mentions seers, who used omens and sacrifices to see into the future, and bards described as lyric poets who sing praise and satire to the music of an instrument like a lyre. Athenaeus (*c*.AD 200) quotes Posidonius on poets and says that they recited 'praises' to large crowds; the bards told stories recited in song. Ammianus Marcellinus agrees that the bards sang the praise of famous men to the music of a lyre.[29]

Poets in Ireland performed publicly, perhaps accompanied by music or even chanting their compositions; some of the words used for reciting poetry contain the word for singing (*canaid*); a poem is often introduced by the Latin word sang (*cecinit*). Professional musicians such as the harper, piper and *timpán* player appear in the sagas; and there are also references to humming and singing (*sianán*), and the music of the Fianna is like the humming of the bees (*dord* or *dordán*). There is no Old Irish word for dancing, and there are no plays or theatre as found in Greek tradition, but the sagas are written with such a strong, dramatic flavour that they provide theatrical entertainment in themselves.[30]

The *file* did survive the arrival of Christianity and they appear in the sagas and composed some of the earliest sources. The word originally meant a person who can see, a seer, and it is used in Modern Irish for the word 'poet'. His role in society was quite different from the modern-day poet. He was like a Public Records Office, recording traditional lore (*senchas*) such as history, genealogy, place names and sagas; one of his main duties was to praise his patron as well as to satirize and prophesy.

When written documents appear in Ireland, the poet is ranked with the king and the bishop at the highest level of society, and it is stated that every area (*tuath*) must have a poet. It is said that 'A tribe is not a tribe without an ecclesiastical scholar, a churchman, a poet, a king.'[31] Seven grades are mentioned, the highest being the *ollam*, for which there is no real English equivalent or translation. One could not become a poet unless he was the son and the grandson of a poet, training took up to twenty years, echoing the period for the druid on the Continent. The poets were supposed to know 350 stories, and a proverb says, 'There is no fort without a king; or a *file* without a story'; they used the stories to add substance to their poems.[32]

The *ollam* was entitled to a retinue of twenty-four people to accompany him – which shows how rich one had to be to maintain an *ollam*. They could become very wealthy; the highest payment for a poem was a chariot and the least that was expected was a three-year-old heifer and a cauldron. In an anonymous stanza, a ninth-century poet faults a patron for giving him a cow instead of a horse.[33] The rules for the metres that they used to compose their poetry were standardized countrywide; this may be because the profession was hereditary and because poets were in close contact with one another as they were allowed to travel freely, unlike the rest of the community.

Poets are quite often blind, as was the great bard Homer; oral transmission meant that sight was unnecessary for learning; it could even be an advantage as there was no distraction. Some rituals, like heron-killing mentioned above, needed closed eyes, and one eighteenth-century account describes poets still composing in the dark.[34] Some of the stories have powerful poets as characters and they seem to be promoting themselves – for example, Aithirne, who is known for his powers and ability to terrify.[35] He threatens the one-eyed king, Eochaid mac Luchta, who gives Aithirne his single eye, but God restores the sight of both eyes as a reward. He also had an argument with the river Mourne because it did not give him a salmon for his supper. He recites a satire against it but the river rises up and follows him; he composes a praise poem and the river returns to normal.

Eochaid Dallán Forgaill is recognized as the author of the earliest poem in Old Irish, the lament for Colm Cille (†597) entitled the *Amra Choluim Cille* (The Lament for Colum Cille) probably composed shortly after his death. This shows that there was a friendly relationship between these two men at a very early stage and that the native and Christian traditions were already bound closely together. Their relationship is also mentioned in an earlier incident known as the meeting of Druim Cett (AD 573/5); this was held to decide whether poets should be expelled from Ireland. The kings thought that there were too many of them and that they were too expensive to support but Colm Cille (abbot of Iona since 563) led the movement to defend them.[36]

As stated already, there is no epic poetry in early Irish literature, but verse is used very widely – for laws, genealogy, calendars of saints and even history. There is also religious poetry; verses are found inserted in the annals and genealogies; and then there are the self-standing poems on history, liturgy, praise, satire, place names, the lore of women and deaths of heroes. A small number of lyric and nature poems, prayers, hymns and personal poems also survive.

There are few references to female poets or druids, but female seers are mentioned in a Gaulish inscription on a woman's grave (c.AD 90).[37] Tacitus mentions a female prophet called Veled who lived in a high tower, and that people could not approach her directly; one of her relatives was chosen to talk to her and then brought the replies back – like a messenger of the gods.[38] There are female prophets in some early Irish texts as well, and references to them as *bandraí* (female druid) or *banfhile* (female poet), as will be seen in the chapter on Poets and Poetry.

The Arrival of Christianity

Christianity arrived relatively silently in Ireland and, as M. Richter says, the process 'eludes the observer. The fifth and sixth centuries, which are when this happened, are very poorly documented; thus it is impossible to follow how exactly Christianity was established.'[39] The only accepted contemporary writings are from Patrick himself, and even the date of his arrival is uncertain. There were very few foreign missionaries, and the next saints to appear are Irish – Colm Cille and Brigit – as are most of the others that follow, such as Brendan, Enda and Ita. We have access only to what the clerical scribes decided to record, and it is to be presumed that they had a vested interest in ignoring the more directly pagan elements of the tradition.

Reading and writing developed within the Christian environment of the monastery. The monks or laymen known as scribes worked in the monastery's scriptorium (writing room) where they compiled the manuscripts (literally 'hand written') and everything recorded comes through this Christian channel, for the monks and their monastic superiors decided what would appear in these books. New words appeared in the language – such as *léann*, originally *léigenn* from the Latin *legendum* – and refers to ecclesiastical learning to distinguish it from the native word s*enchas* (lore). The terms for reading and writing also entered the language; for example, the modern Irish verb *scríobhaim* ('I write') from the Latin *scribere*. Unlike today, most people did not read or write as it was not considered necessary for anyone other than the scribes and learned classes of the *file* and the monk. The law describes what was the fitting education for the son of a king; it included such skills as playing chess, swimming and riding a horse but not reading or writing.

There are a number of unusual features about the Irish and their writings: it seems that they were the first to speculate about the meaning of their own language and they were so confident about their native language that they began writing in Irish at a relatively early stage, in contrast with other vernacular languages. After the eighth century, the Latin hymns nearly die out because the scribes begin to write in Irish and they were prepared to accept the pagan authors of Rome and mythology in general. F.J. Byrne says: 'saints such as Columcille, Columbanus and Adomnán never dreamt of any danger to their faith from their classical studies. It is very strange, yet typical of the early Irish Church, to find so starkly ascetic a figure as St Columbanus delighting in the composition of verses redolent of pagan mythology.'[40] They were also prepared to read and record the apocryphal texts that were frowned upon in Europe. As a result, more apocryphal texts survive in Ireland than in any other Western European country, and some of the sources go back to the Gnostic gospels and literature of Egypt.[41]

When writing begins, as might be expected, the texts are written in Latin and connected with the Church. But they become bilingual (Irish and Latin) at an early stage. Irish did take over as the main written language but it never fully replaced Latin. The scribes translated Latin texts, such as the lives of the saints, into Irish, and, showing a considerable interest in historical material, they used both prose and poetry to record annals, genealogies, king lists, chronology and synchronism; the bulk of Irish literature consists of this record rather than sagas and poetry.

The first written documents are from Patrick himself, but his *Confessio* (Confession) gives little information on his life and he describes himself as humble, unworthy and badly educated.[42] These were followed by biographies of saints such as Patrick, Brigit and Colm Cille including two seventh-century lives of Patrick – one by Tírechán and the second by Muirchú. There is also a third from the ninth century, called the *Vita Tripartita* (Tripartite Life).[43]

The first biographies include a description of Patrick confronting the pagan king, Laegaire son of Niall of the Nine Hostages, at Tara. Patrick lights his Easter fire at Slane before a fire is lit at Tara, and his druids warn Laegaire that unless they put it out the fire will outlive their pagan fire forever. Laegaire is feasting at the banqueting hall, compared with that of king Nebuchadnezzar of

Babylon, when Patrick enters and confronts the 'great, fierce, pagan emperor of the barbarians reigning in Tara, which was the capital of the Irish.' Patrick celebrates Easter and destroys the pagan festival, and Laegaire eventually becomes a Christian. In the second biography, Laegaire refuses to become a Christian and insists on being buried in pagan fashion – that is, upright and fully armed, in the ramparts of Tara facing his hereditary enemy, the king of Leinster. The king of Leinster is likewise buried in the Liffey plain facing Laegaire.[44]

Branches of Literature

Apart from the sagas, the scribes recorded a vast array of material including genealogies, ecclesiastical literature, topography and onomastics along with annalistic and historical texts. The earliest manuscript that still survives is known as the *Cathach Choluim Cille* (The Battler of Colm Cille), written in Latin, and Colm Cille is said to be the scribe himself. In the eighth and ninth centuries, the famous illuminated manuscripts like the Book of Kells (a Latin copy of the four gospels), the Book of Durrow and Book of Lindisfarne are created. To date, the first known manuscript that is mentioned and known to contain early narrative saga material is *Cín Dromma Snechta* (The little book of Druim Snechta). It no longer survives, but a list of contents can be put together from references to it in later manuscripts, and it must have contained the germ of the early literature. Latin and Irish were combined from an early stage and were still used in the eleventh-century macaronic (that is, using two languages) hymn by Mael Íosa Ua Brolcháin (†1086) where he has alternate lines in Latin and Irish.[45]

As noted above, one of the earliest poems written entirely in Old Irish is the *Lament for Colm Cille* that was composed on the death of the saint (†597) by his poet friend, Eochaid Dallán Forgaill. The author is not a churchman, but he had learned Latin and must have trained in a monastery. This shows that, at this very early stage in the development of written Irish literature, both traditions had combined and that the Irish language was already being used in a Christian context. There was also a life of Colm Cille written, in Latin, by Adomnán (*c.*700); he was also responsible for *Cáin Adomnáin* (The Law of Adomnán), in Irish, that covers many subjects but, most notably, it gave women a Christian legal protection from being killed in battles.[46] One of the earliest Latin stories to combine religious belief with secular saga is the *Navigatio Sancti Brendani* (The Journey of St Brendan). It is related to other such tales written in Irish about the Otherworld in its different manifestations and will be discussed in the chapter on the Otherworld.

Some scholars took Latin manuscripts to the Continent, and these contain some of the earliest Old Irish words as glosses (notes or explanations) on the original texts. One of them has some Irish poems including one to the scribe's cat, Pangur Bán. This most famous of Irish cats has a Welsh name *pangur*, which means a fuller. The cat's name thus means 'white fuller' – he must have been a very white cat. The fuller was white because of his profession – treating cloth with white clay that stiffened it.

There was an extensive early legal system in Ireland now called Brehon law from the Irish word for judge (*brithem*). This was also written down in the monastic environment; during the conflict between Patrick and Laegaire at Tara, a poet showed Patrick the native law and the saint decided that whatever did not conflict with God's law could remain. Brehan law recognized divorce, re-marriage and even the fact that a man could have two wives at the same time.[47] There are about eighty texts covering all sorts of topics such as property and trespass, bees, cats and dogs. The language can be difficult, and some of the texts seem to be guidelines rather than complete law tracts. They tend to have a very sensible attitude on such topics as slander: in modern times any type of comment can be made about an individual once they are dead, but the early law protects the dead, and the slanderer must still compensate the family.

There are a number of texts that deal with place names and personal names (onomastics) such as the *Dinnshenchas* (Lore of Famous Places) written in prose and in verse giving explanations, origins, stories and mythologies of the most important place names in Ireland. The metrical version of the *Dinnshenchas* begins with five poems on Tara, and the sixth is about the naming of Achall (the modern day Skryne) across the Gabhra Valley from Tara. Personal names and their meanings, whether real or imaginery, are found in *Cóir Anmann* (Fitness of Names), but explanations are found in the sagas as well. For example, a pre-historic king of Munster, Fiacha Muillethan (Fiacha Flat Head), son of Eogan, got his unusual name because his mother sat on a rock to delay his birth so that he would be king.[48] The text *Sanas Cormaic* (Cormac's Glossary) gives the ety-mology, the meaning of words. It is probably based on continental Latin mate-rial, but many of the explanations are suspect.[49] The *Banshenchas* (Lore of Women) is found in both prose and metrical form. This twelfth-century text gives exhaustive lists of women, their spouses and offspring (mainly Irish but also from biblical and classical sources), from the pre-Christian period, followed by those from the Christian period up to the arrival of the Normans.[50]

There are also a number of gnomic or wisdom texts that give instructions or advice; for example, *Audacht Morainn* (The Testament of Morann), containing advice on how to be a good king and *Tecosca Cormaic* (The instructions of Cormac), said to be written by the king of Tara, Cormac mac Airt. He advises his son on various topics, and his advice on women is one of the most misogy-nistic pieces of literature in the language, for example:

They are crabbed as constant companions ...
Silly counsellors,
Greedy of increase,
They have tell-tale faces ...
Better to whip them than to humour them,
Better to scourge them than to gladden them,
Better to beat them than to coddle them,
Better to smite them than to please them ... [51]

There was a tradition of collecting proverbs and subjects in differing numbers, such as duads, triads, tetrads (fours) and heptads (sevens). The Triads collect nuggets of information and wisdom on a range of eclectic subjects: 'Three darknesses into which women should not go: the darkness of mist, the darkness of night, the darkness of a wood.'[52]

Genealogy was an important element of this lore; the most important families in the country were recorded in all major manuscripts and their genealogy probably formed part of the reportoire of the poet. The genealogies are written in a combination of prose and poetry, and some of the oldest surviving material appears in these texts.[53] Annals are an account of (usually) historical events in chronological order; they probably began as ecclesiastical records that were expanded to include information on all historical events. Latin was used, to begin with, but the Irish language came to be used afterwards although Latin words or phrases occasionally appear.

Apparently the Irish did not view their past chronologically (with dates) before the arrival of Christianity: everything simply happened in the past. When the historical chronological material came from continental sources the scribes set about creating a history of their own for Ireland. There were a certain amount of historical events available to them to create this history, but it was not enough to fill the gaps, so they used the literature and turned it into history. Dates were applied to the story cycles; the Ulster Cycle was dated to the first century AD to coincide with Christ's death, the Fenian Cycle to the third century AD, and the Mythological Cycle was used to bring history back thousands of years to the time of Adam and Eve in the Bible. One of the texts that came about as a result is the *Leabhar Gabhála* (The Book of Invasions) that was completed in the twelfth century and links the Irish with the Israelites. The leader of the Irish, Nél son of Féinius Farsaid, was living in Egypt when the sons of Israel escaped from the Pharaoh. Nél and Moses met and Nél gave the Israelites wine and wheat, and Moses was grateful. This strange encounter is followed by an even more bizarre event where Gaedel Glas son of Nél was bitten by a snake. Moses cured him and declared: 'I command ... that no serpents dwell in the land of his progeny.'[54]

Oral Tradition and Written Literature

The transition from oral tradition to written literature is as silent as the coming of Christianity, and this has led to heated debates on the origins of the written literature and how much it has taken from the pre-existing oral tradition. It is difficult today to imagine what it is like to learn without writing, books, note-taking, blackboards, computers etc. The teacher simply speaks, and the message is taken aurally by the pupil to be committed to memory rather than to writing. The pupil needs help in memorizing the material; mnemonics and alliterative poetry are regarded as being particularly helpful. Even today we know that it is easier to memorize poetry written in rhyming verse than passages of prose.

At some point, a decision was taken to create manuscripts and to compose stories featuring native, traditional characters such as Cú Chulainn and Finn mac Cumaill, with probably native plots. The writers had to find a style suitable for the written versions of stories rather than the oral tellings, and the earliest stories of the scribes are short and pithy. From the eleventh century onwards the scribes began to translate long Latin texts and they learned how to compose longer texts in Irish as a result. They did include the themes from the imported Latin literature and adapted this new material to suit their own needs. By the time they compiled the surviving texts, the Christian and native learned classes had already merged and all the literature was 'recorded, adapted or composed' by these literary people. Some modern critics acknowledge the existence of pagan, pre-Christian material not 'the detritus of a lost mythology' which grew from those two traditions, native and Christian.[55]

S. Ó Coileáin outlined the views of scholars in an article written at the end of the seventies.[56] J. Carney used the term 'nativist' to describe those who saw the written texts as based on the older, oral tradition, and the stories as native, without much outside influence. He said that the sagas were primarily of written origin, had little or no oral background and were influenced by non-native literature that came to Ireland after the advent of Christianity.[57] J. Carney is termed then as anti-nativist and K. McCone follows this approach in his *Pagan past and Christian present* and says that 'early medieval Irish writers tend to view it as a seamless garment' and that the boundaries between the different traditions are 'blurred'.[58]

Some of these *file* probably became scribes and wrote down what they decided was worthwhile, and presumably they wrote down their own works as well.[59] So the scribes themselves are seen as the conduits of the tradition. But this raises the question of the blind poets and how their poetry found its way into the manuscripts; there must have been dictation by the poet to the scribe who actually writes the poem down although this is never mentioned. There seems to be a pride in their own tradition, even among churchmen, rather than an inferiority complex about the pagan past, and they saw their identity as 'the marriage of two cultures'.[60]

Ogam, Writing and Manuscripts

The earliest form of writing, called Ogam, appears mainly on stones that are found all over the country but with particular clusters in the counties of Kerry and Cork in the south of the country. They appear to be mainly commemorative stones, and as they usually contain only personal names they tell us little about the language. Ogam had twenty characters; these are called by tree names such as *Beithe* for the letter *B* (birch tree) and *Sail* for *S* (willow), and they are represented by a series of slashes and dots used to indicate the letters.

The god Ogma is credited with inventing the script; its real origin is obscure but is probably related to the arrival of Christianity. The Irish had their explanation for the invention of Irish; it is said that Fénius Farsaid, a man versed in three languages (Latin, Greek and Hebrew), went to Nimrod's Tower (the Tower of Babel) with seventy-two scholars to study the languages, and as a result Irish was created as well as *Bérla Féne* (the Language of *Féne*). The Irish see it as being taken from the best languages of the world, which shows their pride in the language.[61]

The oldest written form of the language is called Old Irish (600–900), and it evidences linguistic connections with Latin and Greek and the other European vernacular languages. They are all members of the Indo-European family of languages that develop later into continental languages such as Spanish, Italian and French. The similarity with Latin can be seen in the word for 'mother' – *mater* in Latin and *máthair* in Irish.

The first Irish manuscripts were written in Latin, but some significant practices are credited to the Irish scribes; to help them read what was a foreign language, for example, the division of words and the use of capital letters and punctuation.[62] An Irish manuscript was usually a book, with leaves/pages made of parchment. The parchment was made from sheepskin, goatskin or the more expensive calfskin vellum, the preferred skin in Ireland. This made producing a manuscript very expensive; about 500 cows would have been needed to make the Book of Kells, for example. From the sixteenth century onwards paper was preferred because it was cheaper. The books vary in size, script, quality, neatness and content, and they came about in different ways. The written word gave way to the printing press, and Johannes Gutenburg established the first one in Mainz in 1450; the first one in England was set up by William Caxton in 1476. Printing in Irish was late in coming to Ireland, only becoming common practice from the nineteenth century onwards.

The Irish hand by T. O'Neill, with an introduction by F.J. Byrne, is one of the very few good books on the topic of scripts and manuscripts. The body of the book contains a page describing each of the major manuscripts and a reproduction of one page from each in chronological order. In the past, access to the viewing of manuscripts was quite restrictive, but the Internet has opened this possibility to everyone with a computer. This means that the pages of the great manuscripts can be viewed in detail thanks to the work done by ISOS (Irish Scripts on Screen).[63]

The scribes had to adapt the Latin alphabet to the Irish language, and the letters might not represent the sound exactly. The description of the writing is referred to as the 'hand', and the handwriting of the various scribes differs one from the other and may therefore be distinguished and recognised. The pages are referred to as *folio* (singular) and *folios* (plural) and the terms *recto* (right) and *verso* (reverse) are used to refer to the front and the back. A page could contain different columns of writing instead of writing fully across the page as we do today; there could be two, four or even more columns. They are usually referred to as: a, b, c or d, and then the line number on the page is added. This is the type of reference used, for example, in referring to the genealogies: LL 136 b 37 refers to the genealogies in the Book of Leinster, page 136, column b and line 37.

Wax tablets and slates were used as 'note books' with a type of metal stylus (pen). The most common writing instrument was a quill – usually a goose feather, but apparently crow feathers were used for the finer work. The shape of the quill point dictated the writing style to an extent. Inks were made from substances such as oak gall and iron gall; this seemed to ensure that the writing did not turn brown although the later manuscripts have turned from black to brown. Styluses were also used for marking margins and lining the pages to keep the writing straight and drawing the outline of the complicated drawings found in the letter initials. The scribes tested their new quills in a practice known as *probatio pennae* (testing the pen) sometimes using their own names as the test writing.

The work was carried out in the scriptorium in a monastery and the books were kept in a *tíag* (leather satchel named from the Greek word *theca*) and could be hung on the wall. It is thought that training may have begun at a very young age and that the best scribes may have been teenagers. It has been shown today that it is difficult to learn this style of writing properly at a later stage in life.[64] There are references to the scribes writing outdoors, as in this lyric poem:

> A hedge of trees surrounds me,
> A blackbird's lay sings to me;

Above my lined booklet
The trilling birds chant to me.

In a grey mantle from the top of bushes
The cuckoo sings;
Verily – may the Lord shield me! –
Well do I write under the greenwood.[65]

The Irish used a series of abbreviations (*noda*) that are unique to them and different from those used by continental scribes. They did inherit a number of them from the Latin manuscripts, and some of these look quite unusual and strange today such as an inverted c, (ɔ) for *con*, an inverted e (ə) for *eius*, ⁊ for **et** (and) – which can still be used today as it was in the old name for the Postal Services in Ireland (P⁊T) etc.[66]

The first known manuscript to contain secular material was the one called *Cín Dromma Snechta*, Co. Monaghan, but this no longer exists. It may have been written in the eighth century (although not all are agreed on this) and it may be as late as the tenth century. The monastery at Druim Snechta was connected to another one at Bangor, and this area may be where the writing of manuscripts first began; a lot of the earliest material comes from there.[67] Two more lost manuscripts that are mentioned as sources from time to time are the *Lebor Buide Sláni* (The Yellow Book of Slane) and the *Saltair Chaisil* (The Psalter of Cashel). It is difficult to judge just how many manuscripts have been lost, but the discovery of a ninth-century Latin manuscript in an Irish bog in 2006 proves that they were sometimes hidden, and there may be more secrets to come to light in the future.

Some manuscripts are known by a title, like *Cín Dromma Snechta* or *Lebor na hUidre* (The Book of the Dun Cow), but others may be known by the shelf in the library in which they are kept – for example, Rawlinson B 502 or the Book of Uí Mhaine, which is known as D iv 2. Some of them have had a very long and complicated history; some have been a manuscript as an entity from the very beginning, and others have been put together over the centuries. They may have been written by one scribe or by a series of scribes, one taking over from the other in a rota system. And manuscripts may have been added to at a period later than their original compilation.

Some of the earliest examples such as the *Cathach*, the Book of Durrow and the Stowe Missal are written across the page as we would today and not in columns as are such manuscripts as the Book of the Dun Cow, the Book of Leinster etc. The Annals of Inisfallen are written in three columns, the Annals of

Ulster in two columns, and the Annals of the Four Masters are written across the entire page.

The manuscript pages may be numbered in different ways; the first is the method we use to paginate today with a number for each page, or secondly with a number for each leaf and then a reference to whether it is the right side (*recto*) or the left side/reverse (*verso*) of the same leaf. Then the columns may be referred to as **a** and **b**, and then the lines themselves are numbered. This gives rise to such references as, for example, 27^r b 34 (= page 27, reverse, column 2, line 34). Thirdly, the columns themselves may be numbered (this is quite a lot simpler).

The oldest manuscript that survives today is the *Cathach* (champion, battler). The book has a metal shrine (*cumdach*) and consists of fifty-eight pages containing the psalms.[68] It has been attributed to Colm Cille, who is described by his biographer, Adomnán, as frequently writing even on the day of his death. The sixteenth-century life of Colm Cille tells the story of the copied manuscript that was the cause of a battle. Colm Cille is said to have copied a manuscript that belonged to St Finnian, and, when Finnian said that he wanted the copy Colm Cille would not give it to him. The high king of Tara of the time, Diarmait mac Cerbaill, gave the famous verdict, 'To every cow its calf and to every book its copy'. Colm Cille refused to return the copy, and his stubbornness gave rise to the battle of Cúl Dreimne near Bulbulban, Co. Sligo in 561, a battle fought between his own people, the Northern Uí Néill, and the Southern Uí Néill led by Diarmait mac Cerbaill. Although the king was defeated, the price that Colum Cille paid for keeping the book was very high, as the saints of Ireland gathered to condemn him and he was sent into exile to Iona as punishment for his behaviour.[69] In the eleventh century a cover was made for the manuscript, and the book stayed in Donegal until 1691 until it was brought to France; it returned to Ireland in 1813 and eventually reached its present home – the Royal Irish Academy.

The Book of Armagh has the earliest extant Irish prose narrative as distinct from Latin texts and early glosses. This is the manuscript that contains the writings of Patrick himself and the early Lives of the saint by Muirchú and Tírechán. There were at least two different hands involved in the writing, or else the scribe Ferdomnach, who gives his name and wrote during the abbacy of Torbach, was writing at different times of his life. Ferdomnach and Torbach are related to another scribe, Mael Muire, who was involved in writing a later manuscript *The Book of the Dun Cow*. The king of Ireland and Tara at the time, Donnchad son of Flann (fl. 937), ordered that a cover be made for the manuscript. It travelled far and wide after that; eventually in 1707 Arthur Brownlow had the book in Lurgan, Co. Armagh, and the family put it up for sale in 1853 when Dr William Reeves bought it and then sold it to Lord John Beresford, archbishop of

Armagh. He presented it to Trinity College and it remains in that library as MS 52.

Lebor na hUidre is abbreviated as LU; its principal scribe, Mael Muire ua Célechair, was killed by intruders in 1106, according to the Annals of the Four Masters. He was descended from a family who lived in Co. Louth originally although they had settled in Clonmacnoise since the eighth century. Co. Louth was the homeland of Cú Chulainn and the scene of most of the action of the *Táin*. R.I. Best recognized three hands, A, M and H, M being the principal scribe, the Mael Muire mentioned above. But this manuscript has one strange feature in that parts of it were erased and rewritten; the scribe responsible for this is called the Interpolator, but there is no agreement as to whether the Interpolator is a different scribe or Mael Muire himself rewriting the material.

The book contains a mixture of ecclesiastical and secular material in Irish including such Ulster Cycle tales as the oldest copy of the *Táin*, *Mesca Ulad* (The Intoxication of the Ulstermen), *Fís Adomnáin* (The Vision of Adomnán), *Scéla Laí Brátha* (Tidings of the Last Day) and *Scéla na hEséirgi* (Tidings of the Resurrection). It is now in the Royal Irish Academy.

The so-called Book of Leinster, usually abbreviated to LL, is probably the manuscript that was originally known as *Lebor na Nuachongbála* (from Noghoval in Co. Laois). It is dated to *c*.1160, but in fact the writing was done over a period of time. There is a diplomatic edition available,[70] as is the case with LU, in six volumes (which shows how much material this manuscript contains). It is one of the most important early collections of secular material, and concentrates on Leinster. It contains a mention of the king of Leinster, Diarmait Mac Murchada, being banished from his kingdom, and of the coming of the Normans and Diarmait's subsequent death in 1171.

The manuscript has a copy of the *Book of Invasions* and an account of the creation of the world followed by a large quantity of poetry including *The Lore of Famous Places* and genealogies that begin with the kings of Ireland but are then followed by those of the kings of Leinster, the Uí Cheinnselaig and Uí Failge (also of that province – indicating its provenance and its interest). There is also a large collection of Ulster Cycle tales.

The Ó Mórda family brought the book with them to Ballyna in Co. Kildare when they lost their lands in the seventeenth century. Edward Lhuyd bought it in 1700 and it went to Trinity College in 1782. By this time it was being called the Book of Leinster or the Book of Glendalough. It was separated into parts, for some of its content ended up with the Franciscans; and it may have lost other material as well. It is still housed in Trinity College as MS 1339.

Leabhar Leacáin (The Book of Lecan) was compiled by the well-known scribal family Mac Firbhisigh between the years 1416 and 1418 at Leacán in

Co. Sligo. This family was also responsible for the production of *Leabhar Buí Leacáin* (The Yellow Book of Lecan) and of the huge book of genealogies compiled by Dubaltach Mac Firbhisigh. Three scribes were involved in the writing of The Book of Lecan – Gilla Ísa Mac Firbhisigh himself along with two of his pupils, Murchad Ó Cuindlis and Ádamh Ó Cuirnín. Mac Firbhisigh was an *ollam* to the Ó Dubhda, who was the king of the Uí Fhiachrach. It contains such material as *The Book of Invasions*, the *Lore of Famous Places* and *The Fitness of Names*. It contained a large collection of genealogies, particularly those of the families who were associates of Mac Firbisigh, and also a wide selection of hagiographical, biblical and historical material.

The book passed to Henry Piers, secretary to Sir Arthur Chichester, lord deputy of Ireland; then it seems to have been bought by James Ussher, archbishop of Armagh; and in 1688 it appeared in Trinity College, it disappeared again and eventually arrived in the Royal Irish Academy.

Some manuscripts have comments in the margins that give more personal insights into the scribe's lives. These come from the manuscript known as Laud 610.

> May God forgive him who makes us write on a Sunday night, namely Edmund Butler. We are in Pottlerath tonight.
>
> May God forgive the owner of this book for making me write on a Sunday night, namely Edmund Butler. I am Gilla na Naem Mac Aedagáin in Cill Fraích on the banks of the Nore.
>
> I think it long for Edmund to be out in the frost while I wait for him without my dinner.
>
> Unhappy is he who bears witness against a friend unless he be eager to do so. The two things that come of it are envy and reproach.
>
> Upon my word it is a great penance for us to keep to water on Good Friday, considering the good wine that is at hand in the house of Pottlerath.[71]

An Example of the Language about 1000

This is the beginning of the *Loinges mac nUislenn* (The Exile of the Sons of Uisliu) that tells the story of Derdriu:

> *Cid dia-mboí Longes mac n-Usnig? Ni ansa. Bátar Ulaid oc ól i taig Fheidlimthe maic Daill, scélaigi Conchobuir. Baí dano ben ind Fheidlimthe oc airiuc don tshluaig ósa cinn is sí thorrach. Tairmchell corn ocus chuibrenn ocus ro-lásat gáir mesca. A mbátar do lepthugud, do-lluid*

*in ben dia lepaid. Oc dul di dar lár in taige, ro-gréch in lenab inna broinn
co-closs fon less uile.*

(Why was the exile of the sons of Uisliu? It is not difficult. The Ulstermen
were drinking in the house of Feidlimid mac in Daill, Conchobar's storyteller. Feidlimid's wife was attending upon the host, standing up and she
pregnant. Drinking horns and portions [of food] circled around, and they
uttered a drunken shout. When they were about to go to bed, the woman
came to her bed. While she was going across the middle of the house, the
infant in her womb screamed so that it was heard throughout the whole
enclosure.)[72]

CHAPTER 2

The Mythological Cycle

It has often been observed that in their literature the insular Celts, and particularly the Irish, show a remarkable concern with the physical configuration of the land upon which they live. Every river and lake and well, every plain and hill and mountain has its own name, and each name evokes its own explanatory legend.[1]

The gods and goddesses are the principal characters of the stories in this cycle, and the events take place in the Time of the Gods. In Irish literature, the Tuatha Dé Danann (people of the goddess Danu) are probably the primary gods, and they are said to have retreated underground after the arrival of the Gaeil, the children of Míl (the Milesians), according to the *Book of Invasions*, which contains a lot of information on gods and goddesses. They are presented as supernatural humans along with the other supposed invaders of Ireland – a woman called Cessair, Nemed, Parthalón and the Fir Bolg. The *Lore of Famous Places* also contains a lot of mythological information.[2]

The monuments of Ireland, such as Brú na Bóinne (Newgrange), Knowth and Dowth and Temair (Tara), are populated in the literature by the gods and goddesses of the Tuatha Dé Danann – for example, Oengus in Brú na Bóinne, Bodb in Síd ar Femen, Co. Tipperary and Midir in Brí Léith, near Ardagh, Co. Longford. Modern folk tradition still refers to the fairy folk living underground in fairy mounds throughout the countryside. Due to the lack of pre-Christian material, it is difficult to establish with any certainty the functions of Irish deities; the mythological tales probably contained material that would have threatened the new religion. The names and relationships of many gods and goddesses still exist, but there is little information available on the original beliefs of the people; and, because the scribes are the Christian monks, the gods and goddesses appear as supernatural beings rather than deities.[3]

The Greek and Roman writers have given accounts of the supposed Celtic deities, but it is not easy to establish a connection between the names they use and those of Irish deities. Caesar mentions the main gods and goddesses as being Mercury, Apollo, Mars, Jupiter and Minerva. Lug may be the god that he describes as Mercury; he was known in Ireland and all over Europe (some of the place names associated with him include Lyon and Laon in France, Leiden in Holland, Leignitz in Silesia and Ludgate in London). In Welsh he is called *LLeu* and appears in the guise of a shoemaker. Archaeological evidence agrees, and shows him as young, beardless, athletic and handsome, and he is Cú Chulainn's divine father, who is also described as beardless. He is described as multi-talented (*samildánach*) and kills Balor of the Evil Eye with a slingshot.

The god Nuadu, called Nodens on the Continent, is found as Nuadu Necht. He is seen as the ancestor of many Irish dynasties, and is worshipped as the fisher-god Nodens in fourth-century Britain at the elaborate temple at Lydney in Gloucestershire. Because he lost his arm in the first *Cath Maige Tuired* (The Battle of Moytura), he is called Nuadu Lámairgit (the silver arm). Place names like Mag Nuadat (Maynooth, the plain of Nuadu) came from a person of this name.

On the Continent, Ogma is found as Ogmios on inscribed tablets – an old man, bald and grey with darkened skin and wrinkled by the sun. He carries a club and a bow and is linked to eloquence; in Ireland he is said to have invented the Ogam alphabet.

Smiths were essential to society and had a supernatural aura because of their relationship with the magical properties of iron and fire. The principal smith is Goibniu (Modern Irish *gabha*), who is found with his two associates, Luchta the wright and Créidne the metalworker; all three provide arms for the Tuatha Dé Danann in *The Battle of Moytura*. Goibniu is called the Gobbán Saer (Gobbán the Wright), a renowned builder, in the later folk tales. The Dagda (good god) is not found on the Continent and seems to be uniquely Irish. He is also called Eochaid Ollathair (horse-like, the great father) and described as an old man wielding a club (rather than Lug's more sophisticated spear). He is associated with a cauldron of plenty that never empties and therefore with fertility and fecundity. His son Oengus is also called In Mac Óc (the young boy); he seems to be the same as Maponos (the divine youth) who is connected with north Britain and also with healing springs in Gaul.

There are as many goddesses as gods in the early Irish pantheon as most are presented as couples. The goddesses of the land and fertility are associated with animal life and the health of the land; they are found all over Europe.[4] Danu may be the ancestor of the Tuatha Dé Danann; her name is now confused with the goddess Anu, whose name is found on the Kerry mountains as Dá Chích Anann (the two breasts of Anu).

The goddess Brig(it), daughter of the Dagda, appears in the literature. Caesar mentions Minerva as patroness of art and crafts, and Brigit may be her closest Irish associate. She is found widely in the Celtic areas, and her name may mean 'the exalted one'. The word 'Brigantia' is found on Gaulish and British inscriptions as well as on rivers – Brigit in Ireland, Braint in Wales and Brent in England. There were three sisters called Brigit, and they were worshipped by poets and associated with healing and the smith's craft; these triadic groups are quite common in this mythology.[5] The Welsh chronicler, Giraldus Cambrensis (Gerald of Wales), who came to Ireland with the Normans, says that she and nineteen nuns took turns guarding a sacred eternal fire surrounded by a hedge where no man could go. She was seen as a war goddess, the protector and tutelary goddess of the Leinstermen in battle and as the sovereignty goddess. Her Christian feast day is still celebrated on 1 February in Ireland.[6]

The earth herself was revered as a goddess. The rivers, lakes, wells, plains, hills and mountains have names – many of them are of gods and goddesses: Loch Neagh comes from Loch nEchach (Lake of Eochaid < horse); the Isle of Man is named from Manannán mac Lir, god of the sea. Rivers have goddess names such as Boann (Boyne, the fair cow) and the Eithne (Inny). Some of the principal sites – Carmun, Tailltiu, Tlachtga (the Hill of Ward) and Temair (Tara) – are ritual areas named from the deaths and burials of various goddesses associated with fertility and the earth. These were places of assembly and also entrances to the Otherworld at Samain when the doors opened to admit human beings to the other realm.[7] Emain Macha (the twins of Macha) is named from Macha, a goddess who died while racing horses and giving birth to twins. One of the most abiding motifs in the literature is the relationship between this goddess of the land and the male king; their union is seen as a marriage.

Some of the goddesses appear as triadic groups: Éire, Fótla and Banba and triplicity is also found in three-headed statues. Another triadic group, the Mórrígan, along with her two sisters, Badb (crow, raven) who is found on the Continent as Cathubodua (crow, raven of battle) and Macha/Nemain, are associated with war or death and appear as black birds on the battlefield. They seldom participated in the battles but depended on the terror that they inspired as they shape-shifted, created panic and tempted the heroes with sex.[8] This may be another face of the sovereignty goddess who welcomes the king/hero to his destiny and then turns on him at the end of his life. These deities may interfere in the affairs of humans: the Mórrígan and Lug appear in the *Táin*, and a supernatural birdman helps king Conaire Mór.

There are up to four hundred gods and goddesses mentioned in continental inscriptions. On sculptures the gods sometimes appear in zoomorphic images (animal form) or accompanied by bulls, horses, dogs and horned animals associated with their cult. The horned figures may be a stag, a ram or a bull, such as the one that is found on the rock carving at Val Camonica in northern Italy from the fourth century BC. It is Cernunnos (the horned or peaked one), and the name is applied to all images that resemble it. Others appear as antlered gods seated cross-legged with a torc (a necklace) around their necks or as a ram-headed or ram-horned serpent and less frequently as a bull or a stag. The Gundestrup cauldron, found in Denmark in 1891 and dated to the first century BC, is made from silver and bronze and covered with images including a ram-headed serpent, a horned man who may be Cernunnos and a drowning scene.

The bull signifies sovereignty, bravery, manliness and strength, and two bulls are central to the main Ulster Cycle saga the *Táin*. On the Continent an altar in Paris has the image of a bull with a crane on his head and two others on his back, accompanied by the inscription *Tarvos Trigaranus* (a bull with three cranes). The wild boar and the bear are found in the names Dea Arduinna (the boar) and the Dea Artio (bear) that is echoed in the name Cormac son of Art (son of the bear).

The horse is the animal that appears most often in inscriptions, iconography and personal names. The native word (*ech*) is the basis for the male names Eochu/Eochaid. A female version is used in *Roech* (great horse), mother of the great Ulster hero, Fergus mac Róich (The strong man the son of the great horse). Étaín of *Tochmarc Étaíne* (The Wooing of Étaín) is called *Echraide* (horseriding) and there was a Gaulish divine horse or horse goddess Epona. The horse is one of the most important cult animals among the continental Celts and in Ireland. Excavations on the Hill of Tara have revealed the bones of both horses and dogs that show evidence of being eaten. The valley between the Hills of Tara and Skryne is called the Gowra (Gabhra) Valley from the Old Irish word *gabor* (white mare, goat).

It is very difficult to regain the beliefs of the pre-Christian Irish, but there are some hints in the continental accounts. Worship occurred primarily outdoors rather than in large man-built temples; the writer Lucan, describing a grove destroyed by Caesar close to Marseilles, says that the trees were so interlaced that they kept out the sunlight, and that the altars were heaped with hideous offerings. The priests were afraid to go near it, and the images of the gods were primitive and made from tree-trunks.

The information on druids and their practices is equally sparse, and their use of oral tradition alone hid their beliefs from the general public. Caesar says that they believed that, when someone died the soul moved to another body (reincarnation) and that they did not fear death, such was their firm belief in the afterlife. Archaeology shows that grave goods are included in burials both on the Continent and in Ireland. Caesar also accuses the Celts of human sacrifice although the Romans had only recently abandoned the practice. One of the sacrificial methods mentioned was putting the victim in a huge wicker image of a man and burning it.

There were four ritual festivals celebrated in the pre-Christian period, and they still survive in modern Ireland but with a Christian veneer: Samain (summer's end) is now the winter feast of Hallowe'en and All Soul's Day; Imbolc is Brigit's Day; Beltaine is Mayday; and Bilberry Sunday was Lugnasad. The first-century Coligny calendar, from eastern France, which seems to have calculations based on five solar years, mentions Samonios (probably Samain) that may be the beginning of the New Year and winter. Beltaine is seen as the beginning of summer and the second half of the year.

At Samain the border between this world and the Otherworld opens, and there is freedom of passage between the two; the dead may appear to the living, and human beings may enter that mysterious other side. Many stories happen at Samain. This festival is still celebrated widely with bonfires, and children and adults dressing up and playing certain party games. It was called *oíche na bpúcaí* (the night of the *púca*, an impish spirit) and *oíche na sprideanna* (the night of the spirits), and many divination activities and mischievous tricks were carried out. Food like colcannon (potatoes, green cabbage and onion) was served as well as stampy (cakes made of potato and of flour).[9]

The modern Irish word Lúnasa, from the older Lugnasad, comes from *Lug* + *násad* (literally Lug's festival) and seems to reach back to a Gaulish festival at the modern Lyon, in Roman Gaul, to honour the emperor Augustus. Two great assemblies were held in Ireland: the first was the fair (*oenach*) of Carmun celebrated by the king of Tara at Lugnasad, the second, the feast of Tailltiu dedicated by Lug to his foster mother Tailltiu.

Lugnasad is now associated with the fair of Lammas and Christian festivals with names like Garland Sunday when people traditionally pick bilberries and climb Croagh Patrick. This is a time of plenty when the harvest is brought in, and celebrations and open-air assemblies took place in high places such as mountains. Normal sexual restraints were set aside even into the post-Norman period, and this was a time of matchmaking and courtship.[10]

Imbolc is now St Brigit's day (1 February) and is connected to the importance of milk; marriages in early Ireland tended to be made between mid-January and early March and the first children appeared between mid-October and February when sheep came into milk. The Christian feast day is marked by making Brigit's crosses; the shape and size vary according to where they are made. They were believed to prevent illness and cure sick animals, and were placed in the home and in outhouses. Brigit's cloak (*brat Bhríde*) was also associated with healing.[11]

The meaning of Beltaine, now the first day of May, is obscure, but it may mean 'the fire of Bel'; there was a Gaulish god Belenus and *-taine* may come from *tene* (fire); this was originally a time of sexual permissiveness. The festival became associated with other European flower festivals and then dedicated to Mary mother of Jesus. The May bush was brought into the house, fires were lit and the May dew was considered a cure for illnesses and a guard against the magic that might happen at this dangerous time of the year.[12]

Myth is very difficult to define; originally it was understood as something that was believed to be true, or as sacred sagas about real events. A myth indicated something that people of a given time believed to be true regardless of its historical truth. But the meaning changed to 'that which cannot be' and with the arrival of Christianity it came to mean 'falsehood'. The French mythologist M. Eliade described myth as:

> a sacred history; it relates an event that took place in primordial Time, the fabled Time of the 'beginnings'. In other words, myths tell how, through the deeds of Supernatural Beings, a reality came into existence, let it be the whole reality, the Cosmos, or only a fragment of reality – an island, a species of plant, a particular kind of human behaviour, an institution. Myth, then, is always an account of a 'creation', it relates how something was produced, began to *be* ... The actors in Myths are Supernatural Beings. They are known primarily by what they did in the transcendent times of the 'beginning' ...

> In short myths describe the various and sometimes dramatic breakthrough of the sacred (or the 'supernatural') into the world. It is this sudden breakthrough of the sacred that really *establishes* the World and makes it what it is today. Furthermore, it is as a result of the intervention of Supernatural Beings that man himself is what he is today, a mortal, sexed and cultured being.[13]

M.L. Sjoestedt wrote: 'Some peoples, such as the Romans, think of their myths historically; the Irish think of their history mythologically; and so, too, of their geography. Every strange feature of the soil of Ireland is the witness of a myth, and, as it were, its crystallization ... Hence it is easier to describe the mythological world of the Celts than to define it, for definition implies a contrast.'[14] The theories used to interpret mythological material are to be found at the end of this chapter.

The main surviving sagas are: *Aisling Oengusa* (The Dream of Oengus), *Cath Maige Tuired Chonga* (The Battle of Moytura of Cong) (1), *Cath Maige Tuired ocus Genemain Bres meic Elathain ocus a Ríghe* (The Battle of Moytura, the Conception of Bres and his Kingship) (2), *Tochmarc Étaíne* (The Wooing of Étaín) and *Altram Tige dá Medar* (The Nourishment of the House of the two Vessels).

Cath Maige Tuired Chonga (The Battle of Moytura of Cong), the first of two sagas with this title, tells of the battle between the Tuatha Dé Danann and the Fir Bolg (men of bags?) for Ireland. During the course of this tale Nuadu loses his arm. It ends with Bres becoming king of the Tuatha Dé Danann (the main theme of the second saga of this title) and his death is said to take place after he took a drink while hunting in Sliab Gam. Nuadu succeeds him as his missing arm has been replaced.[15]

Cath Maige Tuired (The Battle of Moytura), the most important surviving story of the cycle, is discussed in detail in the chapter on Sovereignty.[16] Ostensibly, the story describes a battle between good and evil, a war of the gods between the Tuatha Dé Danann (The People of the Goddess Danu) and the Fomoirí (anglicized Fomorians, possibly meaning the People from under the Sea) who are often described as being one-armed, one-legged and one-eyed. At another level, it is a saga of three kings – Nuadu, Bres and Lug – each displaying different aspects of the nature of sovereignty and their effects upon the people ruled by these kings.

The saga also includes an explanation of important aspects of Irish life such as true kingship, the power of rightful satire, keening, place naming, fertility, and when to plough, sow and gather the crops. It confirms the position of the people of arts (*áes dána*), particularly the poet, in Irish society. It emphasizes family relationships between father/son, father/daughter and the role of proper marriages versus casual sexual relationships. Many of the events in the saga take place at the winter festival of Samain.[17]

The Tuatha Dé Danann make an alliance with the Fomoirí; Balor the grandson of Nét gives his daughter Eithne to Cian son of Dian Cécht, and she gives birth to a son called Lug. The conception of the second king, Bres, is quite different. His mother Ériu daughter of Delbaeth sees a ship sailing towards her and on board a beautiful man who asks her for an hour of love-making. She agrees without even asking his name and when they are finished she begins to cry. He asks her why and she explains that she regrets leaving him regardless of how they met and that she does not know his name. He tells her he is Elatha mac Delbaith king of the Fomoirí and that she should call her son Eochu Bres. The child grows twice as fast as other children. His mother gives him land, and the Dagda builds him a fort called Dún mBrese. The Tuatha Dé Danann give the kingship to Bres, their own 'adopted son', so that he would improve the relationship between the Tuatha Dé Danann and the Fomoirí. But the choice is illegal; Bres is not entitled to inherit from his mother but only from his father.

Bres is not a suitable king; he shows this by making a number of bad decisions. He allows the Fomoirí to impose tribute on Ireland and reduces the primary warriors, Ogma and the Dagda, to stonemasons and servants. The Dagda is further insulted; not only is he unhappy in his work but afterwards he must confront the idle blind man, Cridenbél, 'whose mouth grew out of his chest'. He threatens to satirize the Dagda unless he receives the three best bits of food on his plate. The Dagda agrees but his 'appearance was the worse for that' and he asks his son, Oengus, for help. Oengus advises the Dagda to place three pieces of gold in the food: these would then be the best bits but would kill Cridenbél. Bres would be forced to decide how Cridenbél should die and would make a bad judgment. The Dagda follows his advice and Cridenbél dies. Bres declares that he died from poisoned herbs, but when his stomach is cut open the pieces of gold are visible and the Dagda is vindicated.

Bres is stingy and does not provide entertainment for his people (generosity is essential in a good king). But his worst decision is to insult Cairpre son of Étaín, the poet of the Tuatha Dé Danann, by his meanness. Cairpre is put in a 'dark, little house' where there was no fire or bedding, and he was given three dry cakes to eat. When he gets up the next day, the poets satirizes Bres and proclaims: 'Bres's prosperity no longer exists'; this was the first satire in Ireland. The king asks for seven years' grace and travels with his mother, Ériu, to the father he has never seen. When his father, Elatha, questions him about his reign, Bres admits that he was unjust and arrogant. But, in an act of misplaced loyalty, Elatha agrees to help his son (in contrast with the proper help received by the Dagda from his son Oengus).

Nuadu's silver hand was given to him by Dian Cécht, the god of healing. Miach, Dian Cécht's son, replaces this with a real hand of flesh in an act of filial disloyalty and Dian Cécht kills him. In contrast, his daughter, Airmed, obeys her father and survives to preside over the healing herbs of their craft.[18]

The Tuatha Dé Danann immediately restore the cured Nuadu as king, and his first act is to hold a great feast at Tara recognizing the necessity for generosity and reversing all of Bres's evils. But the festivities are interrupted by the arrival of a stranger who declares that he is Lug, the son of Cian and of Eithne, daughter of Balor. He is said to be multi-skilled, and when the doorkeeper asks him for his art, Lug lists his talents as follows: builder, smith, champion, harper, warrior, poet, historian, sorcerer, physician, cupbearer, brazier. He asks if they have anyone in the hall who possesses all those skills. To prove his abilities the *fidchell*-board is brought to the door and Lug wins all the games.[19] He is admitted to the hall and given the sage's seat. To further test him, Ogma throws a huge flagstone down the length of the hall knocking down a wall; Lug tosses it back and repairs the wall again. Then Lug plays the three types of music for them on the harp: sleep music so that they sleep for a day; 'sorrowful music so that they were crying and lamenting'; joyful music 'so that they were merry and rejoicing.'

As a result, Nuadu and the Tuatha Dé Danann hold a meeting and decide to give the king's seat to Lug. He then spends a year conferring with Ogma and the Dagda along with Dian Cécht, a leech and the god of healing, and Goibniu the blacksmith on how to defeat the Fomoirí. He also engages the wider group and speaks to the druids as well as to physicians, charioteers, smiths, wealthy landowners, and they 'conversed together secretly.'

The full power of the Tuatha Dé Danann is shown when Lug lists all the skills they possess. In turn, Lug questions Goibniu the smith, Dian Cécht the leech, Créidne the brazier, Luchta the carpenter, Ogma the champion, the Mórrígan, sorcerers, cupbearers, druids, Cairpre the poet, Bé Chuille and Dianann the witches (*bantuathaid*) and the Dagda. Lug uses the Dagda in two separate episodes with women to ensure their loyalty to the Tuatha Dé Danann cause. In the first encounter, the Dagda arranges to meet the Mórrígan at Unshin in Corann. As a result of their sleeping together, the place is called The Bed of the Couple.

Their union leads to the rebirth of the Tuatha Dé Danann, and the Mórrígan helps them against the Fomoirí. The men of Ireland gather a week before Samain, and Lug asks the Dagda to delay the Fomoirí until they are ready for battle. When the Dagda visits them, it is his knowledge of contract, hospitality and his sexual abilities that help the Tuatha Dé Danann. The Fomoirí abuse hospitality by over-feeding and mocking him and then threatening to kill him if he does not eat the enormous meal given to him. When the Fomoirí laugh at the Dagda, they perform a type of illegal satire; but he achieves the delay he required. Later he meets the daughter of Indech of the Fomoirí and, although he wants her, he is impotent because of the size of his belly.[20] Eventually he manages to sleep with her and, as a result of this union, she also helps the Tuatha Dé Danann instead of her own kin.

Just before the battle, Lug collects the various groups around him and asks them what they will provide; Goibniu the smith promises that he will replace their swords for seven years. The others list their skills: Créidne the brazier; Luchta the carpenter; Ogma the champion; the Mórrígan; sorcerers; cupbearers; druids; the poet; the witches Bé Chuille and Dianann and the Dagda.

When the battle is seen to go against the Fomoirí they send Ruadán, the son of Bres, and of Bríg, daughter of the Dagda, to spy on the Tuatha Dé Danann. He is chosen because, like Lug and Bres, he is the product of a mixed marriage. He is asked to kill Goibniu and get a spear from a woman who is grinding weapons. Ruadán wounds Goibniu with the spear, but Goibniu pulls it out and throws it back, killing him. His mother keens her son and it is said that this is the first time that keening was heard in Ireland. Goibniu is healed in a well. Lug escapes from the guard placed on him by the Tuatha Dé Danann; he chants a spell while circling them on one foot and with one eye closed. Shortly afterwards Lug and Balor meet in the centrepiece of the battle; Balor's evil eye opens only on the battlefield, and anyone who looks at it would offer no resistance. Lug casts a sling stone, sending the eye through his head so that it looks at the Fomoirí.

The Tuatha Dé Danann win the battle, and the real meaning of the victory is shown in the meeting between Lug and Bres; Bres asks for mercy but Lug will not decide on his own and gets advice from their wise men. Bres promises that the cows will always be in milk, but this does not free him. Finally he is spared when he reveals the secrets of agriculture: he has power over crops and herds and he lists the days that certain farming activities should take place (these are still used by Scottish farmers).[21] The story ends with two incomplete prophetic poems uttered by the Mórrígan – one on peace and the second that gives a view of the end of the world.

Tochmarc Étaíne (The Wooing of Étaín) is presented as three stories where gods and humans constantly move between this world and the Otherworld.[22] Étaín is the female ancestor of the ill-fated Conaire Mór, a prehistoric king of Tara whose life-cycle is found in the tale *Togail Bruidne da Derga* (The Destruction of the Hostel of Da Derga).[23] She is reborn on a number of occasions, either under her own name or under pseudonyms such as Mess Buachalla. This has been used to suggest a belief in reincarnation in pre-Christian Ireland.

The first story begins with the birth of Oengus son of the Dagda and his occupation of Brú na Bóinne (Newgrange). This also survives as an independent story, *De Gabáil in tSída* (About the Taking of the Fairy Mound), and the theme is also the subject of a poem.[24] The Dagda, also called Eochaid Ollathair (Eochaid the Great Father), is said to 'control the weather and the crops', and he falls in love with Boann (also called Eithne) the wife of Elcmar of the Brú. The Dagda sends Elcmar away so that he can sleep with his wife. Nine months go by as if it was a day and a night; Elcmar never notices that his wife has given birth to Oengus son of the Dagda, and the baby is spirited away to the house of the god Midir at Brí Léith (near Ardagh, Co. Longford). He stays in fosterage until he is re-united with his father the Dagda, who promises that he will have Brú na Bóinne as his inheritance despite the fact that the god Elcmar lives there. He also advises him on how to achieve his aim by visiting the Brú at Samain and threatening to kill Elcmar and to ask for the possession of the mound for a year and day because 'it is in days and night that the world is spent'. This came to pass, and the Dagda gives the dwelling of Clettech to Elcmar instead.[25]

Midir visits Oengus, and a row breaks out between two groups of youths; Midir intervenes, and one youth takes out his eye with a holly spit. With the eye in his hand Midir goes to Oengus who brings him to the god, Dian Cécht, to be healed. Oengus asks Midir to stay for a year but he will only agree in return for certain rewards: an expensive chariot, a mantle and also the fairest woman in Ireland – Étaín Echraide (horse-riding) daughter of Ailill of Ulster. Oengus finds the girl and pays her weight in gold and silver in compensation for her.[26]

Midir and Étaín stay with Oengus for a year; when Midir returns home it emerges that he already has a wife – Fuamnach of the Tuatha Dé Danann, who was raised by a druid.[27] She makes them welcome initially, but as soon as Étaín sits in a chair, Fuamnach touches her with a 'rod of scarlet quickentree' and turns her into a pool of water. The pool becomes a worm that turns into a purple fly as big as a man's head with eyes like precious stones and a fragrance that would turn away hunger and thirst. Fuamnach vows to further injure her and stirs up a wind that blows Étaín around Ireland for seven years until she arrives at Brú na Bóinne to Oengus who welcomes her. He covers her in a purple cloak but Fuamnach blasts her into the air until she lands on a roof in Ulster and falls into a cup in front of the wife of the warrior Étar, and the woman swallows the fly. As a result a daughter is born who is again called Étaín, and it is said that there is a space of 1,012 years between the first conception of Étaín by Ailill and this conception. Étaín grows up to be a most beautiful woman. While she and her companions are swimming a horseman appears and speaks to her in a poem, calling her both Étaín and Bé Finn (fair cow). This is Midir although it is unclear at this point.

The second section of the story concentrates on the relationship between Étaín and her second husband, Eochaid Airem, king of Tara and Ireland, and his brother, Ailill Ánguba, and on Midir's attempts to claim back his wife. Marriage, the requirement for marriage by a proper king and the tempting of a wife to infidelity may underline this part of the saga.

Eochaid Airem is the king of Tara; the men of Ireland refuse to pay their taxes because he has no queen. He sends messengers looking for 'a woman that none of the men of Ireland had known before him.' Étaín is found at Inber Cíchmaine, and Eochaid marries her 'for she was his match in beauty and form and lineage, in splendour and youth and fame.'

Eochaid has two brothers; the first is Eochaid Feidlech who appears in the Heroic Cycle as the father of Medb and her siblings; the second, Ailill Ánguba, who falls in love with Étaín and is constantly staring at her no matter how hard he tries to avoid doing so. The doctor tells him: 'You have one of the two pains that kills a man and that no physician can heal, the pain of love and the pain of jealousy.'

Ailill is dying, but Eochaid goes on a circuit of Ireland, leaving Étaín to look after his death, dig the grave and make the lamentations. Ailill improves as she looks after him, and he admits his love for her. She visits him every day and after twenty-seven days he is nearly cured; and although it is never stated that she will sleep with him this is understood when she promises to meet him on the hill above the court.[28] She tries to meet him on three different occasions, but Ailill cannot stay awake long enough to meet her. A man similar to him appears each time and tells her that Midir of Brí Léith was her first husband and asks her to leave with him. She says that she will not change the king for a man she does not recognize.

Midir admits that he put the idea of love into Ailill's mind and took away his carnal desires so that her honour would not suffer. She agrees to return to him if Eochaid tells her to go. When she returns home, Ailill is cured, her honour is not tainted, and Eochaid is delighted to find his brother well again when he comes back to Tara.[29]

The third story opens with Eochaid watching Mag Breg from Tara; a purple-clad stranger appears beside him although the doors were still unopened. He is Midir, and they agree to play chess using Midir's board because Eochaid's board is in the sleeping queen's bedroom. Midir sets the wager, and Eochaid wins the game. Midir returns the following morning; they play again and Eochaid wins for the second time. As part of the wager, Eochaid asks Midir to complete a series of tasks. Midir offers to play a third time; this time he says that if he wins he will have the right to put his arms around Étaín and give her a kiss. Eochaid agrees that this can happen in a month's time. Midir wins, and Eochaid prepares for his arrival at Tara by locking the court and arranging war-bands and warriors all around. Midir suddenly appears and declares that he has won her fairly and when he puts his arm around her the people 'saw two swans flying around Tara.'

Eochaid will not accept defeat and digs up fairy mounds all over Ireland and meets Midir while digging at the fairy mound of Brí Léith. Midir promises that Étaín will be with them the following day, but when the time arrives he forces Eochaid to choose his wife from fifty women serving drink who all look exactly alike, and when Eochaid chooses one woman he declares: 'That is truly Étaín, though it is not her serving.'[30]

Eochaid brings the woman home only to receive a visit from Midir who says, 'Your wife was pregnant when she was taken from you and she had a daughter, and it is she who is with you now. Your wife is with me and it happens that you have let her go a second time.' Eochaid is horrified that he has slept with his own daughter and that, even worse, she is now pregnant and declares that he and his daughter's daughter will never look at each other. When the girl is born, he orders his servants to throw her in a pit with wild animals but instead they visit the house of Finnlám (Tara's herdsman at Sliab Fuait) and they leave the baby with a dog and her pups where the herdsman and his wife find her and bring her up to adulthood. When the new king of Tara, Eterscél, is looking for a wife, his men come and abduct her and she becomes the mother of Conaire Mór son of Eterscél.

T. Charles-Edwards says that the text works at different levels – the human love-sickness of Ailill and the cunning schemes of Midir to regain his wife. Étaín brings together the worlds of gods and men while they compete for a woman's trust. Midir only managed to recover Étaín because she was willing to leave, and Eochaid had let her go. She was not prepared to allow herself to be bought again.

People turning into swans also appears in *The Dream of Oengus* that was the inspiration for W.B. Yeats's poem *The Song of Wandering Aengus*.[31] Oengus, son of the Dagda and of the river goddess Boann, falls into a love-sickness for a girl who appears to him in a dream. When he finds her, it emerges that she turns into a swan every second year and that she will be in her bird shape at Samain. The only way that Oengus can have her is to become a swan himself. They fly around the lake three times, sending everyone to sleep, before they fly off to Oengus's home at Brú na Bóinne. In the story of the children of Lir the children are turned into swans for 900 years by their jealous stepmother. As well as facilitating the lovers Oengus helps his father in *The Battle of Moytura*. Love-sickness also afflicts lovers in the story of Oengus, Étaín and also Cú Chulainn in *Serglige Con Culainn* (The Love-Sickness of Cú Chulainn).

Altram Tige dá Medar (The Nourishment of the House of the two Vessels) combines the older mythological names and characters with a decidedly Christian theme. The heroine is Eithne, a name commonly used for the sovereignty goddess, and there are numerous saints of the same name, including Laegaire's daughter converted by Patrick.[32] She was born to a steward's wife at the same time as Manannán's wife has a daughter; they are fostered together, and a sun house (*grianán*) was built for them. Finnbarr Meda of the Tuatha Dé Danann visited, and the women were brought to him. Finnbarr makes the strange remark: 'Who is that who is sitting on her heel [?] ... and I had like to name her "heel-sitting" [?].' After this, Eithne can only drink the milk of a dun cow that she milks herself.

Manannán explains that Finnbarr insulted her and that she no longer belongs to their people. Eithne is left in that state until the kingship of Laegaire son of Niall of the Nine Hostages when Patrick arrives in Ireland. The food, the milk of that one cow, was celebrated as the Nurture of the House of two Vessels. One day Eithne and the women are swimming in the Boyne; the other women get their clothes but Eithne does not see them leaving because the magic of the *Féth Fiada* (a magic mist or veil that makes people invisible) has left her. She meets Patrick, who introduces her to books that she reads as if she had always been able to read. A cleric catches a salmon, and she can eat this, grilled with honey. Oengus sets out to look for her; Eithne sees him but she has made the decision to stay with the Christians. Patrick has a conversation with Oengus about the faith, and, when Oengus returns to the Otherworld without Eithne, the Tuatha Dé Danann lament her loudly. At her own request, Patrick baptizes and names her; she dies shortly afterwards, and Cell Eithne at Brú na Bóinne is called after her. Patrick orders that the story be told only to a few good people so that it would get a proper hearing; no one is to sleep or speak during the telling, and if the story is told when a man brings home a wife it will bring good luck to the spouse and children. In the later saga of the children of Lir, the saint Mo-Chaemóc listens to them and ends their extended, suspended animation in the shape of swans.[33]

Addendum – Theory

An exceptional approach to mythology is taken by M. MacNeill, *The Festival of Lughnasa*, where she approaches myth through the legends and rituals of Irish folk tradition.

Comparative mythology fell into disrepute in the 1920s; solar mythology, a belief that the gods represented light and the power of the sun, went out of fashion; but there is a certain resurgence with theories on fire gods.[34] J. Frazer put forward the theory of the myth of the dying god, where the god or hero is killed as a sacrifice to maintain the youth of the world, and this may apply to the figure of Cú Chulainn in this literature.[35]

G. Dumézil used myths from different traditions and said that one could not understand Indo-European culture without learning about the deities, rituals and myths of all the traditions. He considered that myths were based on the moral order of human life and that real life gave rise to features considered 'sacred'. Myths were socially 'real', and the gods represent the significant groups within society. He maintained that Indo-European ideology included three social groups (he called them 'functions') that were organized hierarchically and that the gods represent these in the sagas. The three groups/functions are priests, warriors and the herdsmen or those who work the land with fertility and generosity.

He points to a war between the combined first and second groups against the third as a major theme in mythology and the victory over the third group means that it is merged into the social order of the other two. The three groups are represented in *The Battle of Moytura*: the priests are Nuadu and Lug, Ogma is the warrior, and Bres represents fertility and the knowledge of growing crops. He said that the one-eyedness and the one-armedness of Lug and Nuadu respectively were connected with the first function.[36] Cú Chulainn is Lug's son and seems to imitate him.

One of Dumézil's disciples, S. Wikander, drew attention to the *berserkir* group, 'berserk' comes from this word. These are usually young men who live outside the boundaries of civilised society, also referred to as the *männerbund* (band of men), who were separate from society and known for recklessness. They are best represented in early Irish literature by Finn mac Cumaill and the Fianna.

It is difficult to give a brief overall view of the theories and the beliefs of the structural anthropologist C. Lévi-Strauss; his critics fault him for being difficult to understand, and indeed some of his observations have been described as 'nearly dizzying'.[37]

C.S. Kirk outlines C. Lévi-Strauss's structural approach to myths; the essence of his belief is that myth is a way of communicating like economic exchange or kinship exchanges. He likens myth to language where the sounds mean nothing on their own and are only understood when they are combined and related to other sounds; one myth cannot be understood without all the variations and this gives the true message. For example, the violins would not be enough to give the full flavour of a musical score: the whole orchestra is needed.[38] Along with this he believes that myths mediate between two polar extremes such as black and white, good and evil, high and low, raw and cooked, culture and nature. J.F. Nagy gives a short and precise explanation of C. Lévi-Strauss's methods: 'Briefly … every story has something to say about every other story within the tradition. Every tale, accordingly, can be treated by the mythologist as a multiform of every other, just as every story, in both a thematic and a structural sense, "flows into" every other.'[39]

CHAPTER 3

The Heroic Cycle

Nonetheless, the Ulster Cycle as an independent witness to ancient Celtic Europe can only be discounted fully if we suppose either that pagan Ulster had no native heroic narratives or that the impact of Christianity and literacy was such as to bring pre-existing tradition to a screeching halt, a total disjunction. For a country which was never part of the Roman Empire and for a literature set in that country's own pagan past and expressed in a vernacular language established in prehistory, any such scenario of absolute discontinuity would be what we call in the US 'a hard sell'.[1]

The stories of the Heroic or Ulster Cycle are set mainly in Ulster and the centre is Emain Macha (The Twins of Macha) anglicized as Navan Fort, just outside the modern town of Armagh. The political group of the Ulaid ruled the area in prehistory but had long since been overthrown. As Emain Macha is situated on the edge of the present-day Armagh, it may be that the writers and compilers of this cycle were the Armagh clerics. The tales are set in an era of martial conflict between Connacht and Ulster, but at the time of writing Emain Macha was not and had not been the centre of power for centuries. This genre of literature is also found in Latin, Greek, English, French, German and Nordic countries, and it generally describes an environment that is a throwback to a Golden Heroic Age, without any historical or chronological context. This is the largest cycle, with about seventy-five stories and a large cast of characters, both male and female, including fifty-three warriors.[2]

The king at Emain Macha is Conchobar mac Nessa accompanied by his wife, the queen Mugain. The main hero is Cú Chulainn, son of Deichtire daughter of the king and of Sualdam mac Róich, and his wife is Emer. Sualdam is the lesser known brother of one of the major warriors, Fergus mac Róich, who features extensively in the cycle. Also appearing in the stories are Laeg, Cú Chulainn's charioteer, Laegaire Buadach (the victorious), Conall Cernach, Celtchar mac Uithechair, the learned man Sencha, Blaí Briugu a hospitaller, the female satirist Leborcham (skinny, bent one), the druid Cathbad and Bricriu Nemthenga (of the poisoned tongue) who causes all sorts of arguments. The

Ulaid are seen as enemies of the king and queen of Connacht, Ailill and Medb, during the action of the main text *Táin Bó Cuailnge* (The Cattle Raid of Cooley). (This is abbreviated to the *Táin* from now on.) There are a group of Ulaid with the Connacht camp led by Fergus mac Róich, an exile from his native Ulster. Fergus and Medb are probably mythical in origin, and the gods and goddesses interfere in the action of these sagas from time to time. When the scribes were writing down the stories, the *Táin* is presented as the central saga and many of the other stories are linked to it either directly or indirectly as part of the *Remscéla* (the introductory tales) that are said to precede the main text.

Many of the story types mentioned in the tale lists appear in this cycle: death tales, battles, adventures, feasts, visits to the Otherworld, cattle raids, wooings and destructions. The stories were written for an aristocratic audience, and it is also the aristocrats of society that appear for the most part – little information being given about the lives of ordinary people, although functionaries such as cup-bearers, musicians, charioteers, poets do appear. There seems to be a deliberate attempt at creating a largely pre-Christian society, but some stories mention Christ and Christianity. This cycle dominates the initial period of creative writing of the eighth and ninth centuries and through the period of re-working of the ninth to the twelfth centuries.

There are many similarities between these stories and the classical descriptions of the continental Celts in the accounts of such writers as Julius Caesar and Diodorus Siculus. Some of this material has been taken from the accounts of the writer Posidonius, whose original writings are now lost but which were used as a source by many later chroniclers.[3] The main features include a fondness for feasting, single combat at a feast, a lack of fear, head-hunting, fighting in and from chariots, the warrior's arms, clothing and decoration, their vanity and dedication to appearance.[4] Their clothes are described, including helmets with horns that are said to add height to the warrior. They may have used a stiffening agent in their hair in Ireland; Diodorus Siculus says that the Celts used lime to create a bouffant style.[5] K. Jackson speculated that the Irish remembered their continental, Celtic past and that the stories were written down in the seventh century based on oral tradition. He also said that the events in the Ulster Cycle are not historical but 'extraordinarily similar to that of the Gauls and Britons in the couple of centuries before they were absorbed by Rome'.[6] It is difficult to accept that oral tradition was responsible for the cycle, particularly in view of the uncertain genetic connections between the Irish and the part of the Continent supposedly inhabited by the Celts. J. Koch says that the Irish did not know of Posidonius because they do not acknowledge their descent from the Gauls.[7]

Diodorus Siculus said that the Celts praise themselves in an exaggerated way and are given to self-dramatization. Aristotle commented on their lack of fear and excessive bravery, while Strabo wrote: 'The whole race ... is madly fond of war, high-spirited and quick to battle' and he tells the story of a group of Celts who visited Alexander and while they were drinking he asked them what they feared most, thinking that they would name himself. But they said that they were afraid of nothing except that the sky might fall down on them. A similar boast is found in the *Táin*: when the warriors set out before the last battle, they swear to Conchobar: 'We will hold out, until the earth gives under us, or until the heavens fall on us and make us give way.' [8] The continental accounts also say: 'some of them so far despise death that they descend to battle unclothed except for a girdle', and in the *Táin* a charioteer says, 'They are rushing naked to the battle, with nothing but their weapons.' [9]

The use of chariots in the continental sources agrees with their frequent use in Irish literature although there is little archaeological evidence for them in Ireland. They are fully described in the heroic sagas, and both Patrick and Brigit travel in chariots. The practice of head-hunting, the taking of heads, hanging them from the horses and keeping them as souvenirs is referred to in both the continental and Irish sources. The writer Posidonius mentions the practice of hanging the heads of the enemy from the necks of their horses as they left the scene of battle and then putting them on the doorway of their houses. On his first day as an adult defender of Ulster, Cú Chulainn beheads three giants and ties the heads inside the chariot. [10] Cú Chulainn's head is parted from his body and buried on the top of Tara. [11] Conchobar mac Nessa is killed by a calcified brain taken from a skull that becomes lodged in his head and eventually is dislodged. [12]

The theme of feasting and the champion's portion (*curadmhír*) appears in two texts; *Fled Bricrenn* (Bricriu's Feast) and *Scéla Muicce Meic Da Thó* (The Story of Mac Da Thó's Pig). [13] The best hero was entitled to this and warriors could fight to the death on its account. The continental writers also describe warriors fighting in single combat that could result in death and state that the winner received the thigh portion of the meat.

The plot of the first text is repetitive, as the three warriors, Conall Cernach, Laegaire Buadach and Cú Chulainn, battle with various forces until Cú Chulainn is finally declared the victor. The host, Bricriu of the poisoned tongue, plans this contention and spends a year building a house modelled on the Tech Midchuarta at Tara. He also engineers a contest between the wives of the champions where each woman defends her husband in the *Briatharchath* (the war of words), and Cú Chulainn's wife, Emer, wins out and displays her usual wisdom. [14] Bricriu is humiliated when the women try to enter the house, because he had told them that the first one who enters will be the queen of the province. Cú Chulainn lifts the house for Emer but cannot replace it, and Bricriu and his wife are thrown from their tower onto the dungheap; he is unrecognizable as he enters the house.

There are episodes echoing other texts: Medb rebukes her husband Ailill because he cannot make up his mind; the scene is very similar to the conversation between Mac Da Thó and his wife below. The text says that he 'put his back against the wall, and he was troubled in his mind ...; for three days and three nights he neither ate nor slept.'

The second story has the better plot and shows similarities to the *Táin*. The Ulster and Connachtmen are vying for a dog rather than a bull – a pointless battle that leads to the death of the prized animal and the naming of a landscape. Cú Chulainn is totally absent from this text. A lot of the violence is recounted second-hand, and there is little actual bloodshed.[15]

Mac Da Thó was a hospitaller (*briugu*) in Leinster, the owner of one of five famous hostels of Ireland and of a hound called Ailbe. Messengers come from Ailill and Medb in Connacht and from Conchobar in Ulster, looking for the hound. Mac Da Thó cannot decide who should have the hound and his (unnnamed) wife advises him to give a feast, invite the two groups and allow them to fight it out themselves. He goes three days without food or drink and he cannot sleep and he is tossing and turning at night. His wife speaks to him in verse and says that 'he has need of advice but he speaks to no one.'

At the feast Cet mac Mágach of Connacht is the first to take the knife to cut the pig. A series of Ulster warriors challenge him; he replies to Oengus mac Lám Gábaid that he injured his father and that finishes his challenge. Eogan mac Durthacht and others follow, but Cet deals with them by boasts and heroic deeds that surpass their achievements. The final confrontation happens with Conall Cernach of Ulster and Conall boasts that he is the better hero. Cet agrees but contends that if his brother Anluan were there that he would surpass him. In a dramatic moment, Conall Cernach replies: 'Oh, but he is!' and taking Anluan's head from his wallet he throws it at Cet's breast so that a mouthful of blood splatters over the lips.

Conall Cernach cuts the pig and begins to distribute the meat, but the Connachtmen are unhappy with their share and the fighting begins and spills out onto the green. Mac Da Thó brings out the hound to choose one group, but the dog is killed by a charioteer, Fer Loga. The area is named after him, Mag nAilbi (Moynalvey), and, in a scene reminiscent of the bulls at the end of the *Táin*, other place names are explained from the distribution of its body parts. Fer Loga jumps into Conchobar's chariot and threatens him. Conchobar gives him what he wants in return for his life. Fer Loga says, 'Take me with you to Emain Macha, and every evening send the women of Ulster and their beautiful daughters to sing in chorus "Fer Loga is my darling".' He returns a year later and he has two of Conchobar's horses with golden bridles on each of them.

There are similarities to the *Táin* and the story may be poking fun at it and the cycle in general. Dogs were extremely important animals in early Ireland; the physician, harpist, the queen and, notably, the hospitaller were expected to have one, and they were one of the entertainments at a gathering. The hound Ailbe was related to two other dogs that appear in *Aided Con na Cerda* (Slaying the Hound) and *Aided Cheltchair meic Uithechair* (The Death of Celtchar mac Uithechair).[16]

K. McCone points to a much more serious message in the text; in the book of Genesis, the folly of the man in following the advice of the woman is seen as the male abdicating his responsibility. He analyzes the story of Mac Da Thó's pig along with the other two stories about dogs; each involves the killing of a ferocious hound, but the outcome is different in each case. Cú Chulainn kills the hound and earns his adult identity as a warrior. Fer Loga slays Mac Da Thó's dog Ailbe and bests Conchobar and is treated like a real warrior for a year. In the third, Celtchar's faithful hound, Daelchú (black hound), runs amok; he is killed by Celtchar himself, who also dies in the process.[17]

Another feature of this and other texts is the overwhelming hospitality, generosity and gift-giving that is found in other societies as well.[18] The plots of both stories are also based on a lack of truth that motivates their action. Mac Da Thó shows a cavalier attitude to truth when he follows his wife's advice and promises the hound to both parties, and he does this in private where there are no witnesses.[19]

Many of the stories in the cycle are deliberately connected, directly or indirectly, with the *Táin*. It is presented as the main story of this cycle and the linked stories are referred to as introductory tales (*Remscéla*), many of them included by T. Kinsella in his translation, *The Táin*.[20] Certain stories fill perceived gaps in the *Táin* itself and explain such events as the debility that falls on the Ulstermen, how the story was found and why Fergus and his followers are exiled in Connacht.

The story of the pangs of the Ulstermen explains why they were afflicted with the debility that prevented them from defending Ulster and the meaning of the name Emain Macha. A rich Ulsterman, Crunniuc son of Agnoman, lived alone with his sons, as his wife was dead. A woman came to them and began working in the house and slept with him and they lacked nothing while she was there. A fair was held in Ulster and everyone attended, Crunniuc included. The (unnamed) woman warned him not to boast about her, but despite his promises he boasted about her running abilities, and she was forced to race a chariot while pregnant. The crowd ignored her cries and she cursed them. When the king asked her name, she said she was Macha; and when she had twins, a son and a daughter, Emain Macha (the Twins of Macha) was named from them.

During the birth she said that everyone who heard her screams would suffer from the same pangs for five days and four nights when they were in trouble – everyone except the young boys, the women and Cú Chulainn. Another explanation for the debility is found in a story about Cú Chulainn who is said to live with the fairy woman, Fedelm Foltchaín (fairhaired), wife of Elcmar, for a year. When the Ulstermen see her naked, they are affected by the debility.[21]

There are a lot of theories about the underlying meaning of the debility, and it has been compared with the custom where the man suffers a *couvade* and goes through childbirth with the woman or with a collective rite in honour of the mother-goddess.[22] It has been interpreted as 'death or winter sleep' where the land and its people must be brought back to life by a hero, the young Cú Chulainn in this case, symbolizing the coming of spring and fertility and the triumph over death and decay.[23]

Faillsigiud na Tána (The Revelation of the *Táin*) shows how the story was lost and found again. The loss is explained in the *Táin* when Cú Chulainn kills Roan and Roae, the two poets who were to chronicle the events. It was found when the poets of Ireland are gathered about Senchán Torpéist trying to remember the story. Two of them, Emine, grandson of Ninéne, and Muirgen son of Senchán pass the grave of Fergus mac Róich and raise him from the dead. He tells them the story in its entirety. This scene is reminiscent of a continental account of the Celts who are said to have spent the night near the tombs of their dead heroes awaiting visions from the dead.[24]

De Chophur in dá Muccida (The Conception of the two Swineherds) gives the background to the two bulls and how they were conceived.[25] It begins with an argument between Ochall Ochne the king of the fairy mound of Cruachu in Connacht and Bodb the king of the fairy mound of Femen in Munster. Both of them had pig-keepers; Friuch, called after a boar's bristle, was Bodb's keeper; and Rucht, called after a boar's grunt, was Ochall's keeper; they were friends and practised pagan arts and shape-shifting. They would travel to each other's lands to feed their pigs, but people made trouble between them so that they became enemies. As a result of competition between them that goes too far, they were dismissed as pig-keepers and they shape-shift as birds of prey, water creatures, stags, warriors, dragons and finally maggots. They are drunk by the cows who give birth to the two bulls, Finnbennach the white-horned bull of Connacht and the Donn (brown) of Cuailnge, who appear in the *Táin*.[26]

The Ulster hero, Fergus, is exiled in Connacht with his warriors during the *Táin*, and this is the subject, directly or indirectly, of a number of stories. *Coimpert Conchobair* (The Conception of Conchobar) says that he gave the kingship temporarily to Conchobar because he wanted to marry Nessa, Conchobar's mother, and the Ulstermen refuse to take him back.[27]

He also appears in *Táin Bó Flidais* (The Cattle Raid of Flidais), where Flidais, wife of Ailill Finn, is in love with him. She joins him on the *Táin*, and her cows are used to support the men.[28] Another version says that, while he was king of Ulster for seven years, the sun did not rise over the edge of Emain Macha, and that his kingship was called 'the black reign of Fergus'; but the text also praises his generosity. His huge size is emphasized; he ate and drank for seven men and it took seven women to fulfil his needs until he met Medb.[29]

The first account shows him in a distinctly bad light; the second is ambivalent; but the following version rehabilitates and 'whitewashes' his image, giving rise to 'the most stunning tale ever written in Irish' including the triangular relationship theme that appears in a variety of Irish stories and other literatures.[30] *Loinges mac nUislenn* (The Exile of the sons of Uisliu) begins with a feast organized for the Ulstermen by Feidlimid Dall, Conchobar's storyteller. Feidlimid's (unnamed) pregnant wife walks across the floor and the unborn child screams in her womb. Cathbad forecasts that a beautiful girl will be born and that high-kings will woo her; she will be called Derdriu, and disaster will follow her. The men want the baby killed but Conchobar orders that she be fostered secretly until she is old enough to marry him. No one is allowed to visit her except Leborcham, the female satirist.

On a snowy day in winter, Derdriu sees her foster father skinning a calf, and a raven drinking the blood. She says to Leborcham that she wishes that she had a man with those colours (white skin, black hair and red lips), and the satirist tells her, 'He is nearby, Naíse son of Uisliu'. Shortly afterwards the two young people meet, and he comments on the fine heifer walking by; when she says that she chooses a young bull like him rather than Conchobar, Naíse rejects her. She takes hold of his ears and and says: 'These are two ears of shame and derision unless you take me with you!'[31] As a result, Naíse, his two brothers Ainle and Ardán, with warriors, women and hounds flee from Conchobar. They stay in Ireland but are forced abroad to Scotland; when the king of Scotland wants her for himself, they move to an island in the sea.

Conchobar is persuaded to allow them to return, and he sends three guarantors, namely Fergus mac Róich, Dubthach and Fiacha son of Fergus, to give them safe passage to Ulster. But when they return, on Conchobar's orders, Fergus is invited to many feasts by the Ulstermen, thus becoming separated from the others. When the brothers arrive at the green at Emain Macha, the warrior Eogan mac Durthacht breaks Naíse's back and the rest of the men are hunted and killed. Derdriu is brought, hands tied, to Conchobar.

Conchobar keeps Derdriu with him for a year, and for that period she 'did not laugh or smile or have her fill of food or sleep.' She recites two poems in praise of her life with Naíse and his brothers in the wilderness, extolling the food, drink and music that they experienced.

The king asks her whom she hates the most; she replies, Eogan mac Durthacht and himself. Conchobar says that she will spend a year with Eogan. The following day they visit a fair at Emain Macha, and Derdriu is in the chariot behind Eogan. She had sworn that she would never see her two companions, Conchobar and Eogan, in one place. She sees a boulder and hits her head against it so that the stone makes fragments of her head and she dies. When news of the murders reaches Fergus, there is a slaughter as he takes revenge before leaving Ulster for Connacht with three thousand exiles, and for sixteen years there was 'crying and trembling' in Ulster every night.

In *Táin Bó Fraích* (The Cattle Raid of Fraech), Fraech (heather) is said to join the *Táin* with his cows. He is the son of Idath, a Connacht king, and of Bé Finn, sister to the Boann (river Boyne), and is the most beautiful warrior in Ireland. His mother gave him twelve white, red-eared cows from the Otherworld; these he kept for eight years without taking a wife. Finnabair, daughter of Ailill and Medb of Connacht, loved him, and when he decides to visit her, his aunt gives him wonderful presents: cloaks, tunics and silver shields with rims of gold from the Otherworld. Ailill and Medb welcome them, and they all play chess (*fidchell*), the board being described as follows: 'There was a board of white bronze with four corners of gold. A torch of precious stone gave them light. The chessmen on the board were of gold and silver.' Then Fraech's harpers play for the people:

> They had harp-bags of otter-skins ... Coverings of linen, white as the plumage of a swan, around the strings. Harps of gold and silver and white bronze with figures of serpents and birds and hounds on them. Those figures were of gold and silver. When the strings were set in motion those figures used to turn around the men. They play to them then so that twelve men of their household die of weeping and sadness.

The three brothers Goltraiges, Gentraiges and Suantraiges sons of Boann play three types of music and the brothers are named from the music played by Uaithne, the Dagda's harper. The music puts everyone to sleep. On awaking Boann makes the ominous statement: 'Men will die on hearing them [the three types of music] being played' and they stop playing. Three days pass as one as they play chess. As a sign of her love Finnabair gives Fraech a ring that her father, Ailill, had given to her as a present. When Fraech requests her hand Ailill demands an exorbitant bride price and Fraech declares that he would not pay this for Medb herself. Ailill and Medb decide to kill him in case he kills

Finnabair. Ailill asks Fraech to show them his swimming ability in a river that contains a water-monster. While Fraech is swimming, Ailill sees the ring in Fraech's purse and throws it in the river where a salmon swallows it. The water-monster attacks Fraech and Finnabair hands him his sword so that he can kill the beast. Although he is gravely wounded, his mother brings him to the Otherworld where he is cured completely. Ailill orders Finnabair to return the ring to him but she cannot since it is still in the salmon. Fraech arranges for the salmon to be served on a plate and the ring is restored.

Finnabair is given in marriage to Fraech, and Ailill promises that he may sleep with her when he brings his cows to the cattle raid. He leaves to return home alone, where his mother informs him that his cattle, wife and three sons have been taken. This wife was not mentioned until now. He and Conall Cernach travel to the Alps, where an Irish woman helps them to recover his wife who is guarded by a serpent that jumps into Conall Cernach's belt. When Fraech finds his wife Conall releases the serpent again. He brings his family and cattle home before joining the *Táin*. J. Carney maintains that two stories are combined here, the first about Fraech and Finnabair and the second about the cattle raid, that the *táin* element is necessary to follow the other tales of this type, and that the motifs of love and the ring came from an English saga.[32]

As part of *Tochmarc Emere* (The Wooing of Emer), Cú Chulainn visits the Otherworld and makes Aífe, one of the women who is training him, pregnant. He leaves a ring for his unborn son and says that she is to send him to Ireland once it fits him. He gives him the name Conla and says that he is not to make his name known to any man or to refuse combat. The boy follows his instruction in *Aided Óenfhir Aífe* (The Death of Aífe's Only Son) and visits Ulster when he is seven years old. He arrives in a bronze boat and performs extraordinary tricks; Conchobar says that a warrior should go out to meet him. They send Condere mac Echach, who asks him his name. The boy refuses and they speak, mostly in verse. Then the boy disgraces Conall Cernach and no one but Cú Chulainn will meet him. His wife Emer intervenes, saying that he cannot kill his own son. She has no children and defends the boy as if he were her own, but Cú Chulainn will not listen to her advice. In the wrestling match between them, the boy forces Cú Chulainn so that his feet sink in the stone up to his ankles. Cú Chulainn uses the *gae bolga* to defeat Conla (who is nearly a match for his father), and carries him to the Ulstermen before he dies.[33]

The *Táin* is probably the best known of the early sagas today and, with 4,000 lines, it is the longest tale from this period, the next in length being *The Destruction of the Hostel of Da Derga*. It marks a departure from the style of the stories discussed earlier, and the plot flags in the middle. The oldest version is found in *The Book of the Dun Cow* and other manuscripts, and the second in the twelfth-century Book of Leinster.[34] T. Kinsella based his translation mainly on the Book of Leinster version that includes the Pillow Talk between Ailill and Medb the king and queen of Connacht; this sets the tone for the rest of the saga and places a lot of responsibility for events on Medb and casts her in a particularly malevolent role. The physical route of the *Táin* is found in the first section of *Aspects of the Táin* and there is a map of the route at the beginning of *The Táin* by T. Kinsella. It is possible that the story retains a vague historical folk memory of the early fifth-century downfall of the Ulaid at Emain Macha, since the enemy is seen as coming from Connacht or Tara.

The basic plot is relatively simple, the main episodes being: the Connachtmen's march northwards to take a bull; fights at a ford; a final battle between two armies; and the fight of the two bulls. The story is expanded by dozens of fights at fords between Cú Chulainn and Connacht warriors, scores of onomastic legends, the use of the 'watchman device', and long lists of characters and descriptive passages.

The Book of Leinster version begins with the Pillow Talk where Ailill and Medb argue about their respective wealth and marriage. Ailill says, 'It struck me ... how much better off you are today than the day I married you.'[35] Medb boasts that her father, Eochaid Feidlech, gave Connacht to her, a legal impossibility as women could seldom inherit land. She hints at her mythical origins, saying that she 'never had one man without another waiting in his shadow' and she chose Ailill because he was not 'greedy or jealous or sluggish.' Ailill says that he succeeded his mother in the kingship – another highly unlikely scenario, as a man cannot inherit through his mother. Both of them count their possessions until it emerges that Ailill has a great bull (Finnbennach) which had been a calf of one of Medb's cows and, refusing to be led by a woman, joined the king's herd.

Medb sends their messenger Mac Roth, with nine companions, to Ulster to get the Donn Cuailnge (the brown bull of Cooley) for her. The Ulstermen at first agree, but the messengers start drinking and a row breaks out and they refuse to send the bull. Ailill and Medb assemble an army; before they leave, they meet the female seer, Fedelm, who warns them of impending defeat, but they ignore her.

The first stage takes them to Cúil Sibrille (Kells) where they spend the night. The snow is so deep that it reaches the men's belts – a sure sign that they are raiding at the wrong time of the year (it is Samain, November). The army has no peace that night and Fergus (one of the Ulstermen in their midst) sends a warning to Ulster. Although Cú Chulainn feels the army's presence, he promises to meet and spend the night with Fedelm Noíchride.

The army passes the time listening to the boyhood deeds of Cú Chulainn as told by the Ulstermen. (These are outlined in detail, below, in the chapter on the Heroic Biography.) At the age of five, he leaves Muirthemne in Louth for Emain

Macha to join a troop of boys being trained by Conchobar. He has his toy shield, javelin, hurling-stick and a ball, playing games as he goes along. He joins the boy's games without permission and they attack him. For the first time, the distortion appears (*riastrad*) – the metamorphosis that occurs when he loses control in battle or conflict:

> it seemed each hair was hammered into his head, so sharply they shot upright. You would swear a fire-speck tipped each hair. He squeezed one eye narrower than the eye of a needle; he opened the other wider than the mouth of a goblet. He bared his jaws to the ear; he peeled back his lips to the eye-teeth till his gullet showed. The hero-halo rose up from the crown of his head.

Cú Chulainn beats the boys at their games and explains himself to king Conchobar. Later he is invited to a feast with the smith Cualu but comes late and the gates are closed before him and the hound is on guard. Cú Chulainn grasps the dog and smashes it against a stone. When the smith complains, Cú Chulainn offers to act as his watchdog until he gets another hound. Then the druid, Cathbad, declares that his name shall be Cú Chulainn. The most dramatic story tells of how Cú Chulainn, who would take only Conchobar's own chariot, persuades the charioteer to take him to the border of the kingdom, where he kills three giants. The distortion overcomes him again, and he frightens the people on his return to Emain Macha. The women expose their breasts to him before he is put in three different vats of water to cool him down.

The army then moves to Mag Mucceda (The Plain of the Pigkeepers). Cú Chulainn fells an oak tree and cuts an ogam message into its side that no one could pass until a warrior had leaped it in his chariot. Fraech, son of Fidach, sent to fight Cú Chulainn, is killed at Áth Fraích and buried at Síd Fraích. Cú Chulainn swears an oath that he will fire a sling-stone at Ailill and Medb, and he kills the squirrel sitting on her neck and a pet bird on Ailill's neck. At this point he also kills Roan and Roae, the two chroniclers of the *Táin*. Meanwhile, in the Connacht camp, Ailill sends his charioteer Cuillius to spy on Medb and Fergus. He finds the couple together and takes Fergus's sword, signalling that he knows what is going on between them. Ailill excuses her on the basis that she does it to help the *Táin*. Fergus does notice that his sword has disappeared.

Mac Roth, the messenger, is sent with terms to Cú Chulainn. Ailill offers him land in Connacht, a chariot with the harness of twelve men, and twenty-one bondsmaids. Cú Chulainn refuses, but they agree terms whereby a warrior will be sent to fight him every day. They send Etercumal, foster son of Ailill and Medb, to him and Cú Chulainn cuts the sod from under his feet, takes his clothes from him leaving his skin untouched and shears off his hair without touching the skin. Etercumal still refuses to leave, and Cú Chulainn cuts him to the navel. One warrior escapes from him (Láréne son of Nos), but afterwards he cannot empty his bowels or eat without groaning.

Cú Chulainn meets the Mórrígan, who wishes to sleep with him; he refuses, a gesture that he will later regret when she attacks him. Lug, his supernatural father, comes to his aid, and looks after him for three days and nights. This is followed by pages of descriptions of Cú Chulainn, first dressed in his warrior clothes, then describing his *riastrad* in detail and finally showing him in all his beauty. All the women of Connacht, Medb included, are craning their necks to get a look at him and Medb climbs on the backs of the men to have a glance. Fergus is sent to fight him but only agrees because he is drunk. He brings no sword with him; it was taken when he slept with Medb. The final combat occurs between Ferdia and Cú Chulainn at Áth Fherdia (Ardee), Co. Louth, which is named after the event. He and Cú Chulainn are foster brothers and they are equal in training from their time in the Otherworld. There is one exception – Cú Chulainn's possession of the otherworldly *gae bolga*. Ferdia is offered the same bribes as the other heroes but on a grander scale. Medb threatens to have him satirized and Finnabair sits beside him with her shirt open at the neck, saying that 'Ferdia was her darling and her chosen beloved of the whole world.' Ferdia eventually agrees to fight Cú Chulainn.[36] The encounter lasts four days; they fight by day and look after each other by night, each allowing the other a choice of weapons for one day. Finally, Cú Chulainn throws the *gae bolga* at Ferdia, it goes right through him and, as he retrieves the weapon, it destroys Ferdia's body.

Now the pangs of the Ulstermen come to an end, and the approaching Ulster army is described by Mac Roth in the formulaic way known as the 'watchman device' (see below; p. 54). The device is used again as the charioteer describes the fighting groups to the wounded Cú Chulainn, including those that are 'rushing naked to the battle, with nothing but their weapons.' Laeg tells him that the warriors have said, 'We will hold out until the earth gives under us, or until the heavens fall on us and make us give way.'

At this point Medb gets her period or else must go to the toilet. Fergus accuses her of picking a bad time but she replies that she will die if she cannot do it. What she releases dug 'three great channels, each big enough to take a household. The place is called Fual Medba 'Medb's foul place' ever since.' Cú Chulainn spares her for he did not kill women, and he takes his anger out on the landscape; he stops at Áth Luain and takes the tops off the hills nearby. As a result they are called the Bald-topped Hills in answer to the three Bald-topped Hills in Meath. The text continues with the statement damning to Medb: 'We followed the rump of a misguided woman,' Fergus said. 'It is the usual thing for a herd led by a mare to be strayed and destroyed.'

The story continues with the fight of the bulls, indicating how important they are to the plot and the topographical outcome of their deaths. Place names emerge from their body parts spread through the countryside such as Sliab nAdarca (the Mountain of the Horn). The Donn Cuailnge is seen passing Cruachu with the remains of Finnbennach hanging from his horns. A list of place names appears, such as Finnlethe (the White One's shoulderblade), Áth Luain (the ford of the loins), Tromma (liver). Eventually the Donn Cuailgne himself falls dead, giving rise to the name Druim Tairb (the ridge of the bull).

Discussion of the Táin

The introductory tale on the finding of the Táin shows that the learned class considered the story was lost and that it should be preserved in writing. Bringing Fergus back from the dead to tell the tale shows the respect that they had for 'revelation', and this is projected into the past.[37] The popularity of the Táin today is linked to the nationalism of the late nineteenth and early twentieth century by H. Tristram, who also maintains that the first written version dates from the eleventh century and is based on pre-existing short pieces that would have been known to the audience.[38] These pieces were probably the two separate traditions that combined to produce the saga – the first concerning Medb, Ailill, Fergus and an attempt to take cattle from Ulster; and the second, the stories of Cú Chulainn, a Louth hero who was known to fight at fords and whose life cycle was known already.

Three seventh-century short texts contain the germ of the plot and they are similar to the story known today. The first is the early poem, Conailli Medb Míchuru (Medb Makes Bad Contracts) that mentions the relationship between Medb and Fergus; the prose introduction says: 'For Fergus turned against the Ulstermen because ... of Medb of Cruachain ... for the body of a woman'. The poem concentrates on the exile of Fergus, to Tara in this case: 'His great wolves gathered at stout firm-bordered Tara; they left the great lands of the Ulstermen, for they parted from a prince given to feasting and drinking.' The second source is Verba Scáthaige (The Words of Scáthach, the shadowy one) who trained Cú Chulainn in the Otherworld; she prophesies his future, including duels, the fight of the bulls, stolen cows and Medb and Ailill's boastings of the wounds he will receive. The third source is the Mórrígan's prophecy, probably seventh-century as well, that mentions the black bull along with the people of Brega and Cuailnge.[39] The Verba Scáthaige poem is listed as being in the lost manuscript of Druim Snechta, but the Táin itself is not mentioned in this list; the tale lists include the *Táin*, but separate episodes are also mentioned as individual stories.[40]

This basic storyline is then expanded by the addition of fights at fords, the watchman device, long descriptive passages, lists of characters and explanations of place names. The boyhood deeds and the combat with Ferdia may have been separate stories and added to the text, but they do not exist independently today. The 'watchman device' is used to describe the practice of one character describing an event to another character who then explains what is happening. On one occasion, the messenger Mac Roth describes the advancing Ulster army, while Fergus explains and names each band from the description that he receives; and this happens repeatedly.

The early Irish probably saw their native tradition as equal to the new Latin texts and may have composed the *Táin* to provide a native epic.[41] The text is written in the familiar combination of prose and poetry. H. Abrams defines an epic as: 'a story that is a long narrative poem on a serious subject, told in an elevated style and centred on a hero or a quasi-divine figure on whose actions depends the fate of a tribe, a nation, or the human race.'[42] The definition applies to the *Táin* except that it is written mainly in prose not verse. The story contains a mixture of references to the pre-Christian and early Christian periods, as emerges when the *Táin* is excavated like an archaeological site.[43]

R. Thurneysen said that it dated from the seventh century, contained a memory of the prehistoric battle between the Ulaid of the north and the Connachta of the west, and was influenced by the *Aeneid* to provide an epic for Ireland.[44] The scenes with chariots are very like Ovid's *Metamorphoses*, and parallels are seen between the youthful deeds of Hercules in the Irish translation *Togail Troí* (The Destruction of Troy) and those of Cú Chulainn.[45]

H. Tristram maintains that the *Táin* was written under the influence of commentaries on the Bible and the Irish translations of Latin texts. She says: 'I believe that the first compilation of the *Cattle-raid of Cuailnge* was ... the product of a singular creative act ... about the beginning or the end of the eleventh century though I do not wish to pinpoint when exactly the compiler set to work.'[46] Others have pointed to the area of south-east Ulster and its connection with the struggle for the ninth-century abbacy of Armagh as a reason for its composition.

The tale might belong to the Heroic Cycle, but the *Táin* has many mythological features. The central role of the bulls is recognized by commentators; the story begins and ends with them, and their deaths baptize the landscape and explain the creation of the land. Bulls are an important part of Celtic names and iconography, and these have come into existence through the swineherds' transformations. R. Ó hUiginn says: 'It is probable that the force of the tale was originally cosmogonic, and dealt with certain aspects of the creation of the Irish world.'[47] This is confirmed by an Indo-European myth that tells of a first sacrifice where a primeval being is killed, the body is dismembered, and the cosmos is formed. The creation of the world through the sacrifice of a man and a bull sets the pattern for all future sacrifice and creation. B. Lincoln remarks that this Irish variant has been changed and is only found at the beginning and the end of 'an epic tale of battle and adventure ... Its central act of sacrifice becomes an epic duel between those noble bulls ... ; it remains recognizable nonetheless.'[48]

Apart from Cú Chulainn, who is the son of the god Lug, both Medb and Fergus were probably originally deities, but they both function on a human level within the tale. Medb uses her daughter Finnabair as a prize throughout the *Táin* and as a symbol of sovereignty, as if Finnabair is replacing her mother. The Mórrígan also interferes in the action from time to time.

CHAPTER 4

The Fenian Cycle

'*Fírinne inár gcroí, lúth inár lámh is beart de réir ár mbriathar.*'

The truth of our hearts, the strength of our arms, and the constancy of our tongues.[1]

(Motto of the Fianna)

This story cycle centres on the southern part of the country, mainly Leinster but also Munster, in contrast with the Heroic Cycle that is situated mainly in Connacht and Ulster. The word *fian* means 'a group of warriors' and there are three *fiana* leaders mentioned in the early literature – Fothad Canainne, Ailill Flann Bec and (the most famous) Finn mac Cumaill – and most of the stories that exist concern Finn and his *fian* in particular, but Fothad Canainne does also feature.[2] The main characters, apart from Finn, are his son Oisín, his grandson Oscar son of Oisín, Caílte son of Rónán, Diarmait mac Duibne (ua Duibne) and Finn's enemy Goll mac Morna. There are not as many female characters in these stories as in the Heroic Cycle but Finn and his followers do have relationships, often brief liaisons, with various women. In the older material there is an animosity between Finn and the kings of Tara that disappears in the modern stories. From the beginning, however, Finn is not simply a Fenian warrior/hunter; his role as mantic poet is central to many of the tales, and early Irish seasonal poems are attributed to him.

There are very few full tales from the earliest period; the cycle develops after the twelfth century, and most of the stories of the Fianna such as *Feis Tighe Conáin* (The Feast of Conán's House) and *Cath Gabhra* (The Battle of Gabhra) belong to the Classical and Modern Irish period.[3] From the twelfth to the seventeenth century the Fenian lays (*laoithe*) appeared, and these became the common way to tell the stories of the Fianna both in Ireland and Scotland. There is a large collection in the seventeenth-century *Duanaire Finn* (The Poem Book of Finn) written in Ostend and Louvain. Many of the earlier texts have not been edited or translated for over a hundred years, and they are not as accessible as the Heroic Cycle; the stories of the Fianna may have been considered closer to paganism – which may explain why they did not receive the same epic treatment.

Fénnidecht, 'being a féinnid', can be a temporary state, and *The instructions of Cormac* says: 'everyone is a fían-member until landowning.'[4] The Fianna are young men returning from fosterage and most of them will become responsible adults who will inherit land, marry and settle down. Others, however, may choose this as a permanent way of life and then band together in what is called a *fian* with a *rígféinnid* (chief *féinnid*) and live by hunting, plundering the countryside around them and hiring themselves out as mercenaries. This defines the *fian's* relationship with similar institutions in other parts of the Indo-European world 'for making boys into men and establishing male societies within or outside society proper.' In literature, the Fianna may play an important part in cultural values, in a negative way, by showing what they are not. They fight for social order by fighting on behalf of kings against otherworldly and 'alien' beings (as when the young Finn kills the monster Aillén at Tara), and they mix with poets, seers and others in and outside society.

Early Ireland differentiated between the 'civilized' inhabited areas and the neutral areas in-between, including the forests, marshes, mountains and bogs that are the abode of the Fianna. Several incidents occur when the hero fights the enemy at the entrance to a fairy mound. The Fianna are the permanently unruly warriors and heroes who never fully enter the civilized world but live as outsiders in the same space as poets, animals and mad men.[5]

A. Van Gennep describes the 'life crises' suffered by people who deal with change by rites of passage.[6] While moving from one life stage to another, a person separates from the previous state, spends time in transition and then becomes incorporated into the next point in life. The transitional stage is the most dangerous as it is possible that the person will never move from this in-between position. J.F. Nagy gives his definition of liminality, the transitional stage: 'I refer to the state of being in between separate categories of space, time or identity. A boy who is on the verge of manhood is a liminal figure, as is someone who crosses from one world into another.'[7] In his review of Nagy's *Wisdom of the outlaw*, R.M. Scowcroft shows that many Fenian texts cannot be fully understood without a knowledge of what liminality means: 'A number of Fenian narratives seem to be about liminality, as abstract paintings are often about the structures and principles underlying representational art.'[8] Liminality is discussed in detail in the chapter on the Heroic Biography.

Although there are parallels between Finn and Lug (and the Welsh figure Gwynn ap Nudd = Finn son of Nuadu), they are not related. They both fight one-eyed monsters, but Lug is definitely a god and Finn is not: he dies and 'when he is dead he is dead.'[9] It is Cú Chulainn, Lug's son, who shows most similarities with Finn, and he has been described as 'the hero of the tribe' in contrast with the Fianna 'the heroes outside the tribe.' Although the two cycles are separate, the heroes are intimately connected with a canine image – Cú Chulainn with the domesticated watchdog and Finn with the wolf that roamed medieval Ireland. K. Chadbourne says: 'dogs may arguably be called the soul of the *fían*.'[10]

This association with wild animals borders on anthropomorphism (attributing human characteristics to animals) and lycanthropy (the transformation of a man into a wolf). Some personal names contain the words for deer: Oisín (the little deer) and Oscar (deer-loving), Eltan, an ancestor of Finn, may go back to the word for hind (*eilit*), and Finn meets a woman called Damnat (from the word for stag, *dam*). Women appear as deer in the stories and in folklore; Oisín's mother is often said to be a deer called Blá, on this Scottish and Irish folklore agree, and say that she touched his forehead with her tongue once and he grew deer's fur. When Finn turns down the woman Uaine because she can change shape, she takes revenge by becoming a deer to lure the Fianna on a dangerous hunt.[11]

These half-animal, wolf-like qualities link them to werewolves, and on one occasion Finn meets a woman called Donait who is so impressed with his leaping abilities that she gives him clothes to replace the animal skins that he is wearing while living in trees. The same leaping eventually kills him.[12] The personal name Faelán comes from a word for 'wolf' (*fael*) and the word for 'wolfing' (*faelad*) is used to describe Laignech Faelad a man who becomes a werewolf.[13] The members of the Fianna are related to the plunderer (*díberg*), who gathered as groups of young men living outside society, and who appear to be the Irish equivalent of the Germanic *männerbund* or the Scandinavian *berserkir* (bare shirt), referring to their tendency to go to battle wearing very little clothing.

Another feature of many of the Fianna characters, including Finn, is that they are particularly long-lived and can tell tales that may be incongruous to Christianity. Finn is said to be reincarnated as the king Mongán mac Fiachna (†625) of Dál Fiatach, who is said to be the son of Manannán mac Lir, god of the sea.[14]

Many of the stories here are related to Finn's biography and as such will be discussed in the chapter on the Heroic Biography. There are short texts like *Reicne Fothaid Canainne* (The Poem of Fothad Canainne) and two short anecdotes – one about Finn and the jester Lomnae and another from *Cormac's Glossary* – as well as a story about Finn and the Phantoms.[15] Some of the older tales are not only fragmentary but have no beginning and/or or no end; the stories of Finn's boyhood deeds, his death tales and *The Interviewing of the Old Men* all end mid-sentence or are simply 'open-ended'. As J.F. Nagy comments: 'If the tradition were to allow them to grow up – that is, leave the society of the fían and rejoin their real societies – the tradition itself would disappear, and the magic of ever-continuing transition would vanish.'[16]

Áirem Muintire Finn (The Enumeration of Finn's People) outlines the ordeals that young men go through to become a member of the Fianna.[17] They break ties with their families, there is no compensation for their deaths, and their own actions do not need to be compensated. The tests include one where the warrior's hair is braided and he runs through the woods followed by members of the *fian* with only a forest bough between them at first; if he is overtaken and wounded, he is not accepted. This is also the case if his weapons quiver in his hand or if the braided hair is disturbed by the branch of a tree; and he must also be able to take a thorn from his foot while running.

Finn took control of his band of Fianna from his dead father, Cumall, and they were known as the Clanna Baíscne. His chief enemy was the Clanna Morna, led by Goll mac Morna, who killed Cumall in *Fotha Catha Cnucha* (The Reason for the Battle of Cnucha), which tells how Finn eventually became the leader of the Fianna and gave his maternal family background.[18] The prehistoric king Catháir Mór was then king of Tara, and Conn of the Hundred Battles was at Kells. Nuadu was Catháir's druid, and when he asked the king for land in Leinster he was given his choice and he chose Almu (the Hill of Allen); his wife's name was also Almu and she died and was buried in that place. Nuadu's son Tadg was married to Rairiu, and when Nuadu died, Tadg inherited Almu and became Catháir's druid. They had a daughter, Muirne Muinchaem, and many men came to court her, including Cumall son of Trénmór who was the leader of the Fianna in the service of Conn of the Hundred Battles. But Tadg, knowing that he would lose Almu through this, refused to give his daughter to Cumall so she eloped with him. Tadg complained to the king of Tara, and Conn sent messengers to Cumall asking him to return the girl; but he would not agree.

The battle of Cnucha was fought at Castleknock in Co. Dublin as a result; the army of the Fianna was slaughtered and Cumall fell at the hand of Goll son of Morna. Goll was hit in one eye by Luchet, which is why he was called Goll (one-eyed). Goll killed Luchet, and from this arose the hereditary enmity between the Clann Morna and the family of Cumall. Muirne went to the king Conn; her father refused to take her back as she was now pregnant. Her father ordered his people to burn her, but they were afraid to do this because of Conn. Muirne delivered the baby while under the protection of Fiacail mac Conchinn (tooth son of hound head), whose wife, Bodbmall a druidess, was Conn's sister. The child was first called Demne, and later called Finn (as Cú Chulainn was first named Sétanta). When he was older, he challenged Tadg and took Almu (the Hill of Allen) where he lived for his lifetime.

The *Macgníomhartha Finn* (The Boyhood Deeds of Finn) gives the most complete version of Finn's youth.[19] When Cumall dies, Muirne is left pregnant, and the baby is fostered by Bodbmall, Fiacail mac Conchinn and the Liath

Luachra (the grey one of Luachair). His mother only visits him once. When he grows up, his ability to hunt is the first skill that he shows when he brings ducks home to his fosterers. Shortly afterwards he tries to join a group of boys who are playing hurling at Mag Life, and he defeats them. One of the men tells the boys to kill Finn. This is similar but also very different from Cú Chulainn's arrival at Emain Macha. Finn fails to integrate where Cú Chulainn joins and becomes accepted.

He wanders around Ireland for the remainder of this text, and this knowledge will be of benefit to him at a later stage. When Bodbmall and Liath Luachra say that they cannot hunt anymore, he catches a wild deer and now he is the sole hunter. Shortly afterwards he leaves them, never to return and from then on he is totally alone. In Killarney he joins the king of Benntraige, but the king suspects his identity and he leaves. On a second occasion he becomes an attendant to the king of North Kerry. The king recognizes him and tells him to leave as he may be killed for having him in his company.

He reaches the banks of the Boyne and meets another Finn, a poet, who has been waiting seven years for the salmon because a prophecy said that a Finn would eat the salmon and gain all knowledge as a result. Finn the poet catches the fish and, leaving Finn (Demne) in charge, he tells him not to eat it. When Finn returns, Demne admits that he burned his thumb and then put it in his mouth and gained the 'knowledge that illuminates' (*imbas forosna*). The story draws to a close at Sliab Slanga (Sliab Donard, Co. Down), where Finn meets three women with the 'horns of *síd* women'; the women run when they see Finn and he takes a brooch from one of them as they run into the fairy mound. The woman asks him to return it because it will be a blemish if she enters without it; she promises him a reward ... The story stops at that point and this is the only version.

There are two other accounts of how Finn acquires his prophetic knowledge, the first being entitled by its editor 'Finn and the man in the tree'.[20] The otherworldly character, Cúldub, steals food in both stories; he survives in the first and is killed in the second. Finn is eating a meal at Badamair on the banks of the river Siur when Cúldub from the fairy mound at Femen steals his food. This happens on three nights until Finn follows and catches him on the third occasion; as he catches him, Cúldub falls. A woman coming out of the fairy mound with a dripping vessel jams the door against Finn's finger; he puts his finger in his mouth and when he takes it out, he begins to chant and the 'knowledge' illuminates him.

In the second similar text, Finn is at the Curragh, Co. Kildare, and every day a man of his followers is told to cook a pig for dinner.[21] Oisín cooks first, and when it is ready he passes it on a big fork to his comrades but something takes all the pig. He runs after it until he reaches Síd ar Femen, near Cashel. The door is shut after the thing passes into the fairy mound, and Oisín is left standing outside. Finn asks him what happened to the pig, and Oisín replies that it was taken by someone braver than himself. Caílte cooks a pig, and the scene is repeated. On the third day Finn decides that he will cook the pig himself with his spear shaft in his left hand and the other turning the pig. Something takes the pig, and when Finn gives it a blow he hit his back. Finn follows the thief until he breaks its back because it was going into the fairy mound. Finn stretches out his hand at the doorpost and the door closes on his thumb. He hears great wailing and knows that Cúldub (named for the first time) has been killed.

Fothad Canainne, another *fian*-leader, appears in two short texts. The first is *Bruiden Átha* (The Fight at the Ford) where his enmity with Finn is explained: the Fianna killed his sister, Téit, and her husband.[22] Fothad Canainne himself dies as a result of his involvement with a woman in the text *The Poem of Fothad Canainne*. Fothad was in dispute with a man called Ailill Flann Bec; Ailill's wife was better than his own, and Fothad woos her and agrees to her bride price. Ailill follows them, Fothad is beheaded and Ailill's wife brings the head to the grave. Fothad's head then recites the poem that takes up most of the text.[23]

Finn has numerous encounters with women; it is said of him: 'for indeed [in] every mountain region and every forest that Finn used to frequent with his warrior band, moreover, there used to be a particular woman awaiting him in the nearest [inhabited] land'.[24] There is one tale about his separation from Gráinne daughter of king Cormac and a second about his marriage to her sister Ailbe Gruadbrec (freckle-faced), but the one known today is the modern Irish *Tóruigheacht Dhiarmada agus Ghráinne* (The Pursuit of Diarmaid and Gráinne).[25] There is a story entitled *Aithed Gráinne ingine Corbmaic la Diarmait hua nDuibni* (The Elopement of Gráinne daughter of Cormac with Diarmait ua Duibne) in the tale lists, but no text exists for it. There are similar elopment stories: Derdriu and Naíse; the tales of the kings Cano mac Gartnáin and Rónán and his young wife; the relationship between two poets, Liadan and Cuirithir, who are involved in a triangular relationship with the Church; and the continental version about Tristan and Isolde and their conflict with king Mark.

Finn mac Cumaill's wife has died, and Diorraing, one of his warriors, suggests Gráinne daughter of Cormac as a new wife, but there has been enmity between Finn and King Cormac. Diorraing and Oisín visit Tara, Gráinne seems to agree, and a feast is arranged at the Tech Midchuarta, Tara. There she circulates a goblet with liquor that puts most of them to sleep; she sits between Oisín and Diarmait and says that it would be better if she were given to a younger warrior. Oisín refuses her as does Diarmait until she puts him under taboos 'of strife and destruction ..., the pain of woman in childbirth and the vision of a dead man over water ... .'

The couple leave Tara, taking horses and a chariot with them and reach Áth Luain (Athlone) on the Shannon. They abandon their horses so that they will be less easy to follow, and Oengus of Brú na Bóinne, Diarmait's foster father, comes to their aid, putting Gráinne under his cloak and bringing her to Ros Dá Róshailech at Limerick. Diarmait is left in a building with seven doors that he has built with the enemy surrounding him. He finds Finn at a door and performs extraordinary feats to leap beyond him and his followers and join Oengus and Gráinne. Oengus leaves them and gives Diarmait advice on how to elude Finn.

A warrior, Muadán, joins them for a while and cooks for them each night. Diarmait leaves uneaten cooked food for Finn to show that he has not slept with Gráinne. After Muadán leaves, Gráinne is walking beside him and a splash of water hits her leg and she says, 'That little drop of errant water is more daring than you are.' On hearing this, Diarmait sleeps with her for the first time.

Diarmait meets the Searbhán Lochlannach (The Surly Norseman) who is guarding a tree with wonderful berries; he can only be killed by three strokes of his own club. Diarmait agrees not to touch the berries in return for the right to hunt and chase. Gráinne is pregnant and demands the berries, but Diarmait does not want to break his pact.[26] He approaches the Searbhán, who says that he will not get the berries even if the child 'would go through Gráinne's side.' Diarmait kills him with three blows of his own club and gives the berries to Gráinne.

Oengus negotiates a peace that lasts for sixteen years. Diarmait and Gráinne have four sons and one daughter who is given great lands. Gráinne wants to invite both Cormac and Finn to a feast, but she decides to hold it in her daughter's house. One night Diarmait is awoken three times by a hound and he goes to Benn Gulban (Co. Sligo), where Finn is waiting for him. He tells Diarmait that the hounds have found the wild pig of Benn Gulban and that it is a taboo for Diarmait to hunt that animal. When Diarmait asks him why, Finn tells him a story about his own father, Donn, who had killed the child of a steward. The dead child had been turned into a pig and its life would be as long as that of Diarmait. This was the very pig, and it was forecast that he would be killed by this pig.

Finn leaves Diarmait but returns when the warrior is mortally wounded; Diarmait reminds him that Finn has the ability to save him by bringing him water in his hands. Finn refuses and then relents, but on two occasion he drops the water and on the third, when he arrives back, Diarmait is dead. Gráinne falls from the ramparts of the rath on hearing of Diarmait's death and, as she is pregnant, three dead sons are born to her. Oengus arrives and brings Diarmait's body to Brú na Bóinne.

There are similarities between this and other Irish stories as well as the continental tale of Tristan and Isolde. Tristan brings Isolde from Ireland by ship to be the wife of King Mark of Cornwall, who is also his uncle. Isolde's mother, an Irish queen, had given her maid, Brangien, a love potion that was to be given to Mark and Isolde on their wedding night; those who took it could not be separated for four years. Both Tristan and Isolde drink this by mistake and immediately fall in love. They worry that her lack of virginity will be discovered, so the maid is brought to Mark instead and then Isolde tries to have her killed. The attempt fails and Isolde is relieved as she regretted her decision. King Mark is eventually convinced of the guilt of the couple and they run away to the wilderness. The use of the servant is similar to *Fingal Rónáin* (The Kinslaying of Rónán).

When Mark finds them asleep, he takes the sword that Tristan has placed between them and places a glove on Isolde in a scene similar to that in the *Táin* when Ailill finds Fergus and Medb together and takes the sword to show that he was there. Eventually Mark takes Isolde back, and Tristan is persuaded to marry another Isolde. He never sleeps with her and when they are out riding water splashes up her leg and she says that it is bolder than her husband. Soon afterwards they begin a normal married life. Tristan returns to Brittany, where he was wounded by a poisoned spear; no one can cure him but the first Isolde. He sends a ring as agreed between them, asking her to come quickly. The messenger is told to hoist a white sail if Isolde is with him and a black one if she has refused. When the ship arrives with the white flag, Tristan's wife Isolde tells him that the flag is black, and he dies. The queen, the other Isolde, finds him dead, lies down beside him and also dies. They are buried in graves beside one another, and a rose bush is planted over Isolde and a vine over Tristan's grave, and these grow into each other and cannot be torn apart.

G. Schoepperle believes that the Irish text is the original and points to detailed similarities in the plots: Tristan leaves a sword between the couple to show that they are not sleeping together, and Diarmait leaves uneaten meat. The splashing motif appears in both stories, but it is an organic part of the Irish story; Diarmait is loyal to Finn and reluctant to make Gráinne his lover. But the way the motif is woven into the Tristan story is puzzling and makes less sense.[27]

J. Carney argues that the continental story was the original, and he gives a comprehensive list of other related texts. He says that the original Tristan tale was composed in North Britain; the Derdriu story is the earliest Irish borrowing of the theme and all the Irish versions are 'secondary and inferior adaptations'.[28]

The Derdriu story is outlined in the Heroic Cycle chapter (above) and the couple live a life close to that of the Fianna. Derdriu mentions a cooking pit (*fulacht*) on the warrior plain (*fian-chlár*) of the forest in a poem at the end of the text.[29] *Fingal Rónáin* (The Kinslaying of Rónán) contains a triangular affair and is discussed in detail in the chapter on the Cycles of the Kings; and in *Scéla*

Cano meic Gartnáin (The Story of Cano mac Gartnáin) Cano visits Marcán who is married to Créd. She is in love with Cano and puts everyone at a feast to sleep except herself and Cano. [30]

There is another short tale with a similar theme, *Scél Baili Binnbérlaig* (The Story of Baile Binnbérlach) where a couple who have never met fall in love – Aillinn of Leinster and Baile of Ulster. [31] They arrange to meet at Ros na Ríg in Brega, but while Baile is waiting an apparition appears to him. It lies to Baile, telling him that Aillinn is dead and that they will never meet in this world but will be inseparable once they are dead. Baile dies on hearing this news, and when his men bury him a yew tree grows from his grave. The top of the tree develops into the likeness of his head. The phantom then travels to Leinster and tells Aillinn that Baile is dead, and she also dies and is buried. An apple tree grows on the grave and looks like her head. After seven years, poets cut down both trees to make a tablet so that they can write stories on them, and at Samain they take the tablets to a feast being held by the king of Tara. As the king holds the tablets, they suddenly jump together and they can never more be separated.

There are a number of texts that tell of the death of Finn, and they generally agree that Finn was killed by the sons of Urgriu of Luigne from Tara at Áth Breá on the Boyne or that he died while trying to jump the Boyne. They are discussed in the chapter on the Heroic Biography. [32] Caílte predicts his own death in the poem *Cnucha cnoc os conn Life* (Cnucha a hill above the Liffey): 'I shall die in Temair … my gravestone will be northwest of Temair, until Doomsday.' [33]

Three battles are mentioned in relation to the destruction of the Fianna but they were finally decimated in 'the cataclysmic Battle of Gabhar' mentioned first in the eleventh century. The king of Tara Cairpre Lifechair son of Cormac mac Airt asked Finn for the hunting of Ireland and he refused. The Fianna send messengers to Cairpre in Tara giving notice of battle, and he invites his allies to join him, including another Oscar, the son of Garad. They look for the king at Tara but find him at Gabar; the battle is waged and the Fianna are destroyed. The battle is also mentioned frequently in later sources such as *Duanaire Finn* (The Book of the Poems of Finn). The Gabhra Valley is located between the hills of Tara and Achall (Skryne) in Co. Meath, and the tale lists also mention *The Battle of Achall*. [34]

Acallam na Senórach (The Interviewing of the Old Men) is the longest text of the cycle and breaks off unfinished after about 160 anecdotes and stories. Written in the familiar mixture of prose and poetry, it gives a wealth of information on the landscape and place names as Oisín and Caílte travel the country with St Patrick and his scribe, Brocán, who writes it all down. Although some stories contain mythological and historical material, most are about the Fianna and their exploits. A lot of the incidents are not found elsewhere; and the author may have taken the opportunity to collect references to older traditions; some of the content is reminiscent of the *Lore of Famous Places*.

The first full story that Caílte tells Patrick involves a warrior, Artúir son of Benne Brit, a member of the Fianna, who decides to travel across the sea and to take Finn's three hounds with him (Bran, Sceolaing and Adnuall).[35] The Fianna follow them, and after many adventures they find Artúir, kill his followers and bring him and the hounds back to Ireland. But they also bring back some wonderful horses and all their horses descend from them. Patrick says that the Fianna and their tale have lightened his spirit but that their prayers are being neglected. The following day, two guardian angels, Ailelán and Solusbrethach visit him, and, when he asks if it is God's will that he listen to the stories of these old warriors, they reply that he should have them written down in refined language, 'so that the hearing of them will provide entertainment for the lords and commons of later times.' This releases Patrick from his guilt and allows him to enjoy these pagan tales and to have them written down.

The story also shows the futility of trying to leave the Fianna and to live a new life. Artúir is brought back but the warriors also gain a new strength in the horses that they use from then on, so this attempt did have some positive outcome. The poignant love story of Cael and Créide gives a similar message. While travelling to fight Cath Finntrága (The Battle of Ventry), they meet Cael who had looked for advice from his foster mother, Muirenn, on how to woo Créide. Finn warns him that she is the most 'deceiving' woman in Ireland and that she has hidden all sorts of treasures in her house. They neglect the battle to visit her and Cael recites a poem in praise of her house that persuades her to marry him. The Fianna celebrate for seven days drinking and eating but Finn is worried about the strangers coming to Ventry.

When the Fianna leave, Finn insists that she go with them so that they have her cattle to help them. Tragedy strikes on the last day, when Cael is drowned while chasing an enemy into the sea. All the wild animals of the same age die of grief when his body is washed ashore. The Fianna carry him to Tráig Caeil (Cael's strand). Créide recites a poem of laments before lying down beside him to die. This is a warning to the men of the Fianna; a young man should not excel too early, and women spell trouble for the Fianna. This is also the fate of Diarmait when he leaves with Gráinne.

Towards the end of the text, Oisín and Caílte visit king Diarmait mac Cerbaill (†565) while he is celebrating the feast at Tara. He asks them who killed Cairpre Lifechair, and Caílte replies that it was Oscar son of Oisín and goes on to describe the others who were killed in *The Battle of Gabhra*. The following morning, Diarmait enquires about the significance of the Lia Fáil; Oisín replies that it shrieked under the rightful king of Ireland and of the province, and, if a barren woman came on it, a dew of black blood appeared, but if the woman was fertile, the moisture was many-coloured. Diarmait asks the final question: 'Who raised the stone or brought it to Ireland?' and the reply is never completed: 'A warrior of great spirit took over the kingdom ...'

When the Fianna tell the tales, they always include information on the land-scape that revives a memory that had been forgotten, just as the *Táin* was reclaimed from the past by poets who brought Fergus mac Róich back from the dead to recite it for them. By knowing the places, he knows the settings of events. Like the stories of Finn's youth and his death, this text has no end. J.F. Nagy says that the meeting of the past tradition with Christianity is central to the text: 'It is therefore appropriate that the text itself ... is almost always truncated – as if it could begin, resume, or be put on hold at any point.'[36] But the story has come full circle: it begins and ends with references to *The Battle of Gabhra*. The text has been described as a frame story, but J.F. Nagy maintains that it is well crafted and deliberately flexible to accommodate the complicated content that it wishes to describe. At one point the author tries to explain the nature of storytelling: Patrick describes one episode as complicated, the word he uses is *gablánach* (from the word *gabul*, branch, fork). This implies that one story is piled upon and conjured up by another and that they are all are inter-connected. It is also difficult to move the stories into a Christian, literary form, and the text seems to behave abnormally, unfolding 'a gigantic series of variations on a limited number of themes' instead of a beginning, a middle and an end.[37]

The story *Oisín i dTír na nÓg* (Oisín in the Land of Youth) is a modern text dating from around the eighteenth century, and better known as a result. Patrick asks Oisín how he lived so long, and he replies that he was at Loch Léin after the battle of Gabhra. A mist, fragrant trees and singing birds surround him, and he sees a woman on a white horse who introduces herself as Niam Cinnóir (goldenhaired). They leave for the Otherworld and the sea opens before them as they head to the west. But Oisín gets homesick and, although she does not want him to leave, Niam gives him the horse and warns him not to set foot on the soil of Ireland.

On his return, he recognizes no one, and when he looks for news of the Fianna he finds Almu covered with nettles and weeds. He sees a group of men trying to lift a flag of marble from people trapped underneath; they will die if they do not get the proper help and Oisín cannot refuse. When he dismounts, the horse runs away, his youth fades and he is left a helpless, blind old man. In common with other Fianna, Oisín is long-lived, but his world is gone and he does not fit into the new one.[38]

CHAPTER 5

The Cycles of the Kings

The third category ... consists of the so-called 'King tales', stories set in a period when writing in the vernacular as well as in Latin had become firmly established in Ireland through the activities of learned men within the monastic communities who had an interest in transferring to writing the traditional oral lore of the secular learned classes.[1]

This Cycle is really a composite one that includes a wide variety of approximately a hundred tales about the prehistoric and historic kings of Ireland. It has been described as 'the historical cycles', but the term suggested by Cross and Slover, 'tales of the traditional kings' did not become common usage, and for convenience 'The Cycles of the Kings' will be used here.[2] The historical content of the stories is questionable, as writing only began in the seventh century; the historian F.J. Byrne says that the legends were probably 'distorted' and 'in the absence of contemporary documents the political scene of the fifth century and *a fortiori* of the preceding centuries is lost to history'.[3]

Many of the historical tales are dominated by the relationship between the Uí Néill and the men of Leinster and their battles that centre on Tara; stories about minor dynasties and characters are relatively rare. There are differences of opinion on the historicity of early figures such as Niall of the Nine Hostages and Cormac mac Airt. The only Niall and Cormac we know anything about are the men in the sagas, and as they are discussed in the chapters on Sovereignty and the Heroic Biography, they do not appear here.

Some of these stories amount to origin legends; Labraid Loingsech (speaker of ships/exile), an ancestor of the Leinstermen, being one of the earliest kings to feature. *Organ Denna Ríg* (The Destruction of Dinn Ríg) tells of Labraid's revenge on Cobthach Cael in an iron house.

Cobthach son of Úgaine Mór is king of northern Leinster, but his brother Laegaire Lorc is king of Ireland; Cobthach is wasting away with jealousy. He plays a dreadful trick on his brother Laegaire; feigning death, he lies in his chariot with a razor. Laegaire comes to mourn him, lies down on him and Cobthach kills him. Then he poisons Laegaire's son, Ailill Áine. Ailill himself had a son called Moen Ollam who was dumb (*moen*). When he was playing on the hurling field one day he was hit by a stick and called out. The other boys shouted: '*Labraid Moen*' (Moen speaks) and that was his name from then on. Cobthach gathers the men of Ireland to the festival of Tara and asks them who is the most generous prince in Ireland. When Craiptine the harpist and Ferchertne the poet reply that it is Labraid, Labraid is exiled with his followers.

They travel to Scoriath the king of Fir Morca, who welcomes them. He has a daughter Moriath, who is constantly watched over by her mother who never sleeps. Moiriath falls in love with Labraid, and Craiptine lulls the mother to sleep so that the lovers can meet. When the mother awakes, she realizes what has happened and wakes her husband saying, 'The breath of woman has your daughter.' Scoiriath eventually accepts Labraid and agrees to help him to regain the kingdom of Leinster. They attack Dinn Ríg, and Craiptine sends the people to sleep. Labraid takes the kingdom of Leinster and, having built a house of iron, he invites Cobthach to a feast. The house is secured and warmed with bellows until all within are killed. Another version says that he becomes dumb when Cobthach made him drink his father and grandfather's hearts blood from a goblet and eat a mouse to its tail. This gave rise to the saying, 'Eating a mouse to its tail'.[4]

The story of the *Bóroma* (Cattle Tribute) begins with Tuathal Techtmar who had two daughters, Fithir and Dáirine, by his queen Báine daughter of Scál (shadow). Eochu Ánchenn king of Leinster asked him for one of his daughters in marriage and he gave him Dáirine, the eldest. But Eochu took a dislike to her and returned to Tuathal and told him that his wife had died and took the younger sister in marriage. When the two girls saw one another, Fithir died of shame and Daírine died of grief. Tuathal immediately went to Leinster looking for compensation for their deaths; his price was one hundred and fifty cows, pigs and cloaks.[5]

The tax continued for centuries but Dúnlaing king of Leinster refused to pay it to Cormac mac Airt, who retaliated by going on a hosting to Leinster at Samain. While he was there, Dúnlaing went to Tara and killed thirty (or three thousand) princesses, including ten daughters of Cormac mac Airt. The tale covers an extensive historical period, and the kings of Tara continued to levy the *bóroma* until the reign of Finnachta Fledach (†695). He took the levy twice, but the Leinstermen refused on the third occasion, and the king Bran son of Conall sent the local saint Mo-Ling to ask for the tribute to be ended. Both sides agreed that it will be cancelled until Monday (*Luan*), but Finnachta has been tricked. The *Luan* intended is the Day of Judgment (the Irish believed this would happen on a Monday); Finnachta has bargained away the tribute forever and is killed shortly afterwards. The sequel to the battle, *Cath Almaine* (The Battle of Allen/Almu), set in the eighth century, is discussed below.

There are a number of stories about the prehistoric king Conn of the Hundred Battles, ancestor of the Connachta and grandfather of Cormac mac Airt. Conn is in conflict with Eogan Mór, king of Munster, and they divide Ireland between them until the battle of Mag Léna when Conn kills Eogan and makes peace in Munster.[6]

King Diarmait mac Cerbaill (†565), a direct descendant of Niall of the Nine Hostages, has attracted a number of unusual stories and events. He gave the famous 'copyright' judgment against Colm Cille; the saint had copied a manuscript belonging to St Finnian and when he asked for the copy back Colm Cille refused to give it to him. Diarmait declared 'To every cow its calf and to every book its copy' and a battle followed at Cúl Dreimne in 561 at the foot of Benbulban, Co. Sligo, in which Diarmait was defeated; but Colm Cille was exiled to Iona as a punishment.[7]

Diarmait had an uneasy relationship with the Church and, after he violated the sanctuary of St Ruadán, twelve saints were assembled to curse Tara and they said that it would be desolate forever. In the sixth century, the Church was severing the connection between Tara and pre-Christian practices and assuring that the kingship of Ireland would now be Christian. Although Clonmacnoise revered Diarmait's memory, negative stories persisted into the eleventh century when some of the accounts of his death tale were written.

Diarmait appears incongruously in sagas with characters who are not his contemporaries, and he is linked with crucial literary events such as *The Interviewing of the Old Men*. He is seen in another story of the Fianna preceding a poem on the kings of Ireland (mentioned also in the Fenian Cycle). Brocán, a hospitaller, had three sons and on his death the local king seized their lands and took the youngest son as a hostage. Their mother was Samnach from whom is named Dún Samnaige (Dunsany, Co. Meath). The older brothers rescued the younger one, Oengus, and they settled in the wild areas – attacking the king at every opportunity. The younger brother went much further than the others, and they accused him of being more like his mother's family (she was descended from Caílte). With this, Caílte appeared and brought them to live with him in a *fian* hut until Diarmait mac Cerbaill became the king and he invited them to take their land.[8]

It was during his reign that a crucial decision was made about the extent of Tara's domain in *Suidigud Tellaig Temra* (The settling of the manor of Tara).[9] The nobles of Ireland were disputing the area of Tara's domain and refused to participate in the Feast of Tara until this question was resolved. Diarmait called on the ancients, Fintan mac Bóchra and Trefuilngnid Tre-eochair (three-sufferers three-keys), as his authority, and they confirmed the domain. The story of his death is in the chapter on the Heroic Biography. The sixth-century Diarmait is also associated with the seventh-century king Mongán in *Baile Mongáin* (Mongán's Vision).[10]

There are stories about Diarmait's sons as well. He has a number of wives including Muirenn Mael (bald) and Mugain daughter of Conchrad mac Duach of Munster. Mugain is barren and very jealous of Muirenn, who has children. She is afraid the king might divorce her, so she tries to take revenge on Muirenn who is bald. Mugain tells a female satirist that she will give her anything she wants if she will remove the queen's golden headdress that covers her bare head. Just as the satirist is removing the head cover, Muirenn calls on God and St Ciarán to help her, and gold hair grows on her head. But Mugain still wants children, so she visits Finnian of Mag Bile (Moville) and bishop Aed to ask for their help. They gave her blessed water to drink, and she gives birth to a lamb, a silver salmon and finally to Aed Sláine.[11]

Orgguin trí mac Diarmata mic Cerbaill (The Slaying of the three sons of Díarmait mac Cerbaill) may have been inspired by the actual killing of two sons of Blathmac son of Aed Sláine, the grandsons of Diarmait. In the story, the sons are Dúnchad, Conall, and Mael Odor, and while they are in Leinster they come up against the warrior Mael Odrán (servant of the otter). When they find him first, he is on foot, but then he gets a horse and chases them towards a mill where an old woman is grinding grain. When the mill moves, the three brothers are crushed to death.[12]

Diarmait invades Leinster to avenge the murder, but the Leinstermen refuse to hand over Mael Odrán. The king stops at Lagore in Meath, and Mael Odrán finds his way to the island where the king and his army are feasting. When Diarmait goes out to relieve himself, Mael Odrán comes up behind him. The king asks him for a wisp and Mael Odrán gives him a bunch of nettles and thistles that sting Diarmait. When he reaches for his sword, his enemy gets to it first and threatens to kill him. The two men make peace and return together. Eventually, Mael Odrán acts as a battle commander for Diarmait. Mael Odrán's own death appears in a separate story where a woman is peripherally involved.[13]

Diarmait's grandsons Diarmait and Blathmac, sons of Aed Sláine, joint kings of Tara, also appear in a number of stories. The plot of *Scéla Cano meic Gartnáin* (The Story of Cano mac Gartnáin) occurs during the reigns of Diarmait and Blathmac (†665). This is the biography of Cano, a Scottish prince from Skye who died in 688, and other people also appear such as his uncle Aedán mac Gabráin (†606) and Guaire (†663). It seems to be a collection of incidents in prose and poetry about Cano and other characters.[14]

Aedán and Gartnán are fighting for the kingdom of Scotland when Aedán kills Gartnán at Skye. Cano son of Gartnán escapes to Ireland where he stays with Diarmait and Blathmac and, at a later stage, with Guaire Aidne and Illann mac Scanláin the king of Corcu Loígde. Aedán sends messengers to Ireland to bribe the kings to kill Cano, but the scheme does not succeed because Diarmait's (unnamed) daughter, who loves Cano, overhears her father plotting and tells Cano of the plan. When Cano speaks to the kings, they tell him that he is safe with them. Cano chases the messengers as far as the sea, but at the last minute he allows them to go free, and Diarmait praises Cano for his patience (*ainmne*).

Cano stays with Guaire in Connacht and falls in love with his daughter, Créd, who is married to Marcán the king of the Uí Mhaine. Colgu, Marcán's son, has already made inappropriate advances towards her. When Cano is leaving to stay with Illann mac Scanláin in Munster, Guaire throws a feast for him. Créd puts a sleeping spell on everyone except for Cano and herself, and asks him to be her lover. Cano says that he will marry her when he becomes king, and gives her a stone that contains his soul that came out of his mother's mouth.

Cano stays with Illann in Munster until hostages arrive from Scotland to promise Cano the kingship, and he goes home. But a year later Cano sees a bloody red wave and takes it as a sign that Illann is dead, so he returns to Ireland with Saxons, Britons and Scotsmen to take revenge. Although he returns to Scotland, every year he tries to meet Créd at Inber Colptha (the estuary of the river Boyne), but Colgu son of Marcán stops him every time, as in *The Wooing of Étaín*. On one occasion they try to meet in a different place, Loch Créda, and Colcu appears again. In the ensuing clash Cano is wounded. Créd thinks that he is dead and, in a scene reminiscent of Derdriu's actions, she smashes her head against a stone. She is carrying the stone that contains his life, and this breaks, resulting in Cano's death some nine days later when he returned to Scotland.

Cano shows the kingly quality of patience rather than the usual prince's truth; while he stays with Diarmait and Blathmac he is rewarded when he gets the kingship of Scotland. He also postpones his relationship with Créd until he achieves the kingship of Scotland.[15] A second feature of the story is that the characters frequently explain themselves by giving, taking, or rejecting advice or warnings. In the incident mentioned above Diarmait's daughter overhears a conversation and warns Cano in five stanzas of poetry, in three parts, and she uses a switch while speaking to him as if it were a ritual.[16] Cano shows his wisdom by heeding her warning in contrast with others who ignore women's words (Medb disregards the words of Fedelm the female prophet in the *Táin*).

The life and death of the saintly Cellach son of Eogan Bél of Connacht is the theme of *Caithréim Cellaig* (The Triumph of Cellach).[17] It tells of the murder of bishop Cellach and the revenge taken by his brother Muiredach. The characters are not historical contemporaries: Guaire died in 663 and Eogan Bél in 542/3; there is no record of the two sons, Cellach or Muiredach, but a son named Ailill Inbanda died in 550. During the tale the joint kings Diarmait and Blathmac (†665) reign in Tara, and king Guaire Aidne, who is usually wise and generous, appears here as a vindictive, vengeful character.

Eogan Bél is killed in battle and his son Cellach is named as his successor. He is with St Ciarán at Clonmacnoise, and the saint refuses to release him from his intention to become a cleric. The people persuade Cellach to leave; Ciarán curses him; but when Cellach does not like being king and gives the kingdom to his brother Muiredach, Ciarán cannot lift the curse. Cellach is filled with the Holy Spirit and becomes a respected bishop.

Guaire invites Cellach to visit him, but as it is Sunday Cellach refuses to travel until Monday. He reaches a desert island on Lough Conn, where he becomes a hermit. His brother visits him for advice and he has four clerics with him, but Guaire has persuaded them to murder Cellach. Afterwards animals gnaw his body until two deer take him to a church where he is buried. Each of the killers dies afterwards.

Muiredach's followers increase, but he does not have enough troops to fight Guaire, so he goes to stay with Marcán king of the Uí Maine. He is now called Cú Choingelt from a water monster that he killed.[18] He also stays with Diarmait and Blathmac the kings of Tara; Blathmac has a daughter Aífe, who falls in love with Cú Choingelt and they get married. After some time she reproaches him for not taking vengeance for Cellach, and he returns to Connacht and kills the murderers, who are dismembered and hanged. Cú Choingelt gains a good reputation as a generous king, and he is persuaded to marry Guaire's daughter Gelgéis. This is a successful marriage until Guaire tricks him into coming to a feast with Ciarán of Clonmacnoise, and when Ciarán leaves, Cú Choingelt is killed. Martyrs are unusual in early Irish literature, and a murdered bishop would be well known and remembered, but, as M. Herbert points out, there is no cult of Cellach in the area associated with his life and death.[19]

Mongán mac Fiachna (†625) is one of the most enigmatic and elusive of historical figures but he is the central character in a number of stories and it seems there was an attempt to build a story cycle around this king of the Dál Fiatach in Ulster. He is associated with both Finn mac Cumaill and Manannán mac Lir; and the swineherds in *The Conception of the Two Swineherds* are said to be able to shape-shift like Mongán.[20] Sometimes he is described as a pagan, and he is mentioned with king Diarmait mac Cerbaill, whose religious affiliations are also in doubt. One brief story explains that Mongán will have no children because he is cursed by Eochaid Rígécess the chief poet of Ireland.[21] His conception and birth is forecast in *Immram Brain* (The Voyage of Bran) while Bran is travelling to the Otherworld and meets Manannán who recites a poem which says that his son, Mongán, will be born to Caintigern wife of Fiachna.[22]

This adulterous relationship appears in the stories of his conception and birth. In *Coimpert Mongáin* (The Conception of Mongán), Fiachna Lurgan king of Ulster, goes to Scotland to help his friend Aedán son of Gabrán in a war against the Saxons.[23] While he is away, a stranger tries to arrange a meeting with his wife; the queen says that nothing would persuade her to be unfaithful to her husband. When the stranger asks if she would sleep with him to save her husband's life, she agrees. The man forecasts that the son born of their union, Mongán, will be famous. This happens and the man goes to Scotland to save Fiachna's life and he returns home. His wife gives birth to a son and tells her husband what happened; he thanks her for all that she did for him, and then the story reveals that the stranger is Manannán mac Lir.

The information is repeated in *Coimpert Mongáin ocus Serc Duibe Lacha do Mongán* (The Conception of Mongán and Dub Lacha's Love for Mongán) but this includes his marriage to Dub Lacha (black duck). They were engaged when they were three days old but Manannán took Mongán to the Otherworld and would not allow him to return to Ireland until he was twelve years old.[24]

In the story entitled *Scél asa mberar co mbad hé Find mac Cumaill Mongán* (A Story that says that Mongán was Finn mac Cumaill) Mongán shows his wisdom while arguing with the poet Forgall who has been storytelling every night from Samain to Beltaine.[25] Mongán contradicts Forgall on the question of the death of Fothad Airgtech.[26] The poet threatens to satirize Mongán and his family, and says the land will be barren. Mongán asks for three days to prove himself right or the poet will receive great wealth. At the last minute, a man appears leaping across the three ramparts and tells the poet that he is wrong and that he was: 'with you, with Finn'. Mongán quietens him, but the man continues to describe how he, the visitor, killed Fothad; and the last sentence says: 'Moreover, Mongán was Finn except that he did not allow it to be told.'[27] The poet Forgall had a second encounter with Mongán in *Scél Mongáin inso* (The Story of Mongán here).[28]

Mongán's Vision is connected with the strange circumstances of Mongán's conception and birth as forecast by Manannán in the Bran story above;[29] it is a very short text. When his wife asks him for details of his vision, he refuses to reveal what he saw to anyone. The revelation of knowledge also features in another short text where a young man who is said to be Mongán, a pagan hero, passes the mysterious knowledge to Colm Cille but no one else can hear them.[30] He prophesises his own death, saying that he will be killed with a stone that his mother and he had found on a beach. She crushed the stone to powder and put it in the sea. Waves made it whole again and the Britons found it and kill him.[31]

There are three stories connected with Domnall son of Aed son of Ainmire, king of Tara (628–42). The first, *Fled Dúin na nGéd* (The Feast of the Fort of the Geese), describes Domnall's building of the fort, in the style of Tara, on the banks of the Boyne and the feast that followed where Congal Caech, his foster son, thinks he has been insulted and this gives rise to the battle of Mag Ráith. The text names some of the monuments on Tara that are significantly different from the usual list. There are two different versions of the battle, a short version and a much longer romantic version. A number of events arise from the battle including Cenn Faelad losing his 'brain of forgetfulness' and, as a result, he becomes the first person to learn to write down the native and new learning. Congal Caech appears again and the story says that he was blinded in the king's orchard by a bee. The king, Suibne Geilt, also goes mad during the battle but the shorter version does not mention this event.[32]

Suibne's story is continued in *Buile Shuibne* (The Madness/Frenzy of Suibne) and he appears in Flann O'Brien's *At Swim Two Birds* and S. Heaney's *Sweeney Astray* (1983).[33] Suibne is transformed from king to poet and becomes an isolated shamanic figure who can fly, cross boundaries and live in liminal places. Although the text says he was king of Dál nAraide (around the Antrim and Down border), he is not to be found in any historical sources. At the beginning of the story, Suibne clashes with St Rónán (little seal) while the saint is marking the boundaries for his church. The saint's bell rings and as an angry Suibne runs out to stop him marking the land his wife Eorann grabs his cloak, leaving him naked as he confronts Rónán who is reading his office. Suibne snatches his psalter and throws it in the lake nearby. An otter saves the psalter from the lake, and Rónán curses Suibne, saying that he will wander naked.[34]

The king joins in the battle of Mag Ráith; Rónán also arrives at the battlefield but fails to make peace between the combatants. When Rónán sprinkled Suibne with holy water, the king kills a cleric and tries to kill Rónán, who curses him again, saying that he will fly through the air like his spear and die of a spear-cast. The battle terrifies Suibne, and he flies away like a bird, arriving at the gathering place of madmen at Gleann Bolcáin.[35] He wanders Ireland for years and returns to Gleann Bolcáin, where he meets his friend, Loingsechán who allows him to visit his mill and brings him to his senses; but Loingsechán's mother-in-law, the old woman of the mill, reminds him of his madness and he flies away again after he and the hag leap around the bedroom.

Finally he meets St Mo-Ling of Tech Mo-Ling (St Mullins, Carlow), whose name comes from the Old Irish word for 'leaping', and they continue to meet for the following year. Mo-Ling's female servant, Muirgil, feeds him by putting her heel up to her ankle into the nearest dungheap and leaving milk for him to drink. Animal-like, Suibne approaches to drink the milk. But a woman brings about his death: Muirgil's husband kills him because another woman accused Muirgil of having an affair with Suibne.

At the beginning of *Fingal Rónáin* (The Kinslaying of Rónán), Eithne, wife of Rónán, king of Leinster, dies and he is looking for another wife.[36] His grown-up son, Mael Fothartaig, does not agree with his choice, the young (unnamed) daughter of the king of Dún Sobairche (Dunseverick) in the north, and says that he would be better off with an older woman. Rónán brings his new wife home, but his son has left. Mael Fothartaig returns home and promises to respect her; she uses her maid to tell him of her desire for him, but she first tells Congal, Mael Fothartaig's foster brother.

Congal arranges for the servant to sleep with Mael Fothartaig; the queen agrees but then threatens to kill the servant unless she delivers the message. To escape, Mael Fothartaig goes to Scotland until the Leinstermen warn Rónán that they will kill Rónán unless Mael Fothartaig returns. Mael Fothartaig visits Dún Sobairche and learns from the queen's family that the girl had been intended for him and not for Rónán. When he returns, the servant sleeps with him, and the queen threatens her again. Mael Fothartaig asks Congal for help; Congal sends him to hunt at the Bú Aífe (cows of Aífe) to stay out of the way. (The text says the place name comes from stones that look like white cows from afar.)

The queen thinks that she is to meet Mael Fothartaig, but Congal appears twice. He threatens her with a horsewhip, calls her a whore and 'an evil woman shaming him in ditches and thickets alone to meet a young man'.[37] When Mael Fothartaig did not return that evening, the king asks for him. The queen snaps at him, Rónán insults her, and she responds by saying that Mael Fothartaig could not get the pleasure that he wanted from her and that she had narrowly escaped from him. She says that they will see a sign when they play the verse-capping game that was their custom.

Mael Fothartaig returns from his hunting trip and stands, drying his legs, in front of the fire with Congal beside him. His jester, Mac Glas, is playing in the middle of the house. Ignorant of what has happened, Mael Fothartaig begins the verse-capping: 'Cold is the whirlwind for anyone who hunts at Bú Aífe.' She asks Rónán to listen; his son repeats the half-stanza and she replies: 'It is a futile hunting, without cows, without anyone you love.'[38] Rónán takes this as proof of his son's guilt and orders a warrior to kill Mael Fothartaig. The warrior throws a javelin at him and then at Congal; when the jester jumps, he receives a javelin that goes through his innards. When Rónán bemoans the fact that his son could not find a woman except his wife, Mael Fothartaig swears it is a lie and tells him about her attempts to meet him earlier that day.

A raven descends on the jester's innards as he lies at the entrance to the house; when he grimaces the people laugh at him. Mael Fothartaig tells him, in verse, to gather his intestines and not to give the churls an opportunity to laugh at him. After their deaths, they are placed in a house apart, where Rónán mourns his son. When Congal's brother, Donn, beheads the queen's family and throws the heads at her, she kills herself. At the end of the story, there is an anachronistic reference to the two sons of Mael Fothartaig, Aed and Mael Tuile, who take revenge for the murder. Until this, there is an understanding that he is a young unmarried prince.

There is more scholarly comment on this story than any of the others in this chapter. This human story of triangular relationships has the twist of the unwilling partner similar to that of Joseph and Potiphar's wife in the Bible and of Phaedra and Hippolytus by Euripides (428 BC). Phaedra wife of Theseus falls in love with Hippolytus her stepson, but she repents for her feelings. Although linked by some to the theme of the sovereignty goddess, it is more likely that this is a morality tale on the dangers of taking a young second wife: many wives mean many mothers competing for the future of their sons.[39]

The duplicity of the queen, coupled with the inaction and lack of judgment by both father and son, is central to the plot. The literature is full of references to the folly of listening to women or following their advice, but Rónán's acceptance of a flawed and defective trial of his only son is baffling. The young queen deceives Mael Fothartaig, who disappears when he realizes what she wants, and then she lies to Rónán.[40]

The author's attitude to the young queen is revealed by the fact that she has no name and is usually referred to as Eochaid's daughter and once as Rónán's queen. Mac Da Thó's wife is also nameless. This is very unusual in Irish literature, but the absence of a woman's name and the women's role in triggering story plots have also been noted in the Greek tradition.[41] The appearance of the fool, Mac Glas, and the nasty scene of his death, have been discussed by a number of scholars and it has been noted by T. Clancy that the fool can act as an alter-ego for the king or for his son.[42]

King Rónán was identified as Rónán mac Colmáin (†624), but A. Smyth says he was the king of the small Leinster dynasty of Uí Mháil (Glen of Imaal) in the Kilranelagh area of Wicklow. A. Smyth also notes that the place name, Bú Aífe, that appears in the verse-capping scene above, refers to great rocks on the side of Kilranelagh Hill that do look like white cows from far away; a place where murders took place over the centuries.[43]

Fergal son of Mael Dúin (709–22) is the last king to appear as a central character in this type of story and *Cath Almaine* (The Battle of Almu, Hill of Allen, Kildare) is the last episode of the *Bóroma* saga.[44]

Fergal, the king of the northern Uí Néill of Ailech, sets out for battle against Murchad, king of Leinster, to take the cattle tribute of the *Bóroma*. Fergal has with him Donn Bó, the famous musician and storyteller. The dead Colum Cille, through the abbot of Iona, promised Donn Bó's mother that he would return safely. When Fergal asks Donn Bó to perform before the battle, he says that he will perform the following night; but when the battle is over, Fergal is dead and a Leinsterman combing the field hears 'whistling and sad music ... a droning that was sweetest music.' He finds a head – the head of Donn Bó – and when it is returned to the camp and placed on a pillar 'a piteous drone (*dord fiansa*) rose on high, so that they were all lamenting and sorrowing.'[45] The story ends happily when Colm Cille fulfils his promise to the man's mother and restores Donn Bó to life.

CHAPTER 6

The Otherworld

In nearly all cultures, people have told stories of travel to another world, in which a hero, shaman, prophet, king, or ordinary mortal passes through the gate of death and returns with a message for the living.

The voyage to the underworld ... is often associated with initiatory death and rebirth ... The protagonist of a fantastic journey tale sets forth to find another world by exploring the remote reaches of this world ... He returns to tell of hidden treasures and elusive Edens, of fabulous prodigies, monsters, ghosts, demons, and angels that inhabit the periphery of normal life.[1]

The Otherworld is the main feature of three different types of stories: Adventures (*Echtraí*), Voyages (*Immrama*) and Visions (*Físi*). There is also an Irish word for vision (*aisling*). There are both Latin and Irish tales on this topic, one of the earliest being the Voyage of Brendan, who is credited with many extraordinary voyages. This chapter also deals with a small group of short tales with the title *baile* (frenzy, vision, madness).

These three story types take place in very different environments; the Vision tales describe the Christian Heaven and Hell; The Voyages paint a predominantly Christian picture but carry images of a non-Christian Otherworld; and in the Adventures famous heroes visit places that makes no reference to Heaven or Hell at all. Some of the central characters are relatively unknown; and others, like Cú Chulainn and Cormac, visit the Otherworld as part of their heroic biography; Manannán, god of the sea, appears in many of the stories. Continental writers mention the druids' belief in life after death, and Nicander says the Celts sat by the graves of their dead waiting for them to appear – just as the Ulster poets wait for Fergus to return and relate the *Táin*.

The meaning of the vision is interpreted in different ways: as a Christian message, a pagan vision, a book of the dead or even the equivalent of a 'near-death experience'; some visions describe an event that is very close to Christian ecstatic experiences. J. Campbell describes a hero-quest to the island of the goddess and the return with a life-changing trophy, rather as Christ returned with the revelation of the afterlife.[2] Some heroes never return; others return briefly but find that, like Rip van Winkle, time has overtaken them, and they return to the Otherworld. Some need help to survive the upheaval of their impact on the real world, and others do not survive at all and turn to ashes.

The Location and Nature of the Otherworld

Early Irish stories contain a number of different names for the place that is referred to in English as the 'Otherworld'. There seems to be little difference between the two worlds, and hardly a barrier between them; one can slip easily from one world to the other. It is, in a sense, the perfect realization of this world, a place without death, disease, war, old age, sadness or decay. Modern folklore says the fairies live in liminal places such as lakes, rivers, stones, rocks, woods, trees, caves, underground places, bridges, hills, mountains, ancient earthworks, ruins or beneath the sea. A liminal place is associated with sovereignty, and in many cases the king receives the validation of his sovereignty from there.

The Otherworld may surround human beings but they fail to see it and travelling over water is often involved in getting there. The hero may enter a fairy mound (*síd*, which also means peace), travel across the sea or a lake or emerge from a magical mist. From *síd* comes the Modern Irish word for fairies (*síogaí*). The Otherworld is given names like Tír na mBeó (Land of the Living), Tír na mBan (Land of Women), Mag Mell (The Plain of Delight), Mag Mór (The Great Plain), In Tír Tairngire (The Promised Land) or Tír na nÓg (Land of Youth).

The fact that there are so many names leads to the theory that there may be different Otherworlds; certainly, it is always a mysterious place even if the setting is familiar. It is seen as being in the southern hemisphere, implying a place under our feet, the 'flip side', an Alice through the Looking Glass type of reality. The Otherworld in Ireland may simply be 'the other side' where time passes differently, inhabited by people and animals that may be the same as in the 'real' world but strange – dogheads, catheads, an island that is a fish and everliving saints awaiting the Judgment Day. The continental writer Lucan refers to 'another place' and to the spirits going to 'another realm'.[3]

The same themes and motifs appear repeatedly: a land without death, the concept of there being 'neither yours or mine', a beautiful visiting woman, magic apples or branches and wonderful music. Time may also pass differently, and some who return from the Otherworld find that hundreds of years have gone by; or the opposite – they think they have been away for decades and find that no time has elapsed; and the Otherworld can be a land of paradox, of riddles and of ambiguity. The Otherworld opens at Samain; this makes access to it easier for people who can then experience older times in the present or gain a glimpse of the future.[4] It is a place associated with the assembly (*oenach*) that brought together all the people in one sacred place considered to be the dwelling place of the gods. Such assemblies were held at burial places linked with the deaths of legendary figures such as Tailltiu, Carmun and Cruachu, and the dead may gather there. There are about sixty such sites identified in early Ireland. These places are associated with the festival of Lugnasad, and some of the references are glossed with words that are all linked with a theatre.[5]

The first voyage tale is that of Brendan, who is sometimes credited with the discovery of America. His story, written in Latin, spread throughout Europe and was translated to other languages. One of the names for the Irish Otherworld was the legendary island of Hy Brazil; this appeared on medieval maps from 1325 and was not removed until 1865, and it was noticeably on maps from many continental countries.[6] The belief in this island may have affected Columbus: it is said that he thought that there were large islands mid-ocean and the maps available to him bore this out. He was in contact with Galway in 1492 and had a sailor from there, William Irez, with him. Galway was the centre of Irish lore on Hy Brasil. The belief still persists in modern folklore, and the island is sometimes called Árainn Bheag (little Aran) beside the three Aran Islands in Galway Bay. It is said to appear under certain climatic conditions or every seven years.

The Canarian writer, M. Martínez Hernández, suggests that the seven Canary Islands may be the inspiration for the myth of the garden of paradise in Greek and biblical tradition as well as the Irish Otherworld. Like Hy Brazil, La Gomera has a legend of an eighth island that sometimes appears to the west. He concludes the relevant chapter with a list of wonders that Brendan encounters and identifies them as features on the various seven islands, including steep, craggy mountains, the existence of herds of goats (that is still the case in modern Fuerteventura) and wonderful birds.[7]

The main *Echtra* stories that survive are: *Echtra Conli* (The Adventure of Conla), *Echtra Brain* (The Adventure of Bran) also called *Immram Brain* (The Voyage of Bran), *Echtra Laegairi* (The Adventure of Laegaire), *Serglige Con Culainn* (The Love-Sickness of Cú Chulainn), *Echtra Cormaic* (The Adventure of Cormac), *Echta Airt* (The Adventure of Art) and the later *Echtra Thaidhg meic Céin* (The Adventure of Tadg son of Cian). Two titles – *Echtra mac nEchach Muigmedóin* (The Adventure of the sons of Eochaid Mugmedón) and *Echtra Nerai* (The Adventure of Nera) also known as *Táin Bó Aingen* (The Cattle Raid of Aingen) seen as a foretale of the *Táin* – are mentioned in the chapter on Sovereignty below. Many titles appearing in the tale lists no longer survive, and *Echtra Chonli* is not on the lists.[8]

There are many comments on the fact that *The Adventure of Bran* is referred to as *Imram Brain maic Febail ocus a Echtra*, carrying both the words *immram* and *echtra*. P. Mac Cana says the title *echtra* is older and more correct, and M. Dillon treats them as two distinct genres. D. Dumville also sees them as being quite distinct and views the *echtra* as being set in a mythological framework with pagan deities and creatures of the Otherworld who are able to move to and fro with ease from one world to the next.[9]

The differences between Adventures and Voyages may be outlined as follows:

Adventures (Echtraí)	*Voyages (Immrama)*
1. Period/ characters known/ myth/ heroic	Not previously known
2. Invited to Otherworld	Personal reasons for going – revenge etc.
3. Short voyage in glass boat etc.	Long account of journey & preparation
4. Adventure in Otherworld main element	Adventure only as part of framework
5. Usually remains/ may return	Always returns
6. Usually one jouney/island	Multiplicity of islands

There is only one copy of *The Adventure of Bran* and it consists of 56 stanzas of poetry with connecting prose passages.[10] A woman from 'unknown lands' is said to recite fifty quatrains in Bran's house, which was full of kings 'who knew not whence the woman had come since the ramparts were closed'. But the story proper begins when Bran leaves the fortress; he hears music that puts him to sleep with its sweetness. There is a beautiful silver branch with white blossoms beside him when he wakes up. On returning to his house, a woman 'in strange raiment' appears and sings a poem describing the Otherworld. (There seem to be two different introductions to the text.) She describes a place with no crying or treachery, only sweet music and gold and silver chariots. The sunrise is described: 'At sunrise there will come/ A fair man illumining level lands;/ He rides upon the fair sea-washed plain,/ He stirs the ocean till it is blood.' The woman leaves, taking the branch with her.

The following day Bran takes to the sea with three companies of nine: this total of twenty-seven is a common number describing groups of people. He places one of his foster brothers over each company. They travel for two days and two nights before they meet Manannán, the god of the sea, who is riding in a chariot. The poem shows that the Otherworld surrounds Bran but he cannot see it. Manannán tells Bran that where he sees the clear sea there is a chariot and a flowery plain; the salmon he sees are really calves and lambs. In this land: 'A beautiful game, most delightful,/ They play (sitting) at the luxurious wine,/ Men and gentle women under a bush,/ Without sin, without crime.' He describes the birth of Christ as 'a noble salvation … besides being God, He will be man' and then talks about his own affair with Caintigern, wife of Fiachna, and the birth of their son who will live for only fifty years. He does not name him, but the son is Mongán son of Fiachna king of Ulster. Manannán advises Bran to continue rowing to the Land of Women and that he will be there before the setting of the sun.

They reach an island, the Island of Joy (*Inis Subai*), where the inhabitants are constantly laughing; one of the men enters the island and becomes like them. Shortly afterwards they reach the Land of Women; the queen throws a ball of thread at Bran that sticks to his palm, and the boat is pulled ashore by the thread. There is a large house with beds for each of the twenty-seven men, and a woman is provided for each of them, and time flies by so that what appears to be a year is in fact much longer.

One of Bran's followers, Nechtan son of Colbran, becomes homesick and wants to return. The queen tells them that they will regret the decision to leave, that they should not touch the land and should visit and take the man from the Island of Joy with them; this advice they ignored. The boat arrives in Ireland at Srub Brain, the entrance to Lough Foyle (Loch Febail). When the people ask them who they are, it emerges that hundreds of years have passed since they left and they are now part of the saga tradition themselves. One man leaps out of the boat and turns to ash on touching the land (as happens to Oisín when he dismounts from his horse). Bran tells his tale, writes the quatrains in Ogam, leaves for the Otherworld again; and his wanderings are not known from then on.

There seems to be a deliberate effort to show resemblances between two worlds, and there is room for boat and chariot, waves and flowers, fish and calves. S. Mac Mathúna says: 'This twinning (*emnad*) of opposites, like a coin flipping backwards and forwards, is mirrored in the structure of the text itself. Manannán in his chariot, and Bran in his coracle stand in a reciprocal relationship as they gaze on the respective sides of the coin.'[11]

The Adventure of Conla is very similar as it tells of the experiences of Conla son of Conn of the Hundred Battles; it is one of the shortest of early Irish texts. Conla is at Uisnech with his father when he sees 'a woman in an unknown garment' who is invisible to everyone else.[12] Conn asks her where she is from, and she replies that she comes from the land of the living where there is no death or sin; there all enjoy feasts and peace, and live in a fairy mound.[13] When she leaves, she throws an apple to Conla, rather as the queen throws the ball to Bran. Conla needs no food or drink except for this apple, which always remains whole, and it appears that he can only eat the food that has come from her land.

The woman returns after a month and tells him, 'Living immortals invite you', and warns against druidry as being of little value. She invites him to the other country inhabited by women that they will reach before nightfall. Conla jumps into the ship and they row over the sea and are never seen again. Conn comments that Art is now alone – referring to Art, his only remaining son, who is called Art Oenfher (Art Alone) and who rules Tara after Conn.

There are a number of similarities between this tale and *The Adventure of Bran*: a land of women they will reach before sunset although it is far away; the strange clothing worn by the women; and only Conla and Bran being able to see the women who visit them. Conla pines for the woman after the apple (like Adam and Eve) – just as a strange longing for home seizes Nechtan. Because of this there is some debate as to which story might be the original or whether they came from the same place. K. McCone sees them as two sides of the same coin, and J. Carney says that the Conla tale was composed as reading practice for pupils in a monastery and that it was asking them to give up everything for the eternal life.[14]

Scholars are divided on the function/meaning of these texts and on their Christian or pre-Christian content. M. Dillon says that the story has pagan ideals, but J. Carney disagrees, saying that the story was composed in a Christian literate community of the seventh or eighth century and that it tells of the Incarnation with a 'clear parallel ... drawn between the birth of Christ and that of Mongán mac Fiachna.' He also says: '*Immram Brain* is, from beginning to end, a thoroughly Christian poem. It seems, in fact, to be an allegory show-ing Man setting out on the voyage to Paradise.' He says that the Bran story owes much to a poem called *The Phoenix* from the Book of Exeter where a bird is said to sing the hours as mentioned in the Bran poem. Both the Book of Exeter and the Bran poem contain similar descriptions of the land as being with-out bad weather, death or misery. This is at variance with his view, expressed elsewhere, that '... the author was an Irish *fili* with a good knowledge of monas-tic teaching: he is personally involved in the problem of being a Christian, while at the same time retaining as much as possible of his traditional heritage.'[15]

P. Mac Cana says that the authors harmonized the pagan and Christian Otherworld and combined the birth of the hero, Mongán, with the birth of Christ. The saga uses the pre-Christian Otherworld to put forward a Christian ideal, and he questions whether they could compose stories like this without referring to their own, pre-Christian traditions.[16] J.F. Nagy says that this genre of storytelling did and could exist separately from Christianity and that it was recycled rather than invented by the early learned men.[17]

Stories about Mongán probably existed before this story was composed and were used as sources for the Bran saga along with material about the Lough Foyle area.[18] The tale lists contain titles with the word *tomaidm/tomadmann* 'bursting forth' and all the older references seem to refer to water and lands being over-whelmed. The names Bran and Febal are found in Loch Febail and Srúb Brain, both associated with water. A flooded kingdom and inhabitants fleeing from water appear in a conversation between Bran's druid and Febal's female prophet (*banfháith*) that may contain the seed of the Bran story. In a scene similar to the Christian soul leaving the body, Bran's druid says that his knowledge/faculty of cognition (*fiss*) saw a well when it 'went to the high clouds.'[19]

Flooding appears in a short text where Colm Cille is said to meet a pagan hero, Mongán, and asks him about Loch Febail, where they are standing. Mongán replies that it was once a fertile plain and that men, beasts and mon-sters lie beneath; he has lived for a long time in the form of a deer, salmon, seal and a wolf. But when the saint asks him about 'the heavenly and earthly mys-teries', they speak in secret for a full day; no one hears them and they refuse to share the information.[20] Mongán also gives Colm Cille information on *Tír Tarngire na Finn* (The Promised Land of the Fair), his own land, in a short poem introduced by the phrase: 'Mongán sang to Colm Cille.'[21] Loch nEchach (Neagh) was formed from a well that irrupted.[22]

Otherworld Visits and the Heroic Biography

Both Cú Chulainn and Cormac visit the Otherworld as part of their heroic biog-raphies. Cú Chulainn has three different encounters, the first of which appears in *The Wooing of Emer*. He chooses Emer daughter of Forgall Monach as his future wife, but her father objects and arranges that he visit Scotland and the Otherworld to train with the female warrior Scáthach (shadowy one), hoping that he will never return.

When looking for Scáthach, Cú Chulainn is left alone by his companions, and the various elements of the quest-tale appear; helpers steer him in the right direction before he faces the Pupil's Bridge that is said to have two low ends and a mid-point that is higher. When the hero jumps from one end, the other end lifts and throws him back again but eventually he succeeds. When he completes his training, his return to reality includes crossing a narrow road where he meets an old woman, blind in her left eye, who tries to throw him down the cliff-face; and he uses the salmon-leap to behead her. He marries Emer once he has killed her father. He is now the supreme hero who has survived a life-changing jour-ney and he brings back a visible sign of his visit – the ultimate weapon, the *gae bolga* that he uses to kill his foster brother Ferdia in the *Táin*.[23]

In the second story, *The Love-Sickness of Cú Chulainn*, the events begin at Samain and a 'vision' is mentioned. Cú Chulainn casts a stone at two otherworldly birds, and his aim fails for the first time. He is trying to catch them for his wife, having already caught birds for the other women of Ulster. Shortly afterwards, two women appear to him – Fann wife of Manannán mac Lir and her companion Líban, who horse-whip him within inches of his life. Laughing, they leave him there, and he is unable to speak or move for a year. Fergus warns the Ulstermen against waking him as they might disturb his vision. This is the unpleasant face of the Otherworld, and Cú Chulainn procrastinates and sends his charioteer, Laeg, to report back to him on two occasions before he travels to an island in a bronze boat. Cú Chulainn fights a few warriors and wins Fann, whom Manannán has deserted. On his return to Ireland, he arranges to meet Fann at Newry, but his earthly wife, Emer, finds out and confronts the lovers with fifty Ulsterwomen carrying knives. This affair is the converse of Manannán's brief affair with Mongán's mother, the wife of Fiachna. The love triangle of the story is nearly unique in its treatment of marriage and infidelity. Cú Chulainn brings home nothing but trouble from this visit to the Otherworld, in contrast with *The Wooing of Emer* when he returns with the *gae bolga*.[23a]

J. Carney describes the text as 'a mere jumble of picturesque incidents adapted from earlier literature, and as a whole it has no moral to teach and no consistent underlying philosophy' and belongs to a period when the writers of the sagas were borrowing episodes from earlier tales.[24] T. Ó Cathasaigh says that the storyteller may be trying to exonerate himself by suggesting that demons created the story. The story presents three worlds: the Ulster heroic past, the Otherworld and the conditions necessary for a Golden Age in Ireland. The first is described in the beginning of the story; the second when the rival appears from the Otherworld; and the third is an interlude about Lugaid Riab nDerg becoming king of Tara that is ignored by most translations. When Loeg returns with information from the Otherworld, Cú Chulainn is temporarily released from his love-sickness and he is capable of giving advice to Lugaid.[25] There is a similar adventure to the Otherworld in *Echtra Laegairi* (The Adventure of Laegaire).[26]

In the third story Cú Chulainn and Lugaid Riab nDerg appear together in another text where they also meet two women who appear to them first in bird form: one of them is Derborgaill, who is eventually killed by the jealous women of Ulster for her perceived sexual abilities. Cú Chulainn's skill in reaching his target is quite different: he misses his aim in the love-sickness text and ends up in a virtual nightmare; and in the Derborgaill text he hits her and she marries Lugaid and walks into a nightmare.[27] Cú Chulainn returns from the dead in *Siaburcharpat Con Culainn* (The Phantom Chariot of Cú Chulainn) when Patrick brings him back to convert king Laegaire to Christianity.[28]

In the case of Cormac, he visits the Otherworld in *The Adventure of Cormac* at the invitation of Manannán mac Lir. Over a number of months, Manannán kidnaps Cormac's daughter and son, Ailbe and Cairpre Lifechair, and finally his wife Eithne.[29] A magic mist surrounds Cormac and when it lifts he is in the Otherworld. Cormac has a specific mission to complete; he must fulfil an act of truth, and this he achieves by telling the final story over a pig that can be roasted only by people relating true stories. When he tells of the events that have just occurred, the cooking of the pig is finished.[30]

Cormac falls asleep and when he awakes his family have been returned to him and he receives a goblet of truth that will confirm his judgments. The loss of both his son and his wife symbolizes his loss of sovereignty, but his gift from Manannán is physical proof of his position as king, his return from the Otherworld and his ability to give proper judgments.

Conn of the Hundred Battles appears in a similar story – *Baile in Scáil* (The Phantom's Frenzy). The word *baile* means a vision, frenzy, even madness, but it may also be related to poetic inspiration.[31] The short *baile* stories that survive are associated with supernatural revelations, whether it be the goddess dispensing drink to Tara's future kings or an angel revealing future Irish churchmen. Conn is standing on Tara's ramparts when a stone cries out under his feet. His druids, Mael, Bloc and Bluigne, explain that the stone is Fál, and that there has been a prophecy that his descendants will reign over Ireland. A mist descends; a horseman emerges and brings them to a wonderful hall where a beautiful woman called 'the sovereignty of Ireland' sits beside a vat of ale. The warrior beside her says he is Lug and presents Conn with a list of the future kings of Ireland. He gives the list to the woman so that she can present them with a sovereignty drink. When the house and phantom disappear, the vessel remains with Conn.[32] In *Baile Cuinn* (The Frenzy of Conn) he has another vision, in which the future kings of Tara are presented as drinking the sovereignty drink.[33] In *Baile Bricín* (The Vision of Bricín) St Bricín hears a cry from heaven celebrating Easter and asks God to send him a messenger with news of his sovereignty. An angel gives the names of all future Irish churchmen and foretells Bricín's future. His church was at Túaim Drecáin (parish of Tomreegan on the borders of the counties of Cavan and Fermanagh) – where Cenn Faelad attended when he lost his brain of forgetfulness.[34] It was about twenty miles from the monastery of Druim Snechta.[35]

The Adventure of Art is discussed in the chapter on Sovereignty.[36] *Echtra Thaidg meic Céin* (The Adventure of Tadg son of Cian) was written much later and tends to be excluded from discussions of this topic. Tadg is the son of Cian son of Ailill Ólomm (of the bare ear); when his wife Líban is stolen from him, he goes to the Otherworld and meets many people (including Conla) before he brings her back. Thus the adventures end where they began, in an Otherworld where Conla and his female companion rule a wonderful kingdom that anyone may visit.[37]

The Voyages and the Brendan Voyage

A different world, found in the voyage tales, appears influenced by ecclesiastical sources such as Christian and Judaic material combined with the actual experiences of sailors embellished by their vivid imagination.[38] In the ninth century some monks considered the monastery too worldly and became anchorites and escaped the secular world by leaving Ireland or living in inaccessible places. Irish clerics were making sea voyages from the sixth century onwards, and Christian hermits elsewhere made pilgrimages to search for deserted places. Some of the most common motifs are solitary clerics, 'the everliving ones', hermits waiting for the end of the world on islands and 'the promised land of the saints' that appears like a combination of Heaven, the promised land and the land of the living of native Irish tradition. Sources such as the 'Litany of Irish pilgrim saints' contain references to attempts to reach the Promised Land.[39]

The oldest voyage is probably that of Brendan written first in Latin and then in Irish. St Brendan (†577/583) of Clonfert, Co. Galway, is one of the earliest known saints and is also associated with Munster. In the Latin *Life of Brendan* there are two journeys; the first one fails but the second is successful.[40] The work was translated into many of the vernacular languages of Europe such as Anglo-Norman, Old French, German, Dutch and Norwegian and was probably responsible for the spread of such material throughout Europe.

There are three other voyage tales extant: *Immram Curaig Maíle Dúin* (The Voyage of the boat of Mael Dúin), *Immram Snédgusa ocus Maic Riagla* (The Voyage of Snédgus and Mac Riagla) and *Immram ua Corra* (The Voyage of Uí Corra). The tale lists mention *Immram Luinge Murchertaig maic Erca* (The Voyage of the Ship of Muirchertach mac Erca), but this no longer survives. These are frame tales where episodes can be added in or taken out without damaging the basic structure of the story. The main characters have often committed a sin, and the journey is part of their punishment, but in the case of Mael Dúin he wants revenge for his father's murder. This text appears in both prose and metrical versions.

The Voyage of Mael Dúin, although mainly Christian, contains more secular aspects than the other two, and Mael Dúin is treated like a secular hero.[41] He is the son of a man called Ailill of Munster and a nun; when his father is murdered before his birth, he is fostered with the queen of the district. When he decides to avenge the murder, the druid advises him to take seventeen men but Mael Dúin adds his three foster brothers, and this leads to bad luck. They visit a total of thirty-three islands and although the murderers are on the first island he fails to reach them because of the extra passengers. There are similarities to texts described already: they are drawn to one island by a ball of wool that sticks to their hands; there are seventeen women waiting for them on the island; and time passes in an unusual fashion. During the course of their voyage they also see islands of icebergs, a feature that resembles a geyser and exaggerated islands with unusually large animals. On the second last island they meet the Hermit of Tory, who advises them to forgive the murderers. The story ends without revenge, and they return to a joyful welcome with a thoroughly Christian flavour.

The main characters in *The Voyage of Uí Corra* are three brothers – Lóchán, Einne and Silvester – who are sons of Conall Derg, a prince in Connacht, and his wife Caerderg (red berry), daughter of a church official of Clochar. The couple had lost every child born to them until they made a contract with the Devil where they agreed to have any offspring baptized into the heathen faith. Subsequently, they had three sons and the boys spend their time plundering for the Devil until Lochán sees a vision of Hell. The three brothers are advised to repent by rebuilding churches and taking an overseas journey. A wright builds them a three-skinned boat, and in return they agree that he can join them. On board there is also a jester, a bishop, a priest and a deacon. They allow God to direct them and leave the oars in the boat. Crying men inhabit the first island; when one man goes ashore, he becomes just like them. The jester dies shortly afterwards and is reincarnated as a little bird. There is also an island where all are laughing, and when one of the crew visits it he laughs like the others. They see an island supported by a pedestal, a rainbow river, and a pillar with a fishing-net of white bronze and silver. Finally, they are welcomed to an island by a disciple of Christ who foretells their future: they will be famous as far as Rome. *The Voyage of Snédgus and Mac Riagla* is also a story of atonement.[42]

The Vision Tales

The Otherworld here is the Christian Heaven and Hell; the stories are found in both Latin and Irish and all who visit the Otherworld return to give an account of their experiences. The Latin texts may have influenced Dante's view of Heaven and Hell. The similarity to 'a near-death experience' has been noticed by C. Zaleski, who outlines the following points of the journey: exit from the body, the guide, the journey itself along with the type of obstacles they may meet on the way; fire, the test-bridge, an encounter with deeds; and finally the re-entry to this world. A minority of people are permanently scarred by their brush with the Otherworld or they suffer physical pain while they are away.[43]

Only a fragment of the earliest vision survives; it tells of the journey of Fursa (†649) and, according to Bede, his soul left his body when he was ill and was taken to a great height approaching a fire. In a scene reminiscent of Bran's druid, Fursa looks down on a dark valley and passes through the fire with an angel's help before he returns with a permanent scar from the physical pain that he suffered. There is a second fragment about an angel taking St Laisrén on high after he has been fasting; he is shown Hell, which consists of a sea of fire, and the sinners are to be seen with nails in their tongues ... and the fragment tails off at this point.[44] A longer account is found in the Latin text, *Purgatorium Patricii* (Patrick's Purgatory), written by a monk, Henry of Saltrey, in 1153; although the episode happens at Lough Derg, this is the only Irish connection; the main character is a knight called Owen.[45] He goes to Loch Derg and persuades the monks to leave him alone in the cave, where he is attacked by a group of demons and visits different places set apart for penance.

There is a much more complete journey in *The Vision of Tnugdal* written in Ratisbon, Germany. The author, a monk called Marcus, draws an amazing picture of both Heaven and Hell.[46] This is a remarkably vivid portrait of the Christian Otherworld that appears to set the template for Irish and non-Irish material during the following centuries. It includes elements that must have come from singularly Irish, Christian, pre-Christian and apocryphal sources. The prologue gives the background to the story and dedicates it to 'Lady G ... devoted to God and abbess by God's gift' and says that the vision was seen in 1149.

Tnudgal lived in Cashel; while he was trying to reclaim a debt of three horses from a friend, 'his body immediately collapsed unconscious, as if there had never been any spirit in it' and from Wednesday to Saturday 'he lay dead with no sign of life' except for warmth on his left side; otherwise they would have buried him. When he regains consciousness, he tells them of his vision and promises to give all his riches to the poor.

The vision contains twenty-four chapters and describes the departure of the soul, the coming of the angel guide, the visit to Hell and arrival in Heaven before the soul returns to the body and Tnudgal is said to be standing over his body. They travel a narrow path on a mountain – on one side a sulphurous fire and on the other icy snow and horrific wind. Excruciating pains in their sexual organs attack thieves and robbers and those who commit gluttony and fornication. Finally they meet Lucifer, who is black like a crow with a human body, but he has a thousand hands, a tail and a long thick beak.

The angel takes the soul to the glory of God's friends, but these chapters are much shorter than those on Hell. They reach a beautiful meadow reminiscent of the descriptions of near-death experiences; these people will reach God and are surrounded by plants and flowers; there is a fountain with the water of life; there is no night, and the suns shines constantly. The are travelling upwards and meet St Ruadán (probably the man who confronted Diarmait mac Cerbaill on Tara) and finally Patrick surrounded by famous bishops. The soul begs the angel to allow him to stay, but he is told that he must return and tell his experiences to all his neighbours. When Tnugdal recovers, he gives his possessions to the poor and puts the sign of the cross on his clothes. Then he tells everyone what happened to him, and the author finishes by addressing the enigmatic Lady G again.

The text is very organized, with the World of Darkness and the World of Light each given eleven chapters. Hell includes nature at its most horrific with high mountains, deep valleys, dangerous waters, dragons, frightening bridges – all in direct contrast with the organized World of Light with its lovely meadows and walls dividing the different compartments. The text blends the continental with the Celtic tradition.

Fís Adomnáin (The Vision of Adomnán) may be earlier than the Tnudgal text and they are quite similar in content. The translator has identified it as a possible precursor of the works of Dante, who may have read material of this kind.[47] Perhaps this text influenced the previous one and thus the material reached continental Europe. The pattern of events is similar, as Adomnán's soul leaves his body and meets his guardian angel, who becomes his spirit guide throughout the journey. There is one difference: Tnugdal visits the world of darkness first and then proceeds to the light; but Adomnán begins in Heaven and then descends to the lower Hell.

The description of the Land of Saints resembles the interior of a church with chancel rails, and choir stalls lit by thousands of angels instead of candles. There is a crystal veil between them and the face of the Lord, and, although a circle of fire surrounds the place, they pass in and out without a difficulty. The Lord's throne sits in a city with seven crystal walls, a floor of crystal and thousands of angels with fragrant candles. The throne sits on four columns of precious stones; it gives out wonderful music, with three birds celebrating the eight canonical hours.[48]

There are souls waiting for the Judgment on hills and marshy places, and the angel takes him to an awful city where there are six doors guarded by various angels such as Michael and Ariel. The souls are brought by the angels through these various doors until 'they usher the soul into the presence of God'. If the souls are righteous, the Lord receives them; but if they are unrighteous, they are delivered into the hands of Lucifer. On the way to Hell, they encounter a fire-filled glen spanned by an enormous bridge that is high in the middle and low at both ends. The journey across the bridge depends on the status of the soul. The first company find the bridge easily passable, but the second group find it narrow at first, broad afterwards, and they too pass eventually; but for the last the bridge is broad at first but it narrows so much that they fall into the glen beneath into the throats of the eight serpents. Adomnán witnesses a series of companies and the punishments they suffer for a variety of sins. He sees a fiery wall hiding a land that is seven times worse, awaiting the Day of Judgment. Finally, he returns to his body and teaches this doctrine for the remainder of his life.

The text is recognized as the first attempt between the Vision of Enoch and Dante's *Commedia* to work out the architecture of the Otherworld. D. Dumville also praised the author/compiler: 'He has created in *Fís Adamnán* a minor masterpiece of medieval literature; his work stands head and shoulders above the other visions of the early and central Middle Ages. He was indeed a worthy *Irish Precursor of Dante.*'[49]

Aisling Meic Conglinne (The Vision/Dream of Mac Conglinne) lampoons these traditions, particularly the landscapes that it describes as food, a theme of the entire text. The author identifies himself as Aniér Mac Conglinne of Munster and outlines the blessings that will ensue if the story is told.[50] Cathal mac Finguine the king of Munster has a great appetite because Satan, the demon of gluttony, has possessed him and Aniér decides that he will travel from Roscommon to Cork. But he receives bad hospitality there; a guesthouse with wind, snow and rain around it, no thatch and a blanket with fleas. He starts singing the psalms because the fleas will not allow him to sleep, and is condemned to death by Manchín abbot of Cork and locked in a dark house overnight. It is decided that he should be crucified but he stops for a drink at a well and takes drops dripping from the stem of his brooch until his guards are tired. When he sees a vision in the night, the clerics allow him to recite what he has seen – a satire on Manchín's genealogy back to Adam told in the form of food. Manchín is convinced that Mac Conglinne can cure the king.

Mac Conglinne goes to the house of Pichán, who tells him that Cathal is visiting tonight and that it is impossible to feed him. Mac Conglinne is promised a gold ring and a Welsh horse if he can cure Cathal. When Cathal arrives, Mac Conglinne forces him to give him an apple and then many apples, but the king loses his temper and throws apples all over the house while one eye goes to the back of his head and the other pops out, as happened with Cú Chulainn.

Mac Conglinne asks the king to fast with him.[51] He puts an apron on and, while he prepares the food, the king is tied with cords and the food is placed in front of him. Mac Conglinne passes the food in front of Cathal before eating it himself, and torments him by reciting a further vision of the land of food that contains a lake of milk in a fair plain, a house thatched with butter, with doorposts of custard and beds of glorious lard. Mac Conglinne tells him of a phantom who gives a long metrical genealogy for himself and his family in food, calling himself Wheatlet son of Milklet and his dog Haunch of Mutton and his wife Lard.

Cathal is advised to go home, wash his hands in a well, wipe his teeth and comb his hair, warm himself by the fire and have a white-handed woman of good character give him pieces of food that he is to put in his mouth in a swinging jerk, and his eyes must whirl around in his skull while he is eating them. The demon inside Cathal is licking its lips outside his head. Mac Conglinne passes the pieces from the fire to the king's lips. The demon takes one piece in his claws and takes it to the cauldron on the other side of the fire and it overturns on him. The house burns down and the demon jumps to a rooftree above before flying off to the people of Hell. The king is given a special meal and he is put to sleep in a beautiful bed. On waking up, he rewards Mac Conglinne with cows and sheep, a cloak, a ring and a horse. All the motifs of the Otherworld visit are present – the phantom as guide, boat travel, the visitor with a problem and the solution. This genre also spread throughout Europe, like the Vision and Voyage tales, and influenced continental compositions such as the poem *The Land of Cokaygne*.[52]

CHAPTER 7

Kings, Goddesses and Sovereignty

From Tara one can see mountains or hills in each of the four provinces –
Ulster, Leinster, Munster and Connacht – although the not very distant
sea is invisible ... The king of Tara would truly be lord of the four quar-
ters. Perhaps it is here that we should look for the true significance of
Tara.[1]

The belief that the king was sacred and represented the centre of the universe or
cosmos was an intrinsic part of the Irish ideology of sovereignty and kingship;
as such, it appears as the major theme in many of the early sagas. The equilib-
rium of their world depended upon the king's unity with the proper goddess of
sovereignty, as well as his truth, justice and the prince's truth (*fír flathemon*).
The king was expected to be perfect in every way; a physical disability techni-
cally disqualified him from office. But some historical kings are described as
blemished; Tigernán Ua Ruairc (†1172) had only one eye, and Donnchad son of
Brian Bórama had his right hand cut off in 1019 but continued in the kingship
of Munster until 1063. The prince's untruth (*gó flathemon*) was the direct opposite and could be avoided by adhering to the taboos (*gessa*) laid upon a king.
There were also lucky things (*buada*) that would bring good luck.[2] A good king
brings peace to his land, and his kingship is directly related to and validated by
the Otherworld.

The wisdom text, *Audacht Morainn* (The Testament of Morann), outlines
the qualities necessary in a king; he should be merciful, virtuous, generous, hos-
pitable, honourable, honest and give good judgments; this will ensure riches,
peace, an abundance of fruit and great yields from cattle. There are four types
of rulers: the true ruler (*fírfhaith*) who 'smiles on the truth', the wily ruler
(*cíallfhaith*) who 'defends borders and tribes', the ruler of occupation with hosts
(*flaith congbále co slógaib*) whose 'forces turn away, they put off his needs', and
the bull ruler (*tarbfhlaith*) who is in constant conflict and 'Against him there is
always bellowing with horns'.[3]

The king usually shows his truth by giving proper judgments, and his reign
is peaceful. Good, bad and downright unfortunate kings and their sovereignty

goddess spouses populate the sagas with all sorts of combinations emerging – the right king with the wrong woman, the right king and the right woman, and the wrong king with the right woman. As a result of a bad judgment, a king could lose his position or his honour-price, as will be seen in the case of Lugaid mac Con and Conaire Mór. This could also lead to the destruction of crops, and to famine, war, diseases, bad weather and further disasters.

Most of these stories relate to the kingship of Temair (Tara), and some kings are said to celebrate the *Feis Temro* (Festival of Tara) that was only celebrated once during a king's reign. Tara was clearly the most important ritual and kingship site in the country; it survived well into the historical period where its importance and centrality is sacred and mythological as well as historical and literary. The kingship of Tara was exceptional and quite different from the other petty kingships; it made the transition from a religious centre to being primarily a political kingship; but the creation of a king is usually considered a religious act. Christian writings about the confrontation between king Laegaire and Patrick were concerned with making Tara a centre of Christian kingship. There is a view of sixteen counties and all four provinces from the Hill, and it was central to Irish kingship along with Emain Macha, Dún Ailinne and Cruachu; a place where 'the creation of the world was re-enacted' and they were 'the focal points of religion set in religious landscapes'.[4]

The festival of Tara was probably not commemorated until the king had proven himself to his people and asserted his authority. It came under Christian control relatively early, and Diarmait mac Cerbaill (†565) is reputed to have been the last king of Tara to celebrate it (560) when there may have been a revival of paganism. His death tale tells of his confrontation with St Ruadán of Lothra, who curses both Diarmait and Tara.

The festival probably confirmed the relationship between the king and the goddess of sovereignty, the female embodiment of the land. Little is known of what happened at such a ceremony as there are no reputable contemporary accounts. Giraldus Cambrensis (Gerald of Wales), who wrote of the Normans' arrival in Ireland, describes a ceremony that he claimed to witness in Ulster: the people gather in one place and the man to be inaugurated embraces a white mare that is killed, cut up and boiled in water. He sits in the boiled meat, he and the people eat the meat, and the kingdom is his.[5] There is a reference to a similar event in a story about St Mo-Ling who is offered a horse-steak to eat, but after he has blessed the cauldron and the house it changes into a quarter of mutton. The horse and dog bones found on Tara show signs of having been eaten.[6] Horses were considered sacred by the Celts and the pre-Christian Irish, and the native word *ech* appears in the personal names of gods, heroes and kings; but horses were also important in Indian, Norse, Greek as well as Roman culture.

C. Doherty revisits the scene described by Giraldus and the 'horse-sacrifice' that could only be celebrated by the greatest of kings. In his estimation, Tara was the inauguration site of a world-king. One of the very first kings to be commemorated in early genealogical verse is Labraid Loingsech, who is also known as Labraid Lorc, the king who was dumb (*moen*) until he could speak (*labraid*). In a tenth-century tale the horse and the king are also associated.[7] A bull feast is mentioned during the prophecy of the future king of Tara, Conaire Mór, and *The Love-Sickness of Cú Chulainn* also contains a bull feast where one man eats the meat and sees the future king in his dream.[8]

The best known story is that of Labraid; about a king with horse's ears. The king kills everyone who cuts his hair so that they cannot tell anyone about the ears, but a widow pleads for the life of her son and he allows him to go free on the understanding that he will keep the secret. When the son gets sick, he is advised to tell the story to the first tree he meets, and this was a willow. Craiptine the harper makes a harp from the tree, but when he plays it the song coming from the harp is that the king has horse's ears.[9]

The Battle of Moytura, discussed in the chapter on the Mythological Cycle, is the template for kingship that is carried forward to tales of human kings.[10] The saga is exemplary; the actions of Lug in particular are to be imitated, but his deeds happen in the time of the gods as distinct from later deeds, which happen in human time. The three kings, Bres, Nuadu and Lug, each demonstrate a different type of king – Bres the flawed and doomed king, Nuadu the injured king who is prepared to take the kingship temporarily and step down again when the perfect figure of Lug arrives at Tara. Bres shows the prince's falsehood in his meanness to the Tuatha Dé Danann (he holds no feasts, and entertainers are left idle). Bres makes a bad judgment about the death of the satirist Cridenbél and finally insults Cairpre, the poet of the Tuatha Dé Danann. Cairpre satirizes him, but Bres will not give in and travels to the Fomoiri to visit his father.

Bres has committed an offence against the three sacred functions, as outlined by G. Dumézil – the sacred, martial and fertility; and he has insulted all strata of society – sovereignty, warriors, poets and the people of arts. It is the public humiliation of having given a false judgment that seems to be the necessary 'sin' that causes his downfall, and he is also punished at three different levels: he lost the kingship, lost the battle, and gave up the secret of fertility.[11]

The Tuatha Dé Danann reinstate Nuadu as king; his hand has been restored, and his first act is to hold a great feast at Tara. Lug, who arrives at the hall during the feast and is allowed in, shows that he is truly multi-skilled, the possessor of all the arts. Then he proceeds to prove his talent in each of the three functional areas of sovereignty: he wins at chess, defeats the champion Ogma and plays harp music for them.[12]

Before the battle, Lug is seen chanting a spell while circling the army on one foot with one eye closed, and he meets Balor in a confrontation similar to that of David and Goliath and of Finn and Aillén.[13] But the most important meeting is that of Bres and Lug, when Bres saves his own life by giving Lug the secrets of agriculture – to plough, sow and reap the crops on a Tuesday. There was a belief in favourable days for important farming activities; and Scottish farmers still use this advice.[14] This is the climax of the story as the Tuatha Dé Danann manage to take to themselves the third function of fertility. Now they possess all the skills necessary, and the battle is consistent with G. Dumézil's outline of the conflict between the combination of the first and second functions against the third. After the revelation they retrieve the items taken by the Fomoirí – the sword of Tethra, the Dagda's harp and the cows. The story ends with the two prophetic poems by the Mórrígan.

Another unifying theme of the saga is the proper and improper relationship between fathers and sons. Oengus helps his father the Dagda with a positive resolution of his problem with Cridenbél. Miach outstrips his father by giving Nuadu a fully human arm, and Dian Cécht kills his own son because he has set himself in opposition rather than in a supportive role. Airmed, daughter of Dian Cécht, obeys her father and survives to preside over the healing herbs. Elatha supports his errant son Bres, and his misplaced loyalty leads to the destruction of the Fomoirí.[15]

The story also includes a series of 'firsts' such as the first satire and the first keening. T. Ó Cathasaigh says: 'But the events of CMT happened "in the beginning": Lug is the first king to encompass the three functions, and Bres is the first to suffer satire. They are the paradigmatic figures, and *Cath Maige Tuired* is our most considerable exemplary text.'[16]

This saga may also be related to the Viking invasions; the Fomoirí and the Vikings are associated with one another in the text. The Mórrígan's dire prophecy at the end of the text may refer to the Vikings and the end of their world. Bres' failure may be seen as the 'erosion of native values' and 'social chaos'. There was an attack by Viking kings with a king of Meath on the tumuli in the Boyne Valley, something that had never happened before. It is reminiscent of the 'oppression of the Túatha Dé at the hands of Bres and his trio of foreign protectors.'[17]

Human kings replicate the events of the mythological tale and Cormac mac Airt in particular is associated with fertility and a Golden Age in Ireland. Cormac is the archetypally good human king, but even he is eventually flawed and must abdicate and die. His accession to kingship is found, with variations, in three different texts. The first, *Cath Maige Muccrama* (The Battle of Moytura), is really the story of Lugaid mac Con, king of Tara before Cormac, and much of the plot is set in Munster during the kingship of Ailill Ólomm (Ailill Bare-Ear), whose wife was Sadb daughter of Conn of the Hundred Battles.[18] They had three sons – Eogan, Cian and Cormac – and a foster son, Lugaid Mac Con, of another family.

The theme of stripping bare (*lommrad*) is central to many of the episodes of the story from the very start when Ailill goes to Áine Cliach to attend to his horses but finds that the hill is stripped and no one knows who is responsible. Ailill and his poet, Ferches, visit the hill again at Samain, and Ailill falls asleep. Eogabul and his daughter Áine emerge from the Otherworld carrying a bronze *timpán*. Eogabul runs towards the fairy mound followed by Ferches, who breaks his back. Ailill sleeps with the girl, but she sucks his ear so that there is no skin on it and it stays like that afterwards.

There is a disagreement between the foster brothers, Eogan and Lugaid mac Con, after they capture Fer Fí son of Eogabul, a *timpán* player. But Eogabul plays the three different types of music to them and sends them to sleep so that Fer Fí can escape. When they ask Ailill to make a judgment between them, he rules in favour of his son, Eogan.[19]

The foster brothers engage in the battle of Cend Abrat, and Lugaid goes into exile to Scotland. The king of Scotland tests them by placing a raw, dead mouse on each man's plate and telling them that they will be killed if they do not eat it. Lugaid puts the mouse in his mouth first and the men follow his lead. The king recognizes him as the leader and offers him help from the Saxons and the Britons. Lugaid and the army reach Mag Muccrama, south-west of Athenry, and the name, the plain of the counting of the pigs, is explained. Magic pigs emerge from a cave at Cruachu, called Ireland's door to Hell, and while Medb and Ailill try to count them a pig jumps over the chariot which Medb catches 'so that the skin on its forehead came apart so that the skin was left in her hand along with the shank ... From this is Mag Muccrama.'[20]

Art son of Conn, king of Tara, joins with Eogan son of Ailill Ólomm, but Lugaid defeats them in the battle of Mag Muccrama, and both Art and Eogan are killed. Before they die, both men have left pregnant women behind: Eogan meets Moncha daughter of Díl maccu Chrecga, a blind druid and she gives birth to Fiacha Muillethan (Fiacha Flat Head); Art sleeps with Achtan, daughter of Olc Acha and Cormac is conceived. The victor, Lugaid Mac Con, takes the kingship of Tara and reigns for seven years, taking the young Cormac into fosterage. His actions place him in the category of the 'ruler of occupation', for he has taken the kingdom by force. When Lugaid has to make a judgment he makes the wrong decision as follows:

On this occasion some sheep destroyed the woad (*glaisen*) of Lugaid's queen. It came before Mac Con.

'I say,' said Mac Con, 'that the sheep [should be given in compensation] for that.'

Cormac, a little boy, was beside him on the couch.

'No, foster father,' he said. 'It is more just to give the shearing of the sheep for the shearing of the woad, because the woad will grow [and] the wool will grow on the sheep.'

The people agree that this is the right judgment and Cormac becomes king. It seems wrong that Lugaid is judging a case involving the queen, presumably his own wife. The woad (*glaisen*) plant is significant, as it was grown for dyeing clothes a dark blue/purple colour that was the prerogative of the upper classes, and women were particularly associated with the dyeing of clothes.[21] In this case, the landscape reacts in sympathy: the wall of the house falls down. The episode happened at the *Cloenfherta* (crooked memorial stones) at Tara (called the Sloping Trenches) and the naming of the place is an essential part of the saga: 'It will always be like that – the Cloenfherta of Tara.'[22]

Lugaid returns to his foster parents in Munster and is welcomed by Sadb, who warns him against his foster father who will not forgive him for killing his son. Ailill pretends to welcome him, touches his cheek with his poisoned tooth, and Lugaid Mac Con is eventually killed by Ferches casting a spear at him, piercing his forehead and causing Lugaid to wither away.

The theme of stripping bare, a symbol of bad kingship, unifies the story and appears in many episodes, some of them occurring at times when people leave or try to enter the Otherworld: the stripping of the hill at Samain, Ailill's ear, the pig's skin, the woad that leads to the bad judgment and the withering of Lugaid's cheek. Ailill insulted the people of the Otherworld and commited a crime against the gods by placing his horses on that hill. Lugaid's bad judgment results in the stripping of the landscape; the crops do not grow for a year, showing that the king's role is central to the fertility of the land. Ailill has offended the gods and the Otherworld, and Lugaid has committed an offence against the forces of truth.[23]

In another version, Cormac is said to be thirty years old when he assumes the kingship, arriving at Tara with his father's sword, thumb-ring and royal clothing. He meets a woman crying outside Tara, and the king's steward explains that the king judged that her sheep 'be forfeited in requital for the stripping of the queen's field of woad.' Cormac replies: 'One stripping for the other would be more equitable.' There are two women mentioned in this version, but under early Irish law a woman cannot take a court case.[24] Lugaid Mac Con hands over the kingship to Cormac without any argument.

In the third account, Lugna Fer Trí fosters Cormac and brings him to Tara, where Lugaid Mac Con welcomes them and takes Cormac into fosterage. The judgment scene follows immediately; in it Cormac corrects the king and the people welcome it as a true judgment.[25] There is also a corrected judgment in the story of Congal Caech, who was blinded by a bee in the king's orchard. The Ulstermen decide that the eye of the king's son be given in forfeit, but when the matter is referred to the king he says that the whole swarm should be destroyed so that the guilty bee should be killed. [26]

In *Esnada Tige Buchet* (The Melodies of Buchet's House) Cormac finds his goddess wife Eithne and, as he is already king, the marriage validates his kingship of Tara and it is taken away from the Leinstermen as a result. Cormac lives in Kells first because Medb Lethderg has taken the kingship herself and will not allow him into Tara. The story is discussed below.[27]

There are two very different versions of how Conaire becomes the king of Tara: *Togail Bruidne da Derga* (The Destruction of the Hostel of Da Derga) and *De Shíl Chonairi Móir* (Of the Seed of Conaire Móir); the latter contains the more archaic account. In the *Destruction* saga, Conaire becomes king when he is only a young child.[28] He hears of the prophecy that was made at the bull feast and makes his way to Tara. He meets a flock of birds and attempts to shoot at them, but they remove their bird suits and their leader introduces himself as Nemglan (unclean). He explains that Conaire should not hunt birds because they are related to him. He tells him about the prophecy and that he should go to Tara. He also lists the taboos that will ensure his reign: not to travel righthandwise around Tara and lefthandwise around Brega, not to hunt the crooked beasts of Cerna, not to travel outside Tara every ninth night, not to sleep in a house in which firelight can be seen from outside or inside after sunset, not to allow Three Dergs (Red) to precede him into a red house, not to allow plunder in his reign, not to allow a single man or woman to come to his house after sunset, and finally not to interfere in a row between two slaves/servants. So Conaire's kingship is validated by the otherworldly birdman.[29]

Conaire is accused of being too young, but he defends his youth by saying that, being a young man, he is not corrupt, and promises that he will take advice from wise men. There is no account of his taking a wife, the usual validation of kingship, and it is his relationship with his foster brothers that damages his reign. There is peace until they begin to steal as was their right; their father was a professional plunderer (*díberg*). Eventually Conaire is forced to pass a judgment and says: 'Everyone should kill his son; my foster brothers shall be saved.' The people agree, but the king retracts and admits: 'That judgment has not lengthened my life' and sends the men to plunder in Scotland. From that point all his taboos catch up with Conaire until he dies in the hostel of Da Derga. He has sided with his foster brothers and offended both the prince's truth and the Otherworld.[30]

The account in *Of the Seed of Conaire Mór* is very different and Conaire is helped by his goddess-mother Mess Buachalla, who is descended from the goddess Étaín. Conaire travels across the plain of Brega to Tara with his mother, and the inauguration scene is described at length, including the references to the chariot screeching at the Lia Fáil along with Bloc and Bluigne – the stones that reputedly still stand on Tara.

> There was a king's chariot at Tara and two steeds of the same colour were yoked to the chariot, which had never before been harnessed. It would turn up before any man who was not destined to take kingship of Tara ... There were two stones in Tara, Bloc and Bluigne, and when they accepted a man, they would open before him until the chariot went through. Fál was there, the 'stone penis' (*ferp cluche*) at the top of the chariot's pathway, and when a man was eligible to receive the kingship of Tara, it screamed against the axle of the chariot so that everyone could hear it. But Bloc and Bluigne, the two stones, would not open before a man who was not eligible to hold the sovereignty of Tara. Their normal position was that only a hand could pass between them sideways. Fál would not scream for a man who was not eligible to hold Tara's kingship ...
>
> He stands in the chariot and it moves under him. He goes towards the two stones, and they open before him. He goes to the Fál with the people around him and his mother before him. The Fál cries out.
>
> 'Fál has accepted him!' cry the hosts.
>
> The hosts in Tara ... give him the sovereignty and his father's territories ...
>
> So that Conaire then is the king whom the phantoms brought to the sovereignty.[31]

Nessa is instrumental in making her son Conchobar king of Ulster in *Compert Conchobair* (The Conception of Conchobar). When Fergus mac Róich was the king of Ulster, he had no wife, and Nessa agrees to marry him on condition that he allows Conchobar to be king, and Nessa teaches her son 'to strip every second man, and to give (his wealth) to another; and her gold and silver were given to the champions of Ulster because of the result to her son.'[32] Conchobar retains the kingship, but the people will not allow him to make a judgment in case he makes a mistake and the crops are destroyed. In the second, longer, version of the birth tale, Cathbad is said to rear Conchobar, this is why he is called son of Cathbad although he is really the son of Fachtna Fáthach; and there is no interference here from his mother or promises to marry Fergus mac Róich.[33]

The semi-historical king, Niall of the Nine Hostages, is the classic case of the king born to a slave and separated from the kingship.[34] Eochaid Mugmedón king of Tara had two wives. Mongfhinn daughter of Fidach was the first and official wife, and they had four sons together, Brian, Ailill, Fiachra and Fergus. His second wife, Cairenn Casdub daughter of the king of the Saxons, was the mother of Niall. Mongfhinn hated Cairenn and forced her to carry water from the well even as she was expecting Niall.[35]

Eochaid cannot decide who will succeed him as king of Tara and, when he turns to the blacksmith and prophet, Sithchenn, he advises him to arrange for the forge to be set on fire and the five sons are asked to bring the most important instrument out of the fire so that he can adjudicate on their decisions. Brian brings out the hammer, Fiachra the beer and the bellows, Ailill the arms and Fergus the kindle wood, but Niall brings out the anvil, which is judged the most important. But it is a further test that proves the identity of the future king. The five brothers go hunting and lose their way in the woods. They decide to camp for the night and go searching for water. Each of them meets an old woman guarding a well, and she asks them to sleep with her. Fiachra speaks to her and she promises that he will have a connection with Tara. When Niall approaches, he kisses her and is prepared to lie with her, and she changes into a beautiful young woman.

There are a number of stories that address the negative side of sovereignty. In *Echtra Fergusa meic Léti* (The Adventure of Fergusa mac Léti) the king remained in office for seven years, despite his blemished face which was disfigured when he jumped into Loch Rudraige and saw a water monster. The Ulstermen hid the blemish from him and from the people. His hair was washed 'while lying on his back' so that he would not see himself. But he hit a slave girl with a whip when he thought her too slow in washing him; she retaliated by ridiculing his appearance. He cut her in two with his sword, returned to the lake again, killed the monster and died himself.[36]

In *The Adventure of Art* it appears that the wrong otherworldly woman mates with the older king rather than with his young successor. Bé Cuma (beautiful woman) has been banished from the Otherworld for a sin she committed, and she arrives in Ireland instead of Delbchaem (beautiful shape).[37] Conn's wife, Eithne Taebfhota, has died, and he cannot find her equal in Ireland; Bécuma allies herself with him and this seems to prolong his kingship of Tara. It becomes obvious that Bécuma is evil and that she has a negative effect on the kingdom. Conn's druids tell him that he can negate her malevolent influence by finding the son of a couple who have mated only once; this man he should kill at the entrance to Tara and mix his blood with the earth.

Conn finds the couple, who have produced a son called Ségda Saerlabraid (Ségda free speaker), but, on returning to Tara, Ségda's mother finds a cow to sacrifice in her son's place. Conn's son, Art, eventually sets out on a journey to find Bé Cuma's positive nemesis, Delbchaem. The substitute victim is similar to that of Isaac in the Bible, and B. O Hehir says: 'the entire first half of the extant text of *Echtra Airt meic Cuind ocus Tochmarc Delbchaime ingine Morgain* can therefore be seen as a late and entirely Christian invention.' Both K. McCone and B. O Hehir include *The Kinslaying of Rónán* as an example of the young woman allied with the old king, Rónán, rather than his young son, Mael Fothartaig.[38]

Echtra Nerai (The Adventure of Nera) begins with a feast given by Ailill and Medb at the eve of Samain at Cruachu just after two captives have been cruci-fied.[39] They set a test – to put a chain on the foot of one captive. Only Nera is not afraid of the darkness and of the night when demons appear. One captive asks for a drink, and Nera carries him on his back searching for water. He finds one house surrounded by fire, another surrounded by water, and finally a third with three containers of dirty water. The captive drinks from each of the three containers but squirts the people in the house with the water from the last one and kills them.

Then he climbs back on the cross. Cruachu is destroyed, and Nera follows the culprits into the Otherworld, where he is given a wife, and the king asks him to bring firewood to his house every day. He sees a blind man carrying a crip-pled man to a well every day and checks to see what is inside. Nera's wife tells him that contained within are the *barr Briúin* (the crown of Brian), the *cétach Laegairi* (Laegaire's cloak) of Armagh and the *enech Dúnlainge* (Dúnlaing's tunic) of the Leinstermen in Kildare and that the burning of Cruachu was just a forerunner of what would happen the following Samain if the people of the Otherworld were not contained and destroyed. She helps him to get these three treasures. A. Watson says of the saga: 'Sovereignty must create order in all things. This is why the king's truth is seen as so all important in early Irish soci-ety … If the king cannot embody these concepts, then disaster can befall the tribe which he rules.'[40]

Goddesses of Sovereignty

The sacred marriage to ensure the well-being of the land takes place between the king and the goddess, and Ireland is consistently depicted as a woman, the god-dess of the land. This image persists, particularly in the Bardic and metrical tra-ditions and W.B. Yeats used the image in *Cathleen Ni Hoolihan*.[41] B. Jaski argues that in the ninth and tenth centuries the queens of Tara may still be viewed as sovereignty figures and, even if some of them were not, that they were turned into such by later writers.[42]

The goddess is seen as marrying the king as a beautiful young woman who ages with the king, but she is transformed on meeting a young prince and serially marrying the kings. The use of women as a symbol of the land is not confined to Ireland, and A. Coomaraswamy makes reference to the different faces of sovereignty figures outside the Irish tradition, and gives examples from Cambodia and China, mentioning the goddess Sri. Her nemesis is Kali the goddess of ill-fortune and bad luck, and they are fickle and changeable.[43]

A feature of the relationship between king and goddess is her presentation to the king/hero of a ritual alcoholic drink as a symbol of his future lordship that links him with her and the Otherworld.[44] The most common word for sovereignty (*flaitheas/flaith*) is associated with the word for alcoholic drink (*laith*), and the element appears in female personal names combined with different colours: Órlaith (gold sovereignty), Donnlaith (brown sovereignty) and Gormlaith (blue/purple sovereignty); the last mentioned is often used for the daughters of the king of Tara. The continental sources refer to the woman choosing the man by giving him a drink – in a story about the foundation of Marseilles, for example.[45] In *The Wooing of Étaín* when Eochaid Airem has to choose his wife from fifty identical women, he says that she is 'The best at serving drink in Ireland'.[46]

In *The Phantom's Frenzy* Conn is standing on Tara's ramparts when he stands on Fál, and the cry is heard throughout Tara. [47] The number of cries relates to how many kings of his seed will be kings of Ireland. When he asks his druid to relate their names, he says that he cannot, and a mist descends on them. It rises, revealing a horseman who brings them to a hall where a beautiful woman, 'the sovereignty of Ireland', sits beside a vat of ale. A warrior beside her introduces himself as Lug and gives Conn a list of the future kings of Ireland. He hands the list to the woman so that she can present the kings with a sovereignty drink. The house and phantom disappear, but the vat and the vessel, visible signs of the Otherworld, remain with Conn. The related story *The Frenzy of Conn* gives a list of kings as they are presented with a sovereignty drink. The list gives obscure comments on the kings: 'Corbmac will drink it, a drink of elders, a peaceful warrior. He will perish from a morsel of food.'[48]

The name of the sovereignty figure Medb is taken to mean 'she who intoxicates, the intoxicating one.' The name is found in Indian-Iranian tradition as Madhavi <*madhu* 'a fermented drink', similar to the Old Irish word for mead (*mid*). [49] The word *mid* is also found in the Tech Midchuarta, the banqueting hall at Tara. Medb was considered by early scholars to be completely human until T. Ó Máille's article in 1928 where he pointed out for the first time that she was a supernatural sovereignty figure. The daughter of Eochaid Feidlech, brother of Eochaid Airem, she appears most famously as the headstrong queen of Connacht who serially marries the kings of the province as outlined in *Ferchuitred Medba* (The Husband Portion of Medb). She had six husbands – Conchobar mac Nessa, Tinne mac Conrach, Eochaid Dála, Ailill mac Mágach of the Érainn, Ailill mac Rosa Ruaid and Fergus mac Róich.[50]

The name Medb is originally associated with Tara in the person of Medb Lethderg (red-sided/half red), whose name survives at Ráith Medba. She serially married the kings of Leinster such as: Feidlimid Rechtmar, Art mac Cuinn and Cormac mac Airt.[51] She is mentioned side by side with Eithne also the wife of Cormac and they appear to be interchangeable. Eithne also appears as a Christian in *The Nourishment of the House of the two Vessels* and gives her name to Cell Eithne (the church of Eithne) at Brú na Bóinne. Patrick converts the two daughters of Laegaire the pagan king of Tara – Eithne and Fedelm – and their bones form a church. Many others named Eithne appear in genealogies of the saints.[52] One of the epithets attached to Eithne, and others, is *aitenchaetrach* 'with gorse (coloured) pubic hair', showing their overt sexuality. In *The Love-Sickness of Cú Chulainn*, king Conchobar's wife is called Eithne Aitenchaetrach.[53]

Medb is linked with Fergus in the earliest sources, and the poem *Medb Makes Bad Contracts*, by Luccreth moccu Chíara (*c*.600) that contains the earliest *Táin*-type material shows his relationship with her and his exile to Tara. The prose introduction says: 'For Fergus turned against the Ulstermen because of a woman, that is, because of Medb of Cruachain, for her he fought against his own people for the body of a woman'; and the poem itself says: 'His great wolves gathered at stout firm-bordered Tara; they left the great lands of the Ulstermen, for they parted from a prince given to feasting and drinking.'[54] The Stone of Fál (Lia Fáil), which originally lay flat at the Mound of the Hostages at Tara and now stands upright on the Forrad, was known locally to Irish-speakers in the nineteenth century as the phallus of Fergus (*bod Fhearghusa*).[55]

The figure of Fergus is ambiguous; his behaviour is suspect, and one version of his loss of the kingship of Ulster is through his association with Nessa, who tricked him into giving it to her young son Conchobar. *The Cattle Raid of Flidais* says that, during the seven years of his reign, 'the sun did not rise over the edge of the warlike rampart of Emain' and this was called 'the black reign of Fergus.'[56] It is said that it took seven women to satisfy him if Flidais was not there. He uses his sword, the caladbolg with its sexual connotations, to shape the landscape when he takes the tops off three mountains in Meath then called Maela Midi (the cropped ones/bald ones of Meath), but he is symbolically castrated when he loses his sword (this echoes Delilah's weakening of Samson by cutting his hair).[57] Fergus is hugely productive in genealogies as the ancestor figure of many Munster and Connacht families.

There was a successful attempt to 'rehabilitate' Fergus in *The Exile of the sons of Uisliu*. There was also a text called *Fochonn Loingse Fergusa meic Roig* (The Cause of the Exile of Fergus mac Róich) but only the beginning remains today as three pages of the manuscript are missing. The content cannot be established, but both appear in the Book of Leinster.[58] When accompanying Derdriu and Naíse back to Ireland, he is met by the treachery of king Conchobar, who orders the murder of the three brothers. Fergus leaves Ulster in protest and is presented in a better light. J. Carney says: 'The genealogical tradition shows Fergus in a bad light ... [T]he fiction-writer who created the Derdriu story has done a first-rate job of whitewashing.' This powerful story has lasted through the centuries and with it the 'whitewashing' of Fergus.[59]

By the time Medb appears in the *Táin*, she is no longer a goddess but 'no better than a strong-willed virago with unconcealed leanings towards a multiplicity of husbands and paramours.'[60] In the Pillow Talk of the Book of Leinster text she says that her father 'gave me a whole province of Ireland, this province ruled from Cruachan' and that she asked as a wedding gift 'the absence of meanness and jealousy and fear.' This copy expands her role and blames her for the raid because she was jealous of Ailill's bull and wanted one like it.[61] She makes a number of bad judgments; she ignores the prophecy made by Fedelm and exploits her daughter Finnabair by offering her to all the warriors. P. Kelly says: 'it is the central purpose of the *Táin* to depict her (Medb) in a thoroughly unflattering light.'[62] But her actions may be compared with other women such as Mac Da Thó's wife, who must make a decision due to men's inaction. Although both Ailill and Fergus say explicitly that a woman's counsel should not be taken seriously, they, like Mac Da Thó, follow her advice because they have failed in their own roles as decision makers.[63]

Towards the end of the version of the *Táin* in the Book of Leinster Medb is said to either urinate or menstruate; this stops Cú Chulainn from attacking the army as they try to cross the Shannon. From this is named Fúal Medba (Medb's foul place). The contempt for her is expressed in Fergus's words: 'We followed the rump of a misguided woman,' Fergus said. 'It is the usual thing for a herd led by a mare to be strayed and destroyed.'[64]

The Manifestations of the Sovereignty Goddess

It is recognized that the sovereignty goddess appears in the texts in three manifestations: (i) the old woman who becomes young and beautiful on meeting the rightful king, (ii) the woman who loses her mind and regains it when meeting the king, and (iii) the woman who loses her status in society and regains it on meeting her intended spouse. [65]

The best example of the old woman turning into a beautiful young woman is the story of Niall of the Nine Hostages outlined above. A similar story is told of the five Lugaids, the sons of Dáire Doimthech – one of whom is Lugaid Loígde. A druid prophesied to Dáire Doimthech that a son of his called Lugaid would be the king of Ireland, so he called all five of his sons by that name. After a series of adventures, the five brothers go hunting and arrive at a house where an old woman lives, and she asks them to sleep with her. As soon as Lugaid Laígde agrees, she turns into a beautiful young girl who says that she is the sovereignty of Ireland. The following day the house has disappeared.[66]

In the second manifestation, the woman is insane and ugly, and loses her mind until she regains it when meeting the proper king. This theme appears in the stories of Mór Muman and her sister Suithchern along with the story of Mis and Dub Rois – all associated with Munster. Mór (†633/688), daughter of the historical king Aed Bennán of Eoganacht Locha Léin, loses her place in society and regains it by meeting the proper king. She also has a sister, Suithchern or Ruithchern, who appears briefly in this tale but also in a separate story where she is the main character. [67] Mór hears voices in the air, and as a result she jumps over the embankment and travels Ireland unrecognized and dressed in rags. Eventually she reaches Cashel and cares for Fíngen mac Aeda's sheep. His wife dares him to sleep with her; when Fíngen asks her who she is, her senses return. When she goes to the sheep the following day, the king stops her. The queen laughs but Fíngen says: 'Give her the purple cloak and the queenly brooch.'

She gives birth to their son, Sechnassach, and this shows the fertility of the proper king. When Fíngen dies, Mór goes to Cathal son of Finguine king of Eoganacht Glendomnach (†742). There is a hundred-year gap between the two kings so perhaps the intended king was Cathal mac Aeda Flainn (†628). It is understood from the text that afterwards she went to the king of Eoganacht Áine as this was the way in which the kingship of Munster was arranged: it moved from one branch of the Eoganacht to another.

Her sister appears briefly in this tale in similar circumstances. After Mór married the king, Suithchern, also called Ruithchern (from So/Ro 'great' and tigern 'sovereign'), appears in a similarly dishevelled state and cares for the sheep after her. Mór gives her as wife to Lonán mac Bindig of the kingdom of Éile. According to this story, she is captured by Cuanu mac Cailchine, and in the ensuing battle between them both Lonán and Cuanu are killed.

Suithchern is the main character in another tale where she is described as the wife of Rónán mac Dícholla the king of Uí Liatháin. The story has no title, but the tale list mentions *Aithed R/Suithcherne re Cuana mac Cailchine* (The

Elopement of Suithchern with Cuanu mac Cailchine).[68] The only manuscript containing the saga is badly soiled and illegible in places, but the main points are reasonably clear. Aed Bennán, Suithchern's father, curses her; she visits her sister Mór and Fíngen but they do not recognize her at first because she 'rubbed rye dough all over herself, she carried a pointed spade, a hard leather bag at her side and a worn grey mantle round her and a rough linen cloth next to her skin and she was black and swarthy.'

Suithchern leaves to search for her lover Cuanu mac Cailchine, but instead she reaches Rónán mac Dícholla king of the Uí Liatháin. There is a break in the manuscript at this point, and when the story resumes it seems that she is calling herself Mael Choirn (the servant of the drinking horn?), like other women taking an assumed name. The use of the word *corn* associates her with the sovereignty. Rónán's wife goads him into sleeping with Suithchern, and the transformation occurs as she washes and dresses herself as a queen: the stewardess helps her to remove the rough linen cloth from her and the melting, rotten rags; she began to wash herself, the stewardess combs her hair with bogcotton, and she begins 'to turn a light brown colour so that the wave of the sea or the snow of one night was not brighter than every limb and every inch of her from top to toe.'

From her bag she takes 'a bright purple cloak like a cape and put a diadem of gold about her head.' The cloak is spread over her, and when the king comes to her there is no light so he cannot see the transformation until the following day. He gets rid of his wife and takes Suithchern (Mael Choirn) instead. In contrast with Mór, she lives with the king for twelve years without having a child and without revealing her proper name until the fool, Mac Dá Cherda, recognizes her. As he is about to reveal her identity, she disappears to search again for her lover Cuanu mac Cailchine, but the remainder of the story is unknown; she reaches a crossroads, and the manuscript stops at that point. Suithchern's refusal to reveal her proper name, and her lack of children, indicate that she is not the proper woman or that she is not with the right king. The woman in *The Adventure of Art* takes another's name, Sín refuses to give her name in the *Aided Muirchertaig meic Erca* (The Death of Muirchertach mac Erca), and the woman in the story of debility of Ulstermen asks her husband not to mention her name.

The third example is Mis; although the existing version of the story comes from the eighteenth century, the title *Aithed Muirne re Dub Rois* (Muirne's Elopement with Dub Rois) is in the tale lists. The oldest texts refer to her as the daughter of Maired mac Caireda and wife of Caemgen Conganchnes, and she is associated with Sliabh Mis in Co. Kerry. In the later tale she is the daughter of Dáire Dóidghel and she is said to be very strong and a danger to people travelling the mountains.[69]

Her father died in Cath Fionntrá (The Battle of Ventry) and when she finds
his body on the battlefield she drinks his blood and goes mad on Sliabh Mis.
Her hair grows to the ground, and the nails on both her hands and feet are so
long that she can tear apart the flesh of any animal or human who comes too
close. She can run like the wind and eats raw meat. The king, Feidlimid mac
Crimthainn, sends his harpist Dub Rois to pacify her because she is a danger to
anyone who approaches the mountain. In preparation he brings gold, silver,
food and his harp with him. In a very Freudian scene, by introducing her to
money, music and finally sex, he gains her confidence and she is persuaded to
eat cooked meat and to be bathed so that the hair and nails disappear. He lies
on the mountain waiting for her: 'He lay on his back. He placed the harp on his
body.' He opened his trousers or his pants and revealed himself because he
understood that if he had the opportunity to sleep with her it might restore her
senses. She came in response to the music and asks him to play the harp, but it
is his nakedness that attracts her:

> A glance she gave, she saw his nakedness and the *playthings* and said:
>   'What are these?' she asked of his *bag* or of his *little eggs* and he told
> her.
>   'What is this?' she asked of the other thing she saw.
>   'That is *a branch of the trick*,' he said.
>   'I don't remember that,' she said, 'my father did not have such a
> thing.'
>   '*Branch of the trick*,' she said again, 'what is the trick?'
>   'Sit beside me,' he said, 'and I will perform the trick of that branch for
> you.'
>   'I will,' she said, 'and stay beside me.'
>   'I will,' he said. He lay and slept with her and she said:
>   'Ho, ho, a good trick, do it again!'
>   'I will,' he said, 'but I will play the harp for you first.'
>   'Never mind the harp', she said, 'but do the trick again.'

He shows her how to cook food and gives her bread that he brought with him.
The text describes his cooking pit (*fulacht*), although the term itself is not used:
'Then he built a great heap of fire of old dry wood and he collected a pile of
stones and put them in the fire. He made a wide circle in the ground and filled
it with water. He cut up the meat and wrapped it in prepared coarse grass with
a tightenable straw rope and put it in the hole until it was boiling in the red,
burnt stones in the water. He watched it continually until that part of the meat
was cooked. He took it from the hole and put the fat of the deer in the boiling

water until it melted in the water.' This is followed by a sweat treatment that he uses to wash her: he rubs her in the deer lard so that she was clean and 'sweated streams.' She eventually married him; they have children and live happily together until he is killed.[70]

The use of deermeat, the outdoor life and the association of music with the cooking pit conjures up a scene from a Fenian tale; Mis is living a liminal life in the wilderness similar to Derdriu's description of her idyllic outdoor life and her praise of Naíse's music.[71] Nessa, Conchobar's mother, also lives in the wilderness temporarily when she takes it upon herself to avenge the murder of her fosterers. Her marriage restores her to normal society.[72]

The same thread runs through the stories of all three women – losing their minds and their looks, and the restoration of their sanity and beauty by sexual contact with a man. But they are also physically ugly like the hag in the story of Niall of the Nine Hostages, and they lose their social status like Eithne (see below). Their ability to jump or even fly is reminiscent of the male version of madness in the early sagas, as is their lonely existence in the wilderness. These women are temporarily liminal, inhabiting the same space as mad men and marginalized characters until they meet their rightful king.

The third manifestation is the woman who loses her status in society and regains it when she meets the right man like the international fairy tales about Cinderella and Snow White. As noted above, in *The Melodies of Buchet's House*, Cormac's marriage to the goddess and the birth of his son, Cairpre Lifechair, are symbols of his rightful sovereignty.[73]

Eithne Taebfhota is the daughter of Cathaír Mór king of Leinster and she is fostered with the hospitaller Buchet. Her brothers often visit her and eventually this deprives Buchet of all his wealth apart from seven cows and a bull, and the family move to Kells and live in a shack. When Cormac sees Eithne, she is doing the work of a servant, milking cows, cutting rushes and fetching water, but he falls in love with her without knowing her real status in life.[74] He asks Buchet's permission to marry her when he discovers her identity, but he is refused because only her father can do that. Cormac abducts her, and their son Cairpre Lifechair (Liffey lover) is conceived on that first night that they spend together.[75] Eithne escapes, but Cormac accepts his son when the Leinstermen swear that he is his, and Eithne is accepted as his queen. The bride price that Buchet receives restores his wealth, and there is a great feast to celebrate the marriage. Cormac is already king, so his marriage to Eithne validates his kingship like Eochaid Airem's marriage to the goddess Étaín in *The Wooing of Étaín*. The Leinstermen persuade Cormac to accept his son; therefore it is the Leinstermen who are giving him the kingship. Medb Lethderg is also mentioned as Cormac's wife and that she took the kingship for fourteen months.[76]

Madness in Early Irish Literature

The early literature features madness and mad people in many stories, although the latter may also be wise like Shakespeare's fool. They are said to gather at Gleann Bolcáin in the early period, and Gleann na nGealt is mentioned in later sources; the two places are probably the same, located at Ventry, Co. Kerry.[77] Suibne Geilt is the most prominent male figure to lose his reason and live in the wilderness. A second madman, Mac Dá Cherda, is associated with St Cuimine Fota in *Imthechta na nÓinmhidí* (The Wanderings of the Fools) as they walk the countryside together. Mac Dá Cherda is the son of Mael Ochtraig, king of the Déise on the Suir, and he commits adultery with the wife of his father's druid. The court jester dies, and the druid offers to produce a new one; the king agrees, and the druid throws a magic wisp into Mac Dá Cherda's face, and he becomes a fool (*óinmit*) but he is also filled with God's grace. He could sleep outside in deep winter and the birds would shelter him from the cold with their wings. But above all he reveals secret information about people: it is he who recognizes Suithchern.

He meets St Cuimine Fota of the Eoganacht Locha Léin, and the saint recites poems praying for news of Mac Dá Cherda, the chief fool who delivers true judgments when in his full senses. They speak in riddles to one another, become foster brothers, and when Cuimine gives him communion Mac Dá Cherda dies and goes to heaven.[78]

To return to Suibne, he is called the king of Dál nAraide in *The Madness of Suibne*. He goes mad when a saint curses him and he sees the horrors of battle at Mag Ráith.[79] He chooses to live outdoors composing poetry and living a liminal, solitary life. He grows feathers, and from time to time characters from normal society including his wife and St Mo-Ling of Co. Carlow come searching for him and he is killed while drinking milk from a hole in the ground.[80] The image of the madman may have developed from that of Suibne, and there is a relationship between madness, hearing voices in the sky and leaping as Cú Chulainn does when Fann leaves him in *The Love-Sickness of Cú Chulainn*.[81] Suibne is going through the liminal stage of the rites of passage encountered by hero or king during a life-changing experience but, like the Fianna, he is doomed to remain there, and when he re-enters the real world, he is killed.[82]

Mac Dá Cherda also appears in the story of Liadan and Cuirithir where he passes a message to Liadan from Cuirithir and he gives it in riddles because there are other women around her. Later Cuimine says to her: 'I do not like what you say .../ Cuirithir was here, he was not mad,/ any more than before he came.' And she says in her poem: 'It were madness / for one who'd not do his pleasure,/ were there not fear of the king of heaven.'[83]

In modern folk tradition, keening women (*mná caointe*) are barefoot with their hair hanging loose, clothes in disarray and walking in the wilderness; they belong to the same category as the mad man: 'both categories are in transition and both are temporarily outside the normal structure of society.'[84] In the most famous lament, *Caoineadh Airt Uí Laoghaire* (The Lament for Art O'Leary), Eibhlín Dubh Ní Chonaill says that she took three leaps, referring to the liminal areas of threshold, and gate before leaping onto Art's horse that had returned home, covered in blood, and without his master.[85] In *Caoineadh na Maighdine* (The Virgin's Lament) Mary is said to take three leaps to the foot of the cross, just as Cú Chulainn takes three leaps of madness at the end of the story of his love sickness.[86]

CHAPTER 8

The Hero and Heroic Biography

The psychological dangers through which earlier generations were guided by the symbols and spiritual exercises of their mythological and religious inheritance, we today ... must face alone, or, at best, with only tentative, impromptu, and not often very effective guidance. This is our problem as modern, 'enlightened' individuals, for whom all gods and devils have been rationalized out of existence.[1]

The heroic biography is generally presented as consisting of ten points in the hero or king's life that are worthy of having stories composed about them; in Irish literature it applies to characters from all the cycles and, although the individual is usually male, it can also apply to women and saints of both genders.[2] J. de Vries set out the ten major points of the hero's life as follows: conception; birth; the child being threatened in childhood; youth; upbringing; near-invulnerability; a fight with a dragon or a monster; getting a wife; a visit the Otherworld; exile and return; and the death of the hero.[3] The birth and death tales and the taking of a wife are the most common in this literature, but there is very little about invulnerability or the fight with the monster.

The biography is a pre-existing, worldwide phenomenon of human thought into which the lives of major figures are moulded. Every great hero has a biography, but the pattern is pre-Christian and appears in religions and societies well before the arrival of Christianity. The stories contain the template for a good life; and the life of Christ, known to Christians for over two thousand years, fits the biography with few exceptions (for example, he does not take a wife). The steps in the hero's life can be dangerous, and rites are needed to help people in their passage from one point in their lives to the next. This applies to ordinary mortals as well as the elevated hero or king. In the case of real-life models, the dangerous passages of people's lives are: birth; growing up and maturation; finding a partner or entering the church; becoming a parent; achieving a higher social status; choosing a specialized art/craft; and death. Many of these coincide with points in people's lives where even the modern Church intervenes: baptism (birth); confession/holy communion and confirmation (maturity); marriage/holy orders (finding a partner); and extreme unction (death). The ceremonial times of Samain, Lugnasad, Imbolc and Beltaine may have been associated with these transitional periods in life.

A. Van Gennep sees each step as having three stages: separation from the previous stage, a period of transition (liminality), and finally incorporation into the next stage. The danger point is transition: the possibility is that the next step will not be taken and that the individual will be 'stuck' between one stage and the next. Many modern films and horror movies play on the basic human fear that the dead person will not leave this world (this gives rise to the themes of vampires and the undead). As the individual moves from one stage to the next, he is holy and sacred, and certain rites must be used to help him through this disturbed phase to bring him back to the level of ordinary people again. All life is change, with times of peace in between.[4] Early Irish literature in general and the Fenian Cycle in particular seems fascinated, if not indeed obsessed, with the theme of liminality. The word for this transitional stage comes from the Latin word for threshold (*limen*), and it describes a state of in-betweenness, for example standing on the threshold between two rooms but not in either of them. J. Nagy describes it as 'the state of being in between separate categories of space, time or identity. A boy who is on the verge of manhood is a liminal figure, as is someone who crosses from one world into another. Such figures belong only marginally to one or several categories; they are unclassifiable persons, or, they are classifiable in more than one way.'[5]

Taboos (*gessa*) and boons (*buada*) form part of the heroic life corresponding with negative and positive rituals found worldwide. Although Finn mac Cumaill says, 'I don't like being put under *gessa*,' they are designed to protect the hero from danger and to help him avoid tragedy such as death or an insult to his honour. Taboos are connected with heroic honour, animals, sexual activity, places and food, but others may come from real situations that should be avoided.[6]

Territories and borders are central to liminality, and geographical features such mountains, rivers, lakes, doorways, thresholds and entry to the Otherworld appear in the stories and may be marked by stakes, rocks or ogam stones in Ireland. In the literature, the Fianna and other outsiders inhabit the no-man's-land of deserts, marshes and virgin forests. The person passing from one territory to another finds himself in in-between places that are said to have 'developed into the focal points of socio-religious activity.'[7] Passage through doors, sometimes to the Otherworld, and combats at fords are associated with the heroes; and Chulainn, Finn and Lug are all opposed as they try to join society. The Fianna may be seen as in a state of permanent liminality, but even they have their own structures. They have initiation rites that they must pass before becoming fully-fledged members of the group, and they swear by 'The truth of our hearts, the strength of our arms, and the constancy of our tongues.'[8] But when they try to move to the next stage they are blocked or die. Finn never grows into a proper adult; he is trapped in an adolescent limbo, and the stories depend on 'this element of incompleteness.'[9]

Originally, the stories associated with the heroes may have been more than entertainment and intended to help people through real-life crises. In modern times, they are replaced by professionals such as psychoanalysts and psychologists who help people facing change that they cannot handle. These professions have nearly replaced religion as an aid.[10]

The idea of the hero (usually *laech* in these stories) has changed greatly in modern times.[11] Ideally the hero is strong, and shows courage in the face of the enemy, and his name will live forever, as Cú Chulainn declares: 'Provided I be famous, I am content to be only one day on earth.'[12] But heroes are human; they must die, unlike the (usually) God-father. Along with his need for everlasting fame he is ever fearful of being satirized.

Cú Chulainn and Finn mac Cumaill are warrior-heroes as distinct from the king-heroes such as Cormac mac Airt or Conaire Mór. The case of the king-heroes is reasonably clear-cut, but the relationship between the warrior-heroes, Cú Chulainn and Finn, is complex. Cú Chulainn, son of Lug the ultimate godly hero-figure, has been described as the 'hero of the tribe' and Finn and the Fianna as 'the heroes outside the tribe', and they are two sides of the one coin: 'the warrior-dog and the hunter-wolf.'[13] Unlike other Ulster heroes, Cú Chulainn is not an ancestor, and he kills his only son. But later tradition credits him with a daughter called Finnscoth wife of Erc son of Cairpre.[14]

The hero's fury and loss of control is shown primarily by the distortion (*riastrad*) that happens to Cú Chulainn.[15] This anger can be a danger to his own people; Cú Chulainn is both frightening and strikingly beautiful. He is so dangerous that he must be restrained, as shown in the tales of his boyhood. His unstable relationships with women are also seen in his adventures in the Otherworld below, and Medb intimidates him in the *Táin*.[16] Both he and Finn are related to dogs, but animals are connected with other figures: the wolves look after Cormac mac Airt, and his father's name is one of the Irish words for a bear; Conaire is the son of a birdman who warns him not to hunt birds.

T. Ó Cathasaigh also looks at the similarities between certain heroes and says: 'The parallelism between Lug and Finn is impressive, and it would appear too that both of them are Irish versions of mythical personages who were known and celebrated by the continental Celts.' But there is one importance difference between them: Lug is a god and Finn is human; when Finn dies, he is dead.[17]

The stories of the Fianna have survived to the present day in both Ireland and Scotland. Originally Finn is a loner, the hero-outsider and the epitome of the warrior who never settles into society. In later literature, post-twelfth century, he becomes the mercenary of Cormac mac Airt, defending Tara and later the whole country from successive invaders, and he is involved with all manner of heroes of romantic and imported literature.

Cormac mac Airt is the archytypal king and one of the most important ancestor figures for the northern part of the country. His grandfather Conn of the Hundred Battles was the ancestor of both the Connachta and the Uí Néill but the literature contains much more on Cormac himself. He is the ideal, sacred king of Tara, the human exemplar who follows Lug but is eventually flawed and dies.

1 and 2: Conception and Birth

The elements of conception and birth are the first two obstacles that the hero faces when entering the world. The child is quite often named as soon as he/she is born, or the father has already chosen a name before the birth. In the context of real-life crises, some societies remove the mother from the tribe as she is felt to be unclean and a danger to the rest of society because she is in a liminal space while pregnant. She is later allowed to rejoin society and is 'incorporated into normality.'[18] Christian children are cleansed of original sin by baptism, as it is believed that all human beings come into this world with sin on their souls. In Ireland, there was the practice of 'churching' (cleansing) a mother after the birth when she was re-admitted to church services.

In the Irish tales, conception takes place in unusual circumstances, and the same motifs appear repeatedly: the hero/king is the offspring of a god or an animal/bird; the mother is a virgin; women become pregnant by drinking insects;[19] the child is begotten just before the death of the father; the woman is hidden away and must be found or she is visited by strange men at night sometimes as birds; and there may be an incestuous relationship between the parents. The father and/or the mother may die shortly after the conception of the child, who is left an orphan. Time is out of joint, so that the pregnancy may last years or a day, and the birth itself may also be delayed to give the child luck. Another feature is the appearance of a herdsman who looks after an abandoned female child as with Mess Buachalla and Eithne.

There are a number of stories in which the mother swallows an insect or worm. Conall Cernach's mother swallows a worm with the well water. The worm lay in the unborn child's hand, eating away at him.[20]

There are two versions of Cú Culainn's conception and birth, in one of which he is conceived on three different occasions.[21] There are a number of motifs here: at the first conception, the child is entirely of the Otherworld; the second is as a result of his mother Deichtire swallowing an insect in water and being visited by the god Lug; and the final conception occurs through the human combination of Deichtire and Sualdam mac Róich (brother of Fergus). The story opens with birds laying waste Emain Macha, so that a fertility hero is called for. Horses are born at the same time as Cú Chulainn's first conception. After the second conception, when Deichtire becomes mysteriously pregnant, the people of Ulster suspect incest between her and her father/brother Conchobar.[22] She goes to her husband, becomes pregnant again, and gives birth to Sétanta as forecast by Lug. Some see a similarity with the birth of Christ, but the threefold conception is more in keeping with the triplicity of gods and heroes in native literature and iconography.

Conchobar's mother, Nessa daughter of Eochaid Sálbuide (Eochaid of the Yellow Heel), also drinks an insect in water. She was fostered by twelve foster fathers, but when the druid-champion Cathbad kills them Nessa sets out to revenge them. She is bathing in the river when Cathbad comes between her and her spearshafts. They sleep together and she becomes his wife and bears him a son.[23] There is also a tradition that Conchobar's father is Fachtna Fáthach son of Rudraige and that he was sleeping with her while she was married to Cathbad. This version of the tale says that Cathbad foretold that, if she delays the birth, the child will be famous. She says: 'Unless he comes out through my side, he will not come out any other way until the stated time.'[24]

This delaying of time is found in a number of other conceptions: *The Battle of Mag Muccrama* tells how Eogan son of Ailill Ólomm meets Moncha daughter of Díl maccu Chrecga, a blind druid.[25] Moncha becomes pregnant, and the child born is called Fiacha Muillethan (Fiacha of the broad-crown) from the strange circumstances of his birth. Moncha's father advises her that, if she can delay the birth for one day, the child will be pre-eminent in Ireland. She replies that, even if the child is to come through her side, she will hold on. She sits on a rock in the middle of the ford at the river until the proper time and dies after the most liminal of births. Cummain, Brigit's sister, also gave birth to king Tuathal Maelgarb (Tuathal of rough baldness) while sitting on a stone waiting for an omen, and the stone left marks on his head.[26] Brigit's own birth is full of liminal images: as the sun rises, her mother, a slave, carries a vessel of milk across the threshold and falls with one foot outside the house and another inside and gives birth.[27]

Finn's conception, birth and youth are found in *The Boyhood Deeds of Finn*, an incomplete tale.[28] Cumall is said to have married Torba daughter of Eochaman of the Érainn first and then Muirne Muinchaem (Fair-neck). There was a disagreement between Cumall son of Trénmór and Uirgriu son of Lugach Corr of the Luigne of Tara. *The Battle of Cnucha* tells of the conflict that took place between them in the area of the present-day Castleknock.[29] The conception and birth are referred to only fleetingly; the story says that Cumall left his wife, Muirne, pregnant, and she bore a son called Demne who later was called Finn.

There are different versions of Cormac's conception and birth. In *The Battle of Mag Muccrama* his father Art, on the eve of battle, is introduced to a woman by her father; she is Achtan the daughter of Olc Acha, a smith of the Connachtmen. Art advises Achtan to bring her future son to the men of Connacht to be fostered.[30] In *The Conception of Cormac* the girl is called Etan and she approaches Lugna Fer Trí before the child is born; wolves steal the baby and take him to Uaim Cormaic (Cormac's cave) where he is found by two men, and Lugna prophecies a wonderful future for Cormac and fosters him along with his own children. In *Scéla Eogain 7 Cormac* (The Story of Eogan and Cormac) Art sees Achtan milking and asks her for a drink.[31] After they sleep together, Art gives her his sword, gold thumb-ring and his clothing to give to his future son, similar to what happens in the conception of Bres. Shortly after the birth, a wolf steals the baby and Cormac spends a year with the animal until a famous trapper, Lugna Fer Trí, captures them. When his mother finds him, Lugna Fer Trí advises her to take the child to his father's foster father, Fiachna Cassán, in the north of Ireland. As she makes the border journey, wolves howl around her, and horses protect her as she crosses the mountains. Cormac remains there until he is thirty years old. The appearance of wolves is reminiscent of the story of Romulus and Remus and the foundation of Rome.

Conaire Mór and his mother Mess Buachalla feature in three different sagas – *The Wooing of Étaín*, *The Destruction of the Hostel of Da Derga* and *Of the Seed of Conaire Mór*. Many different motifs are found in the sagas, including incest, the abandoned child cared for by the herdsman, swallowing a fly and a visitor who forecasts Conaire's birth. The goddess, horseriding Étaín, married the god Midir but his jealous first wife, Fuamnach, turned her into a purple fly that flies around the liminal space between two worlds for 1,012 years until she falls into a cup of an unnamed woman who gives birth to a daughter who is again called Étaín.[32]

She in turn marries the king of Tara Eochaid Airem, but Midir returns for her and takes her away. As Eochaid searches for her, Midir presents him with fifty women who look like her, and when he chooses one of the woman, and has slept with her, he finds out that she is his daughter not his wife. Eochaid has made his own daughter pregnant; when their daughter is born, she is left at the house of the herdsman of Tara. She becomes Mess Buachalla, the mother of Conaire Mór son of Eterscél after a visit from a man dressed in a bird suit. Other versions are found in *The Destruction of the Hostel of Da Derga* and also in *Of the Seed of Conaire Mór*.[33] Incest appears in the tale of Cairpre Músc who is the son of another Conaire and Sárait daughter of Conn of the Hundred Battles. He sleeps with his own sister Duibfhinn and they produce a son Corc Duibne from whom the Corco Duibne are named.[34] Incest features again in the family of Eochaid Feidlech, brother to Eochaid Airem; and *Cath Bóinde* (The Battle of the Boyne) tells of his triplet sons, Bres, Nár and Lothar (who are called the Trí Finn Emna, three fair ones of Emain) and his six daughters (who include Clothra, Eithne and the famous Medb). The triplets slept with their sister Clothra and she gave birth to Lugaid Riab nDerg (Lugaid of the red stripes) so-called because he was divided in three with similarities to all three fathers.[35]

Niall of the Nine Hostages son of Eochaid Mugmedón was born to Cairenn, his father's second wife.[36] Eochaid had four sons by his first wife Mongfhinn, and Mongfhinn hated Cairenn so much that she made her draw water until the baby's delivery, hoping this would kill the foetus. Torna the poet takes Niall away and they did not return to Tara until he was fit for kingship. He frees his mother and dresses her in purple clothes. The strange conception of Aed Sláine king of Tara (†604) son of Diarmait is mentioned in the chapter on the Cycles of the Kings.

Some birth tales are more overtly sexual: Findach sees a woman Créd and is so moved that he stains watercress with his semen, she eats it and thereby becomes pregnant. The child is the saint Boethine.[37] The most unusual conception tale involves a judgment by the king of Tara Niall Frassach (†778) where he realizes that two women had sex because one woman's husband could not satisfy her. The unmarried woman became pregnant as a result of the semen being passed from the married woman to her; this is one of the very few lesbian references in early Irish literature.[38]

3 and 4: Account of Youth and Upbringing

The best stories are those about the boyhood deeds of Cú Chulainn and of Finn where borders and territorial passage are central. They are separated from their parents at a young age; the naming of the child and his fosterage are features of these stories in Irish tradition. The heroes grow quickly, mature at a young age, and can perform extraordinary deeds. A. Van Gennep, in his study of these stories, includes a chapter on initiation rites and the importance of territories and boundaries.[39]

There is no account of the youth of the king-hero, Cormac, and there is no martial content in his actions as a young child. Cormac's own name is uncertain, and T. Ó Cathasaigh has speculated that it may come from the Old Irish word *cor(b)* (corrupt) and *mac* (son), a corrupt boy/son, perhaps due to his bestial associations. His rite of passage to adulthood is demonstrated by his ability to tell the truth and make a true judgment. Conchobar also shows greatness at a young age, and his mother helps him to become king of Ulster temporarily at

1 Aerial photograph of Tara, courtesy of Eamon O'Donaghue

2 Writing tablets, Springmount bog, Co. Antrim, courtesy of the National Museum

3 The Stowe Missal, p. 1 courtesy of the Royal Irish Academy

4 Shrine for the Stowe Missal, courtesy of the National Museum

5 The Book of Leinster, p. 159, courtesy of the library,
Trinity College, Dublin

6 The Book of Ballymote, page 189r, courtesy of the Royal Irish Academy

7 The Book of the Dun Cow, p. 59, courtesy of the Royal Irish Academy

8 The Fadden More manuscript (found in an Irish bog July 2006), courtesy
of the National Museum

9 Decorated bone, Lagore, Co. Meath, courtesy of the National Museum

10 Carved head, Drumeague, Corleck, Co. Cavan, courtesy of the
National Museum

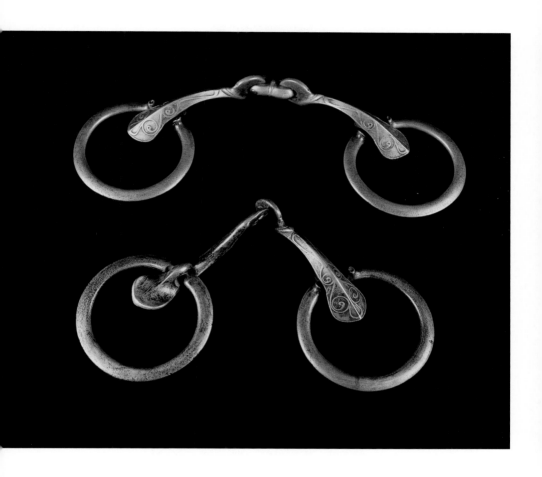

11 Horse bits, Attymon, Co. Galway, courtesy of the National Museum

12 A chess piece, Co. Meath, courtesy of the National Museum

13 A gaming board, Ballinderry, Co. Westmeath, courtesy of the
National Museum

14 Aerial photograph of Cruachu (Rathcroghan), courtesy of the
National University of Ireland, Galway and Marcus Casey

15 Diarmait and Gráinne, courtesy of Jim Fitzpatrick

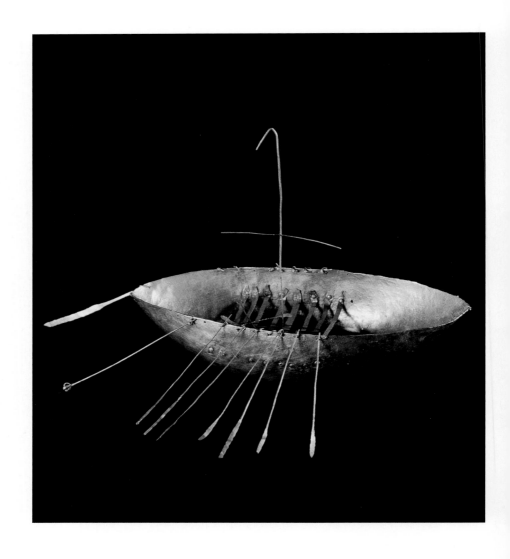

16 Model boat, Broighter, Co. Derry, courtesy of the National Museum

the age of seven in place of the reigning king, Fergus mac Róich. Nessa agrees to marry him on condition that he allows Conchobar to be king, and she teaches her son to be a generous king. The stories of Conaire Mór and Niall of the Nine Hostages taking the kingship of Tara are found in the chapter on sovereignty.

Cú Chulainn and Finn pass from childhood to adulthood by showing their prowess in their own areas. An adolescent going through a life crisis passes through the liminal zone and emerges from the other side. But while Cú Chulainn survives the liminal stage, Finn's attempts to join 'normal' society are rebuffed, and he lives forever in the wilderness.

The boyhood deeds of Cú Chulainn are told in the *Táin* by Fergus and his Ulster companions to the Connachtmen. Many tales have to do with his arrival, opposition and finally acceptance as part of the Ulster society.[40] In the first tale, Fergus describes Cú Chulainn's arrival at Emain Macha as he plays with his javelin and hurley along the way.[41] He rushes onto the green at Emain without making a promise of safety to the boys playing there. He defeats them at their games and is afflicted with his distortion where he changes beyond recognition, for the first time. When he is challenged, he leaps across the chessboard, and Conchobar confronts him. When they recognize him, he is accepted by the boy troop. He compounds his victory by beating one hundred and fifty boys and makes peace with the boy troop. This is in clear contrast with Finn, who drowns the boy troop and then moves away.

Conall Cernach tells the story of how Sétanta is renamed Cú Chulainn as a result of his confrontation with the huge watchdog of Cualu the smith. Conchobar invites the boy to the feast at Cualu's home, but then they forget that he is coming and close the gates and leave the huge hound on guard outside. Cú Chulainn comes to the fort playing with a hurley and a ball, not varying his play even when the hound comes towards him. The people watch in horror as Cú Chulainn kills the dog by smashing it against the nearest pillar or throwing his ball into its mouth and tearing out its intestines. The smith welcomes him but laments the death of his wonderful dog. The boy offers himself as a guard dog in his stead, and as a result Cathbad the druid declares that he shall be called Cú Chulainn.

In his last, and most significant, tale Cú Chulainn asks the druid Cathbad what that day was lucky for, and is told: 'If a warrior took up arms for the first time that day, his name would endure in Ireland.' He takes the king's own arms and breaks twelve chariots until Ibor the charioteer drives him as far as Sliab Fuait (the Fews Mountains), where Conall Cernach was on duty on the boundary. Cú Chulainn persuades him to leave the duty to him and refuses Ibor's request to return to Emain Macha in time for the drinking. Cú Chulainn asks about the landscape that lies before them, and Ibor names every fort between Tara and Kells until they reach the fort of the three sons of Nechta Scéne, where he kills the three monsters who came from the mouth of the river Skayne (Scéne) that runs through Dunsany near Tara (the place mentioned is probably the site known now as Ringlestown Fort). He overtakes a flock of birds in flight and captures wild deer and returns to Emain with 'a wild stag behind the chariot, a swan-flock fluttering above, and the three heads of Nechta Scéne's sons inside the chariot.' He threatens to kill the court unless a man is found to fight him; and the women of Ulster, led by Mugain, Conchobar's queen, strip their breasts to him. He is put into three vats of water when he hides his face from this sight. Mugain gives him a blue cloak, and he sits at Conchobar's knee and that was his seat from then on. Cú Chulainn has achieved his rightful place within his society; he is the ultimate Ulster hero, accepted by the people, controlled by their actions and sitting at the king's knee. Certain parallels may be seen between this scene and Lug's arrival at Tara in *The Battle of Moytura*.[42]

The curious scene of the women exposing themselves may indicate his sexual coming of age.[43] Perhaps he expects praise and becomes angry when he receives none for killing the sons of Nechta Scéne. R. Cormier concludes that 'The scene displays no Christian influence whatsoever: in fact, it appears to enshrine a dark hint from the dawn of civilization.'[44] There are similar scenes elsewhere: a female messenger, Birgad, 'lifted up her dress above the globe of her buttocks' as she approaches Finn.[45] In *Mesca Ulad* (The Intoxication of the Ulstermen) the female satirist Richis strips naked to distract Cú Chulainn, and he hides his face. His charioteer Loeg takes over his role and kills her, thus saving Cú Chulainn's life.[46] These are a kind of female 'full Monty'-type gestures and a vaguely similar episode occurs in an account of the Women's War in Nigeria in 1929.[47]

The Boyhood Deeds of Finn text gives the most complete account of Finn's growth as a hunter and a poet. As his life is in danger, Finn, then know as Demne, is fostered by Bodbmall the druidess and Liath Luachra, who raise him secretly in the forests of west Leinster. His first expedition is against ducks on a lake; afterwards he defeats a group of boys playing hurling at Mag Life, but when they challenge him to plunge them in water he drowns nine of them. His initiation into the world of poetry occurs on the banks of the Boyne, where he meets Finn the Poet who has waited for seven years for the salmon of Linn Feicc (beside the two fairy mounds of Clettech and the Brú na Bóinne).[48] A prophecy said that he would eat this salmon and that all knowledge would become known to him. He leaves Demne in charge of cooking the salmon and warns him not to eat it. When Finn asked if he had eaten any, Demne explains that he burned his thumb and then put it in his mouth. It is clear to both that the salmon was meant for him and that he is the true Finn. As a result he gains the knowledge that illuminates, and this happens whenever he puts his thumb in his mouth. His ability as a poet is shown immediately as he recites the Mayday poem.

He spends time at Dá Chích Anann (Two breasts of Anu, mountains in Kerry) sitting between two strongholds at Samain as the two fairy mounds (*síd*) open with a huge fire at each of them. The fairy people do not notice him and begin to talk to one another. A man comes out of one fairy mound with a kneading trough, a cooked pig, a cooked calf and a bunch of garlic for Samain. He passes Finn on his way to the other fairy mound. Finn threw a spear at him and from the keening in the fairy mound Finn realizes that he has hit someone. His spear is now in the fairy mound and he must get it back. He takes as hostage a woman of the fairy mound and she promises that the spear will be returned in exchange for her.

Finn is elected to watch during the night, he hears a cry from the north, and although he is warned to wake people he goes alone as far as Sliab Slanga (Sliab Donard, Co. Down). He finds three women with the 'horns of *síd* women' on the green. The women cry and put their hands on the mound. They run when they see Finn. He takes a brooch from one of them as they run into the fairy mound and the woman comes out and asks him to return the brooch; it will be a defect if she enters the fairy mound without it; she promises him a reward ... The only version of the story stops here without an ending. He survives his initiation but must remain an outsider: 'Finn is sneaking about in a liminal place and time ... an insignificant and unnoticed figure who has unsettlingly easy access to very private things.'[49]

5: Invulnerability

The invulnerability of the hero is a feature of most of the heroic biographies of the major figures such as Cú Chulainn, Finn, Cormac and Conaire, but it is usually mentioned in passing and in association with the hero's death. The most famous story of invulnerability is that of Achilles, whose mother holds him by the heel as she dips him in the river Styx to ensure that he cannot be killed. Of course, he is finally injured in the heel and dies as a result, giving rise to the phrase 'Achilles heel'. The king in early Ireland is usually bound by taboos to ensure that he will do no wrong or to protect him from harm; these may not be mentioned until he breaks them in his death tale. Cormac mac Airt's druid-smith grandfather places five protective rites about him: against wounding, drowning, fire, magic and wolves.[50]

The hero's life/soul may be hidden in a stone or elsewhere to protect his life as in *The Story of Cano mac Gartnáin*. Towards the end of the story the hero tries to meet Créd but he is stopped on every occasion. When Cano is wounded, she thinks that he is dead and, in a scene reminiscent of Derdriu's actions, she smashes her head against a stone. She is carrying the stone that contains his life and this breaks resulting in Cano's death some nine days later when he returns to Scotland.[51]

Tristan is wounded by a poisoned spear and no one can cure him but Isolde. He sends her a ring, as arranged between them, asking her to come to him. The messenger is told to hoist a white sail if Isolde is with him and a black one if she has refused. When the ship arrives with the white flag Tristan's wife tells him that the flag is black and he dies. Isolde finds him dead, lies down beside him and dies.[52]

Conaire's invulnerability is bestowed upon him by Nemglan; the list of taboos is outlined in the death tale and Cú Chulainn and Finn's taboos are also in their death tales below.

6: A Fight with a Dragon or a Monster

Monsters are not a common feature of Irish sagas, and no fire-breathing dragons appear in the literature. Neither Conaire Mór nor Cormac meets a monster unless Lugaid mac Con (son of the hound) can be seen as such. The guard dog and the three giants that Cú Chulainn beheads could be seen as monsters, and in *The Phantom Chariot of Cú Chulainn* the hero battles with the people of Lochlann and kills a giant.[53]

Finn's encounter with a monster is told in *The Interviewing of the Old Men* where he faces Aillén the otherworldly figure, who burns Tara at Samain (Hallowe'en) for twenty-three years during the reign of Conn of the Hundred Battles. At the age of ten, Finn arrives at Tara and offers to save them from Aillén's attack. Finn is given a spear and a shield to guard him from the otherworldly figure. Aillén was playing the dulcimer, as was his custom, to put everyone to sleep. Finn puts the fringed purple cloak he was wearing into the path of the fire. The fire falls from the air onto the cloak.[54] Aillén runs away and Finn follows, throwing the spear at him. Finn removes the spear from his body, beheads him, takes the head to Tara and puts it on a stake for all to see. As a result of his actions, Finn is made leader of the Fianna in Ireland.

In *The Cattle Raid of Fraech*, Fraech meets a water monster while swimming in a river trying to retrieve a ring thrown in by Ailill, Finnabair's father.[55] He kills it with a sword, beheads it and brings the head to land. He survives the encounter unlike Fergus mac Léti king of Emain Macha, who falls asleep, with his charioteer, by the coast.[56] The fairy folk drag him into the sea; he grabs them and they grant him three wishes. When he asks for a charm for passing under the seas and lakes, they warn him not to enter Loch Rudraige, but Fergus disobeys and when he is under the lake he meets a water monster (*muirdris*). Fergus' mouth becomes distended and he is permanently blemished; but his people hide this from him and they succeed until a servant is washing his head and he thinks that she is too slow. He hits her with his whip and she mocks him about his face so that he cuts her in two with his sword. He spends a day and night under the lake and emerges with the monster's head. Fergus dies and the lake was red with blood for a month afterwards.

The heroes encounter all types of horrendous creatures, particularly on battlefields and many are female, such as the Mórrígan who appears in *The Battle of Moytura*. The beautiful women in *The Love-Sickness of Cú Chulainn* may be related to the figures of the Badb and the Mórrígan; they appear in bird form, threaten the hero with a beating, promise him sex and finally incite him to fight in the Otherworld. In the story of his death, Fothad Canainne is meeting the wife of another man when he is killed in battle and the woman brings Fothad's head to join his body at the grave. He then recites a poem that mentions the Mórrígan along with other frightening creatures referred to as 'terror of the night'.[57] The lore of Waterford (Port Láirge) features an evil female sea creature; apparently a mermaid (*muirduchann*). She lures Roth with her humming (*dord*) and tears him apart, so that the place is named from his thigh-bone.[58]

The Otherworld is inhabited by strange creatures throughout, whether animal or human; for example, unfriendly cats appear in a number of texts. In *Bricriu's Feast* the heroes are attacked by 'three cats ... from the cave of Cruachu' and Cú Chulainn cannot kill them. They finally leave at dawn (Gantz, pp. 238–9). In *Tromdám Guaire* (The Great Visitation of Guaire) the king of the cats attacks Senchán the poet because he satirized cats for not killing mice. The cat carries him away but Ciarán of Clonmacnoise kills the animal.[59]

In the story of the historical king Fergal mac Maeil Dúin (†722) and the conception of his son Aed Olláin in the *Fragmentary Annals of Ireland*, Fergal was having a secret relationship with the (unnamed) daughter of Congal Cennmagar mac Fergusa (Fánad). Her father sent her to be a nun but then he hears that she has a lover. He visits the girl and she hides Fergal under the bedclothes and then sits on the bedclothes herself. A big cat found Fergal and bit his legs and swallowed big pieces of them. Fergal caught the cat and killed it.[60]

7: *The Hero Acquires a Wife*

This element of the biography is an integral part of the human experience and one of the most important transitions from one category to another. One of the couple must move from their family, village or tribe and as they often change residence this must be marked by separation rites. When the two people unite, they are uniting their families, not just themselves, and this is also seen in divorce that may also require separation rites. Marriage may arise from rape or indeed abduction of a woman as a slave or concubine; these relationships are usually considered to be inferior to those of the other women of the tribe, and the same rites may not apply to such unions.[61]

In the case of early Irish literature there are two distinct saga categories that tell the stories of men and women forming relationships – wooing (*tochmarc*) tales, where the man searches and may have to fight for the woman, and elopement (*aithed*) tales, where a woman chooses a man and as a result they must flee from the woman's initial chosen spouse.

There are no marriage ceremonies in early Irish law or literature; the engagement (*airnaidm*) is the defining point of the union. Any children conceived after that point are recognized as being fathered by the man in the relationship. The bridegroom paid a bride price (*coibche*) to the father of the bride (the direct opposite of the dowry system that was found in later Irish society). The texts mention a celebratory feast, and there is no Church involvement at this early stage.[62]

In *The Wooing of Emer* the Ulstermen decide to find a wife for Cú Chulainn, but, when the messengers fail to find a suitable woman, Cú Chulainn goes to woo Emer daughter of Forgall Monach, who lives at Luglochta Loga.[63] He says that he requires a woman who is his equal in age and form and 'the best handiworker of the girls of Ireland', and Emer is said to have six gifts: 'beauty, voice, sweet speech, needlework, wisdom and charity.' From the beginning they speak in riddles, and she says that she was brought up to be 'chaste, equal to a queen in stateliness of form.'[64]

Cú Chulainn returns to Emain Macha, but when Forgall hears of their meeting he decides to stop their impending marriage. He disguises himself and travels to Emain, where he suggests to Conchobar that Cú Chulainn should go to Domnall in Scotland to train as a warrior and that he would be even more skilled if he trained with Scáthach in the Otherworld. Forgall is hoping and assuming that he will be killed while he is there. Cú Chulainn agrees to this suggestion and, accompanied by other warriors, he begins his dangerous journey. (His adventures in the Otherworld are outlined below.)

On his return Cú Chulainn must face Forgall again and he jumps over three ramparts and kills him before carrying off Emer and her foster sister along with their weight in gold and silver. When they return to Emain Macha, Bricriu asks who will sleep with Emer first, as it was the custom that Conchobar had that right. Cú Chulainn explodes with anger, but they reach an agreement; both Fergus and Cathbad the druid will sleep in the same bed with Emer and Conchobar to guard Cú Chulainn's honour and 'they did not part from each other until they died.'

Cú Chulainn also sleeps with the woman Fedelm, and the text says that this gives rise to the debility of the Ulstermen. In a second instance he sleeps with two women and takes one of them, Finnchaem daughter of Eochu Ronn, as his wife.[65] Emer also has an extra-marital affair with the son of the king of Lochlann, Tuir nGlesta. She goes with him to the Isle of Man, the islands of the Foreigners (Gall) and Dún Monaig. Cú Chulainn ransacks the fort, kills her lover and brings Emer back.[66]

In the case of the Fenian Cycle tales, marriage can lead to death instead of moving to another stage; the relationships of Fenian men with women are short-lived and impermanent. They elope rather than form stable unions. Finn is involved with a series of women, and many of them could hardly be described as wives, and he is said to have 'a particular woman awaiting him in the nearest [inhabited] land.'[67] Cú Chulainn kills his only son, but Finn produces many offspring, both male and female. He meets his first woman in *The Boyhood Deeds* – Cruithne daughter of Lóchán the smith. In the same text he wins the love of Donait by showing his ability to leap, but this is what fails him eventually and leads to his death in some tales.[68]

These relationships come to nothing, and he makes two serious attempts at what might be termed 'marriage' or a long-term relationship with two daughters of Cormac mac Airt. The first is with Gráinne (this is mentioned first in *The Separation of Finn and Gráinne*).[69] She tries to avoid the marriage by asking him to bring a couple of every wild animal in Ireland to the meadow at Tara. He persuades Caílte son of Oisgen to catch the animals for him. Gráinne marries Finn, but she is very unhappy; and the remainder of the tale is taken up with their divorce proceedings. There is a short conversation between Cormac, his son Cairpre and Finn, where Finn agrees to divorce Gráinne because he knows how she feels. She tells her father: 'I have a lump of gore under my heart the same size as the grease and fat of my husband and hatred of him so that the sinews of my body are taut.' (*Field Day*, 37)

There is a later and better known story of Gráinne, Finn, and her lover Diarmait that survives as the *The Pursuit of Diarmaid and Gráinne* (this probably corresponds to the title that appears in the tale lists as *The Elopement of Gráinne daughter of Cormac with Diarmait ua Duibne*). This marriage attempt fails as well as Gráinne falls in love with Diarmait and they elope together.

Finn courts Gráinne's sister in *Tochmarc Ailbe* (The Wooing of Ailbe).[70] When Finn arrives for the Feast of Tara, Ailbe is knotting threads of gold into her father's helmet; she is praised for her work in gold or silver, intelligence, beauty, ancestry, wisdom and poetry. This is very similar to the descriptions of Emer shown as the perfect woman or wife. Ailbe is distracted by the arrival of the Fianna, and Cormac notices that her needlework is suffering. This gives rise to a long exchange between father and daughter where she persuades him that Finn will make her a good husband. Cormac and indeed his daughter both use words of wisdom and good judgment as befits the wisest of early Irish kings.

This insight into her views of Finn and her relationship with her father is unusual in such stories. He thinks that Ailbe is too young for Finn, referring to him as 'greybeard', but Ailbe shows her wisdom while replying to him. When asked by Cormac what he brought with him to Tara, Finn replies that he is good at 'old sayings and at pronouncing witticisms.' Cormac is not impressed but allows him to visit Ailbe.

As a test, Finn asks Ailbe a series of difficult questions like the riddles that Cú Chulainn and Emer used in their conversation. For example: 'What is sweeter than mead?' said Finn. 'Confidential talk,' said the girl ... 'What is best in a warrior?' said Finn. 'A lofty deed and a lowly pride,' said the girl. In this telling, they live happily together and Ailbe bears him three sons.[71]

Cormac mac Airt's wooing of his wife Eithne Taebfhota (long-sided) in *The Melodies of Buchet's House* is noted already in the chapter on Sovereignty.

8: The Hero Visits the Otherworld

This element does not apply to the real-life biography, but it is the closest to Campbell's monomyth defined as: 'A hero ventures forth from the world of common day into a region of supernatural wonder: fabulous forces are there encountered and a decisive victory is won: the hero comes back from this mysterious adventure with the power to bestow boons on his fellow man.'[72] Both Cormac and Cú Chulainn bring back extra skills and concrete evidence of their transient visits. Conaire Mór does not visit the Otherworld, and there is no mention of his taking a wife. Many of these stories have been discussed in the chapter on the Otherworld, but there are specific otherworldly incidents as part of the heroic biography.

In *The Adventure of Cormac* the king loses his wife, son and daughter to the otherworldly character who is eventually identified as Manannán mac Lir. He passes a test of truth that restores his family to him, along with a cup of truth that validates his judgments from then on. This may be related to acts of truth in other traditions.[73] Manannán gives Cormac a silver musical branch that contains three apples in return for his family. Cormac follows him to the Otherworld and is surrounded by a magic mist. He is asked to undergo an act of truth; a man roasting a pig tells him that a true story will cook each quarter. Cormac tells the final story, relating the events that have just taken place. This completes the cooking of the pig.

When he wakes up, his family are beside him. He is presented with a golden goblet that will tell the difference between truth and falsity; three lies will break it, and three truths will unite it. Cormac awakes the following morning on the green at Tara with his family and his goblet of truth. The goblet is the reason for Cormac's mission; it is the physical proof of his ability to give good judgments, and it reinvigorates his prince's truth. The loss of both his wife and his offspring seem to indicate his temporary loss of sovereignty and he must recover them to continue as a king.

Cú Chulainn makes a number of visits to the Otherworld; the first is part of his ordeal to win Emer from her father, and the second is in *The Love-Sickness of Cú Chulainn*. He also comes back from the dead to persuade king Laegaire to convert to Christianity in *The Phantom Chariot of Cú Chulainn* where he mentions Dún Scáith (the fort of the shadow) in the land of Scáth (shadow).[74]

Cú Chulainn must visit the Otherworld in *The Wooing of Emer* so that he can win Emer's hand. Her father, Forgall, wants to get rid of him and hopes that he will not come back.[75] He has been told to visit Scáthach (shadow); and a beast that looks like a lion, the 'animal helper', carries him on his back until they reach the 'uttermost bounds of men.' He receives food and drink from a beautiful woman who says that they were fostered together.

Before he reaches Scáthach he survives various trials in a transitional, liminal territory – the Plain of Bad Luck and the Dangerous Glen. Her training camp is on an island, and he must pass over the Pupil's Bridge that has two low ends and a high mid-point so that, when he leaps on one end, the other one lifts up and throws him back. He fails three times before using the 'salmon-leap' to jump on the head of the bridge and managing to land on the island.

Cú Chulainn puts his spear through the door of Scáthach's stronghold and she sends her daughter Uathach (dreadful) to talk to him. After three days she advises him to use the salmon-leap to reach Scáthach where she was teaching her sons, Cuar and Cett. He puts his sword between her breasts and asks for three things: to train him, to marry Uathach without the payment of wedding-gifts, and finally to foretell his future as she was a prophetess.

The story moves briefly to Ireland, where Forgall is plotting to marry Emer to a foster brother of Cú Chulainn, Lugaid son of Nos. But Emer takes Lugaid's cheeks between her hands and tells him that she loves Cú Chulainn and that anyone who took her would suffer loss of honour. For fear of him, Lugaid returns home. This is in direct contrast with Cú Chulainn who is sleeping with Uathach.

Returning to the Otherworld, Scáthach is at war with a tribe ruled by another female warrior, Aífe. To protect Cú Chulainn from harm, Scáthach puts him in bonds and gives him a sleeping potion, just as the Tuatha Dé Danann tried to prevent Lug from entering the battlefield by leaving nine guards around him. Cú Chulainn escapes and fights against Aífe's warriors; as part of the battle he kills the three sons of Ess Énchenn (Ess birdhead) similar to his killing of the three sons of Nechta Scéne in his boyhood deeds. Cú Chulainn distracts Aífe by shouting that her charioteer, horses and her chariot have fallen down the glen. He catches her, throws her on the ground and holding his sword over her, makes three demands; she will give hostages to Scáthach, never oppose her again and bear him a son. This is the boy he kills in *The Death of Aífe's Only Son*.

On his journey home Cú Chulainn must cross another liminal zone, a narrow road where he meets an old woman, blind in her left eye, who tries to throw him off the road. He kills her and realizes that she is Ess Énchenn, the mother of the men he killed. Then he returns to Ireland. (The rest of the story tells of his wooing of Emer and has been discussed already above. A second visit to the Otherworld, *The Love-Sickness of Cú Chulainn* has also been discussed in the chapter on the Otherworld.)[76]

Finn is in constant contact with the Otherworld, and *The Interviewing of the Old Men* comments that the Fianna spend as much time with the Tuatha Dé Danann as they do with humans. A deer that is really a supernatural female leads them to the Otherworld because the Fianna's help was required for a fight with an enemy.[77]

Many of his encounters validate his position as the shaman-poet, and the incidents happen on the threshold of the Otherworld. He brings back the gift of prophecy in *The Boyhood Deeds*, and *Finn and the Man in the Tree* describes him chasing Cúldub, who has stolen his food. He reaches the door to the Otherworld where a woman holding liquid in a container slams the door on Finn, trapping his finger. As a result he puts his finger in his mouth and from then on this is how he accesses his prophetic knowledge.[78] In another encounter he meets with a woman who appears to him as a deer before changing to her human shape. She asks him to look for her two rings in a lake, but he comes out as an old man. When the Fianna see him first, they do not recognize him. In revenge, the Fianna attack the fairy mound, and the lord of the mound, Cuilenn, comes out and offers Finn a drink that will bring back his youth as well as wisdom. His hair remains grey and, when Cuilenn offers to change it back, Finn chooses to have permanently grey hair.[79]

9: *Exile and Return*

This element of the biography is not particularly common in the Irish material and does not apply to Cú Chulainn or to Conaire Mór. Finn is separated from his rightful inheritance and he takes the leadership of the Fianna in *The Interviewing of the Old Men* when he defeats Aillén at Tara.[80] Niall of the Nine Hostages must prove his suitability for kingship; he is the fifth son and the offspring of a slave.[81] Cormac mac Airt attracts many stories about the loss of kingship. He is separated from his rightful position by the death of his father and his fosterage. Both *Cnucha a hill above the Liffey* and *The Melodies of Buchet's House* say that Medb Lethderg takes the kingship for fourteen months and that he lived in Kells.[82] A further loss of his wife, kingship and sovereignty is found in a short text called by its editor 'Cormac's Dream' where he has a vision that Eithne will sleep with Eochu Gunnat of the Ulaid but will return to him again. His druid explains that this symbolizes Cormac's loss of kingship for a year. Eithne is explicitly associated with the sovereignty of Tara in this story.[83]

The Phantom's Frenzy mentions his loss of kingship and says that he was king three times: 'Three times he will be king of Tara in which will die many phantoms, i.e. *síd*-dwellers ... the expedition of Cormac over the ocean,/ three years, hear it far away.'[84] *Cath Crinna* (The Battle of Crinna), mentioned in genealogies, says he was exiled by the Ulstermen and travels to Munster for help. He promises Tadg mac Céin whatever land his chariot can encircle in one day, but bribes the charioteer to avoid the crucial sites of both Tara and Tailltiu.[85]

10: *Death of the Hero*

This is one of the most popular genres of the heroic biography, and there are also many poems that outline the deaths of heroes both legendary and historical. The death tales, the final journey in the biography, are characterized by riddles, broken taboos, the appearance of women, milk and a drink offered or taken by the hero, and the motif of a threefold death where the hero/king is wounded, burned and drowned. Water is often a component in the death tales as it was in the births of certain heroes, and there are also deaths that take place because the hero's soul has been hidden apart from his body and this hiding place is destroyed.

Some of these tales have been described as being 'woman-revenge' and 'tabu-revenge.'[86] The plots are generally quite violent and are described as the best of early Irish stories: 'the most successful tales of the Ulster Cycle are surely those that build up to the inevitable death of someone ... These are certainly written literature, deliberately composed though with some input from oral myth, legend or folklore: they are classic tragedies with no prospect of fairytale happy ending'.[87]

As the final journey for everyone, death and funerals are discussed in detail by A. Van Gennep, who says that transition rites are the most common and complex to ensure that the deceased enter the Otherworld.[88] He also mentions that the most common belief in the Otherworld is that of a world analogous to ours but more pleasant.

The rites performed on the body in various societies are sometimes intended to keep the soul from returning to this world (this seems to be a considerable fear in Irish literature). Many episodes happen at Samain, when the door to the Otherworld is open. Certain societies, including pre-Christian Ireland, buried grave goods including food and drink to help the dead pass over.

In most death tales, women may appear at crucial points in the lead-up to the final scenes of the story. Heroes such as Cú Roí, Crimthann, Cú Chulainn and Conaire die at Samain, some make liminal journeys towards their deaths and spectres haunt the king or hero. The last journey is found particularly in the death of Cú Chulainn.

The motif of the threefold death includes wounding, fire and drowning (*gonad, loisced, báided*), and although it occurs mainly in a Christian context in these sagas it may have been a sacrificial ritual originally, but it is associated with various historical kings.[89] The Gundestrup cauldron from Denmark contains a scene depicting a small figure being immersed in a cauldron.

The liquid that was used positively to confer his kingship upon the king has now turned against him, and it is one of the negative instruments of his death, the goddess may have also turned against him.[90] *Aided Diarmata meic Fergusa Cerbeoill* (The Death of Diarmait mac Fegusa Cerbeoill) includes many of the main motifs: riddles and impossible situations, the presence of a beautiful young woman, a promised last feast and a threefold death. Diarmait (†565) is said to have celebrated the last pagan feast of Tara, and his relationship with the Church is ambiguous.[91]

Diarmait helps St Ciarán to found Clonmacnoise, and in return he is promised the kingship. But Diarmait offends him by burning, wounding and drowning an enemy on the land that he granted the saint, and Ciarán prophesies that Diarmait will die in the same way. This is the first breach in their relationship as he fails to recognize the proper rights of sanctuary. Diarmait submits himself and his descendants to Ciarán again, and his reign is prosperous. The prophet Bec mac Dé (little son of God) makes a second prophecy: he will die by the hand of Aed Dub who will give him a poisoned drink; he will be wearing a shirt of one flax-seed and a cloak of one sheep, and beer from one grain in his drinking horn, and the bacon of a pig never born on the dish, and the main beam of the house, the ridgepole, will fall on his head. Impossible as they seem, they catch up with him like the prophecies in Shakespeare's *Macbeth*.[92]

While Diarmait visits the house of Aed Guaire in Connacht, Aed kills his herald. St Ruadán hides Aed, but Diarmait finds him and hangs him. Ruadánd and Brendan both went to Tara and began cursing Diarmait and Tara: 'May Tara be deserted,' said Ruadán. 'And may there not be a dwelling place upon her forever.'

Diarmait is making a circuit of Ireland when he is invited to a feast by Banbán (little piglet) but his wife Mugain refuses to attend and Banbán offers

Diarmait his daughter instead. She gives him strange presents – the shirt, cloak, bacon and the ale. Then Diarmait sees the ridgepole in the roof and realizes that all the prophecies are coming true. Aed Dub appears and throws a javelin at him, Diarmait goes into the vat of ale and the ridgepole of the house falls and kills him. His body was burned without the head and he is buried at Clonmacnoise.

J. Radner says that the motif is thoroughly Christian and the tale belongs to a wider grouping of riddle deaths like those of Conaire and Cú Chulainn. As these riddles contain such elements as mystery, paradox and seeming impossibility, Diarmait feels that the circumstances are impossible and cannot be fulfilled, but the audience realizes that he has been fooled. The theme is probably connected with the importance of sanctuary in the contemporary Church, and there are instances of the violation of sanctuary in the Annals.[93]

In the second of these tales, *The Death of Muirchertach mac Erca*, the role of the woman is much more prominent as she plots the downfall of this prehistoric king and unlike the story of Diarmait, there is no prophecy of his death. He is less likely to be historical than Diarmait, but he is said to have died about 534/36.[94] Muirchertach is married to Duibsech the daughter of Duí Tenga-Uma (of the brazen/bronze tongue) when he meets a beautiful woman, Sín, while at his palace at Clettech on the banks of the Boyne.[95] When Muirchertach asks Sín what she wants in return for coming with him, she replies that he must never mention her name, that his wife must never be within her sight, and that clerics must never enter the house. When he asks her name, she says: 'Sigh, sough, Sín (storm), rough wind, winter night, cry, wail, groan', and inevitably he will mention all of them. Sín moves in, Duibsech and her children go to the bishop Cairnech for help, and he persuades the king to make a treaty.

Muirchertach returns to Sín; she makes wine from the water of the Boyne, sheep from the stones and swine from the ferns. After a feast of the pigs and the wine from the Boyne they are weakened and unwell the following day. She makes blue men (*fir gorma*) from stones and others with goat-heads, and Muirchertach spends all day fighting them. That night they have another magical feast and he loses more of his strength; when Cairnech visits him, his senses return and he sees the warriors for what they really are – stones and sods of earth. The clerics mark out a church at Brú na Bóinne, and he agrees to dig the trench; he also takes communion and repents to God. But Sín wins him back again, and on the seventh night she was working her magic and it was the 'Tuesday after Samain.' Muirchertach is living an in-between existence, fighting men who are not men and drinking wine that is really river water.

During a huge storm her names are mentioned; the king is having bad dreams and on waking he visits the clerics at the little church. When he returns to Sín, she tells him that he is doomed, and he says that it was forecast that he would suffer the same death as his grandfather: he would burn alive. While he sleeps, Sín arranges a crowd to attack the house and then gets into bed with Muirchertach. He wakes to hear a host attacking the house, which is now on fire. He is wounded and as he gets into a cask of wine he is also drowned.

His wife dies of grief and is buried near the church. With that, Sín appears and explains that she took vengeance on Muirchertach because he killed her father, mother and sister in a battle at the Boyne. She confesses to Cairnech and dies. Cairnech continues to pray for Muirchertach, whose soul was condemned to hell. The Annals say that he was drowned in a vat full of wine at Clettech above the Boyne. Sín appears to be the beautiful sovereignty goddess, and Muirchertach responds in the usual way, but he is showing his unsuitability for kingship through his relationships with the clergy and Sín. Perhaps, both these stories were written to warn warring kings after the death of Mael Sechlainn in 1022 of God's disapproval of the king who lives by the sword.[96]

There are features of this theme in the death of Conaire Mór in *The Destruction of the Hostel of Da Derga*. He is given a long list of taboos that must not be broken, but as he embarks upon his doomed journey towards his death he breaks each of them. There are no riddles here; he finds himself in an impossible situation between a personal loyalty to his foster brothers and his duty as a just king.[97] His foster brothers are professional brigands (*díberga*), and one of Conaire's taboos forbids plunder to be taken in his reign. After an initial period of peace they begin to steal; eventually they are brought to Conaire who says: 'Let every man kill his son and let my co-fosterers be saved.' The people agree. Conaire realizes immediately that he has made a fatal mistake and changes his judgment: 'That judgment has not lengthened my life.'

Although peace returns to Conaire's reign, he breaks his taboos one after another. He makes peace between two servants and spends five nights with each of them; in trying to return to Tara he goes righthandwise around Tara and left-handwise around Brega and hunts the wild beasts of Cerna. As the text states: 'He became the king who was exiled by the phantoms.'[98] The king and his followers decide to travel to the house of Da Derga and meet three red horsemen on the way. A hideous hag is allowed into the hostel, and she insists on being invited to the last supper. Eventually the hostel is set alight on three different occasions with the fire being extinguished with water from the Dodder river that ran through it. Conaire longs for a drink as all the water was used in putting out the fires. Conall Cernach offers to guard the king if Mac Cécht gets the drink, but it takes all night, and as he approaches he sees two men beheading Conaire.

He kills the murderers and pours the water into Conaire's throat. The king's head recites a short poem of praise to Mac Cécht, who goes on to die on the battlefield. In his death tale Conall Cernach is beheaded and it is said that if the Ulstermen drink milk out of his head they will regain their strength.[99]

Although the threefold death is not carried out in a similar way to the previous two tales, the actual elements are present in that Conaire is wounded (beheaded), the hostel is set alight and, instead of being drowned, Conaire is deprived of drink until after his decapitation, when his head is given the water. When he breaks the first taboo, his fate is set; he is overcome by the rest of them and cannot escape. The woman in this case is an ugly hag rather than the beautiful women encountered by Diarmait and Muirchertach. The life-giving water has reached him too late – as happens with Diarmait ua Duibne; the liminal image is a talking head being given a useless drink of water after death. Cú Chulainn also takes a drink from a lake just before his death, and it will be seen that milk and milk-related produce are associated with death: the sovereignty drink now appears in a negative role and some women give poisoned drinks to the hero.

Cú Chulainn's liminal last journey also includes hags and taboos in the versions of his death: *Aided Con Culainn* (The Death of Cú Chulainn) and an early Modern Irish *Brislech Mór Maige Muirthemne* (The Great Destruction of Mag Muirthemne).[1] The women of Ulster, including Leborcham, Niam and Emer, try to stop him leaving on this journey to fight the children of Calatín who use magic to make the plain of Macha seem aflame and weapons fall from the racks. The first cloak he puts on bursts open, and the brooch falls from it; the charioteer refuses to prepare the horses, and the Mórrígan has broken his chariot. He calls on his foster mother (who always has a drink ready for him) before the defining moment when he meets 'three witches blind in the left eye' on the road.

He had two conflicting taboos – not to pass a cooking-place without eating, and not to eat the flesh of his namesake, the dog.[2] The witches taunt him, saying that their meal of hound meat is not good enough for him. One witch gives him the dog's shoulder; he takes it from her hand and puts it under his left thigh. Both the hand and the thigh are weakened. He is now in an ultimately liminal state; if he is struck by the distortion, he will be virtually half-blind, and this meeting has left him effectively one-armed and one-legged. He is in a world where 'right and wrong have merged.'[3]

Erc son of Cairpre wounds Cú Chulainn's horse, the Liath Macha, and it goes into the nearby lake. Lugaid son of Cú Roí wounds Loeg and injures Cú Chulainn so that his entrails come out on the chariot's upholstery.[4] His second horse, Dub Sainglenn, leaves him, and enters another lake. Cú Chulainn then drinks from the lake and ties himself to a standing stone so that he will not die sitting or lying down. The Liath Macha protects him until he dies; the hero's light that shone upright from his head fades. The scald-crow, harbinger of death, sits on his shoulder, and as Lugaid beheads him, Cú Chulainn's sword falls from his dead body and cuts Lugaid's arm off. Cú Chulainn's arm is cut off in revenge and is buried, with his head, at Tara.[5]

There are four versions of king Conchobar's death tale, each very short, and most agree that he was injured by Cet mac Mágach of the Connachtmen who threw the calcified brain of Mes Gegra at Conchobar so that it lodged in his brain.[6] One telling of his death mentions that the women of Connacht asked him to stand so that they might see his shape. Cet hid among the women and threw Mes Gegra's head from a sling. A third of it entered his head and he fell to the ground.[7] His physician says that if the brain is taken from his head he will die; if it is not taken out, he will be blemished. He is now a defective king and lives in suspended animation for seven years; he cannot become angry, have sex, mount a horse, run or even eat properly. On seeing the vision of Christ's death, he jumps from his chair, attacks the wood about him with his sword, and the brain falls out, bringing about his death after a prolonged liminal existence.[8] His son, Cormac Conn Loinges, dies in *Bruiden Da Choca* (The Hostel of Da Choca), where the victims are trapped in a hostel.[9]

There are different accounts of Cormac mac Airt's death, the best known version being that in *The Conception of Cormac* where he chokes on a salmon bone at Speláin's fort at the hostel of Clettech; he is buried at Ros na Ríg looking east to the setting sun rather than in Brú na Bóinne.[10] A similar account appears in the poem, *Cnucha a hill above the Liffey*, where Cormac is invited to a feast at Spelán's fort. A salmon caught in the Boyne is being prepared along with bread, and a bone falls into the bread dough. As Cormac hears the crowd shouting at the games on the green, he chokes on the salmon bone. Cormac's death evokes the story of the salmon of knowledge caught by Finn mac Cumaill, the enduring symbol of wisdom and prophecy seen above. Cormac has gained fame for his good judgment, but his wise voice is silenced forever by choking.[11]

The early text *Indarba na nDéssi* (The Expulsion of the Désse) connects his death with the banishment of the Désse people from Tara to east Munster, where their name still survives. A relatively obscure son, Cellach, abducts a girl of the Désse as his wife, and in vengeance Oengus Gaíbuaibthech, the champion of the Désse, arrives at Tara and while carrying out his revenge he blinds Cormac in one eye. As a result, Cormac has to retire to Achall (the present day Hill of Skryne) and he dies after a year; although no detail of that death is given, it is said to be violent in some versions. Some state that he died in Tech Clettig; this is somewhat in line with the salmon bone version of his death.[12] This is the only version of his death that can be reconciled with the protection rites that Olc Aiche uses in *The Story of Eogan and Cormac*. The druid-smith mentions wounding, drowning, fire, magic and wolves, and this would exclude the wounding by Oengus. Another death associated with Tara is that of Caílte who knows where it will happen: 'I shall die in Temair … my gravestone will be northwest of Temair, until Doomsday.'[13]

Women are involved in the deaths of the Ulster hero, Laegaire Buadach (victorious) and of Fergus mac Róich.[14] Fergus and Medb are swimming in a lake, and Ailill persuades a blind man to throw a javelin at him. Conall Cernach kills Ailill while he is meeting a woman. Mongfhinn (fair hair) wife of Eochaid Mugmedón poisons the drink of her brother, Crimthann mac Fidaig of Munster, but as he refuses to drink until she does; she also dies shortly afterwards. Her death is said to happen at Samain eve, which people call the 'Festival of Mongfhinn'; it is said she was a witch and that women used to petition her because of her magical powers.[15]

There are a number of stories that contain death by inundation where springs or wells spill over to create lakes that kill the inhabitants of the original land mass. *Aided Echach maic Maireda* (The Death of Eochu mac Maireda) explains the origin of Lough Neagh (the lake of Eochu) that bears his name. He died because he did not heed a warning from the Otherworld to leave the area. Instead he builds a house with a flap to cover the well, and he is drowned with his family. His daughter Líban survives and becomes a salmon; her lapdog becomes an otter, and they live for three hundred years until she is baptized by a saint who renames her Muirgen or Muirgelt.[16]

Medb is killed by her nephew Furbaide because he believed that she was responsible for the death of his mother, her own sister Clothra, to get the kingdom of Connacht. He kills her with a piece of cheese from his sling while she is bathing; strange as the method might be, death is linked with water and milk in other death tales. [17]

Cú Roí took Bláthnat, his wife, by force during a siege where he humiliated Cú Chulainn by shoving him into the earth to his armpits, cutting his hair with a sword and rubbing cow-dung into his head. Cú Chulainn spent a year avoiding the Ulstermen. Bláthnat helped him to kill Cú Roí and they agreed that she would pour milk down the river as a sign that she was bathing Cú Roí; the river was called Finnglas (fair/white, speckled). She was de-lousing Cú Roí when, in a scene reminiscent of Samson and Delilah, she tied his hair to the bed where Cú Chulainn beheaded him. Cú Roí's poet Ferchertne killed Bláthnat, but he is killed as well. There is a parallel incident in Welsh literature about the similarly named Blodeuwedd.[18]

Another nasty death tale is that of Derborgaill where women are the cause of another's woman's death as a result of their jealousy of her abilities. In an episode very similar to what happens towards the end of *The Wooing of Emer*, Derborgaill the daughter of the king of Norway is said to love Cú Chulainn. She and her maid come to him in the shape of two birds; Cú Chulainn casts at them and hits her between the ribs with a stone; when she turns into a human being he sucks out the stone. Now they are related and he cannot marry her, so he gives her to Lugaid Riab nDerg who is with him at the time. The plot moves on to the 'pissing game' in the snow when the men made pillars of snow in winter. The women follow them playing a game: 'Let us make our water upon the pillars to see which will enter the farthest. The woman from whom it will enter, she is the best of us to keep.' [19] But they cannot reach far, and call on Derborgaill, who does not want to take part. When she does agree, it pours to the ground and the women turn against her, saying that no other woman would be loved if the men knew what she could do. They torture her until she dies and, in revenge, Cú Chulainn kills one hundred and fifty queens and the place was called Ford of Woman-Slaughter (Áth Bannslechta).

Finally, there are the various and different texts that tell of the liminal death of Finn mac Cumaill; none of these have an ending. There are two fragments on his death; when the Fianna notice him aging, they desert him and he dies at Léim Finn while trying to leap the river Boyne in his old age because he had impressed Donait earlier in his life with his leaping. He also met a woman making curds. The second fragment begins with a hag who prophesies that he will die by taking poison from a drinking horn. He goes to the Boyne to make his leap, but falls between two rocks, hitting his forehead on one, and his brain is dashed in. He is found by fishermen – the three sons of Urgriu and Aiclech, the son of Dub Drenn. The fishermen take his head and their fish to a house to boil and place his head over the fire. One man says that the head should be given a morsel of food. They try to divide the fish into two portions on three occasions but it remains divided in three pieces. In a scene similar to that in the death of Conaire, Finn's head speaks and says that the morsel should be given to him. This is the food that should be placed between the teeth of the dead (*dantmír*). [20]

In Cinaed ua hArtacáin's poem, Finn's killing by the Luigne at Áth Breá on the Boyne is, fittingly, mentioned with that of Mongán. [21] In another version, Finn's wife, Smirgat daughter of Fothad Canainne, is a female seer who makes a prophecy that Finn will be killed after taking a drink from a drinking horn, so he uses a different vessel. One day he takes a drink at a well at Adarca Iuchba (the horns of Iuchba), thus fulfilling the prophecy, and is killed by a place name. [22]

The longest version of his death is the one entitled by K. Meyer *The chase of Síd na mBan Finn* (fairymound of the fair women) *and the death of Finn* but it stops mid-sentence: 'When the children of Uirgriu saw that the hero had been wounded in the earlier combats which he had fought with Fer-taí and his son, Fer-lí, and that he was feeble from loss of blood ...' As K. Meyer said: 'Like all the other versions of Finn's death-story, it is incomplete, breaking off abruptly at the end.' [23]

CHAPTER 9

Poets and Poetry

> I and white Pangur
> practice each of us his special art:
> his mind is set on hunting,
> my mind on my special craft.[1]

The Status of the Poet

The status of the poet is best described by the eighth-century text, *Uraicecht na Ríar* (The Primer of Stipulations). The usual number of classes of poet mentioned is seven: *ollam, ánruth, clí, cano, dos, macfhuirmid* and *fochloc*, most of which are untranslatable; but different sources give different numbers and terms. The use of seven seems to have begun with the Church and then spread to the secular texts (grades of lords for example); but groupings of sixes, eights and nines were also used.[2] The vast majority of the poets discussed here are male, although some female poets are mentioned. The poet must fulfil three essential conditions: (i) to have a proper family background; (ii) to have ability and to study; as well as (iii) being pure of learning, pure in mouth, hand and marital union – he must have only one wife.[3] An unusual text, *The Cauldron of Poesy*, emphasizes the importance of training and ability in composition. It says, for example: 'The Cauldron of Knowledge, it is that which is generated upside down, and out of it is distributed the knowledge of every other art beside poetic art.'[4]

Poets may be blind or even begin life as dumb; others become poets as a result of a trauma that renders them mad – as happened with Suibne and Derdriu. A poet may also be transformed by an encounter with the Otherworld. Conchobar's storyteller, Derdriu's father, is described as 'Dall'; and others include: Eochaid Dallán Forgaill, who composed the eulogy for Colm Cille; Dallán mac Móre (fl. 908) a learned man of Kildare; Lugaid Dall-Écess; Dall Mathgamna (*c.*976); and Ferdomnach Dall (†1110 AU), who is also described as a 'master harpist'. In the later period, Seámus Dall Mac Cuartha and the harper Carolan were also blind. The most common Irish word for blindness, *dall*, can also mean 'dark, obscure', and the words *caech* and *goll* are used for being blind in one eye. The word *caech* also means 'a dimsighted person, empty, winks'. The word *goll* is also used in personal names such as Goll mac Morna, Finn mac Cumaill's enemy, and it is usually associated with evil people who appear frequently in the literature. Blindness can be either real or simulated; it has mythical connotations and can be combined with one-leggedness and one-armedness. Both the god Lug and Cú Chulainn chose temporary one-eyedness, imitating their ancestor Balor of the evil eye.[5] The druidic practice of heron or crane-killing (*corrguinecht*) included reciting spells and satires while standing on one leg, one arm lifted up and one eye closed.

Some poets were dumb at birth. Amairgen, Conchobar's poet, was dumb until he was 14. His first words were riddles and his teacher decided to get rid of him because he would be a great poet.[6] Morann Mórbretha (Morann of the Great Judgments) was born with a caul, and he looked as if he had no mouth. A man from the Otherworld advised that the child be put in the sea and that nine waves pass over him, and his first poem praises God's creation.[7] Moen Ollam (dumb poet) could not speak at all, but he was eventually called Labraid (speaker) when he began to speak.[8] The charcter Uinche Ochurbél (key or clue, solution, guide) was also dumb, and he spoke for three days and nights before and after Samain each year, and he used recite like any prophet (*fáith*).[9] Harpers and poets are linked together as being quintessentially Irish; and one triad says: 'Three things for which Ireland is pre-eminent: a witty quatrain, a tune on the harp, shaving a face.'[10] Harp music can kill or affect people's mood as in the three types of music – happy, sad and sleep music – that appear in a number of texts. Harpers may use their music to send people to sleep when necessary – a magically overpowering sleep (*suan*) as distinct from ordinary sleep (*cotlud*) that can be controlled by humans. Only the harper can produce this sleeping music (*suantraige*).[11]

The Celtic poet, along with saints and other marginalized characters, may be portrayed as a mantic seer or shaman (from the Sanskrit *sramana* 'lord, master') even into the late period. The central elements of shamanic initiation include: 'ceremony: suffering, death, resurrection', and the body may be dismembered and then renewed. He ascends to the sky and speaks to the gods or spirits of dead shamans; and a supernatural female guide may accompany him through his ordeal. Finn is the classic figure of the outsider poet who comes in contact with the Otherworld on many occasions; but one brush changes him utterly. He becomes an old man so the Fianna do not recognize him, but when his youth is restored he chooses to have his hair remain grey – a visible sign of his encounter.[12] On another occasion, Finn is attacked by a plague that leaves him mangy and bald (*mael*). Druids are also described as bald probably because of the way in which they cut their hair (long at the back and shaved at the front).[13]

One of the main functions of the poet is to know about the past and the future, and Finn has access to supernatural knowledge that he gained by contact with the Otherworld; he is known for accessing it by chewing his finger. In the earliest version, the door to the Otherworld is slammed on his finger just as a woman emerges holding a container of liquid. He puts the finger in his mouth and acquires the knowledge. The later story tells how he burnt his finger while looking after the salmon, taken from the otherworldly Boyne river. He put the finger in his mouth and from then on whenever he does this he is enlightened.[14] He has now fundamentally and permanently changed, both physically and mentally. The knowledge comes from hazel nuts that fall into a well in the Otherworld; the salmon in the well eat the nuts and swim down the river Boyne. The process of *imbas forosna* (knowledge that illuminates) describes a poet chewing the raw flesh of a pig, a dog or a cat; when he falls asleep, he dreams of the future.[15]

Certain societies believe that the dead wander among the living, and if they touch them the living may get sick or die. If a shaman can die and return, he is very powerful. M. Klass mentions the Tsembaga Maring of Papua New Guinea where illness and death are thought to come from the Otherworld; the shaman uses an intermediary, known as the smoke woman, who makes contact between the living and the dead. This is echoed in the use of words like *scáil* (shadow) and *scáthach* (shadowy one) for otherworldly figures in Irish literature.

There may be an association between the shamanic abilities, poetry and madness, as in the case of Suibne who goes mad but also becomes a poet, thereby being set apart from others. He now lives in the wilderness (the same liminal place as Finn), and loses his social identity, even his clothes, because his wife inadvertently tears his cloak as she tries to stop him leaving. He meets St Mo-Ling, whose name comes from the word for leaping (*lingid*), he grows feathers, sits on the tips of trees, and flies in a way reminiscent of shamanic journeys. A druid is said to fly in an early text about Bran; it says that his knowledge 'went to the high clouds' in an episode described by J. Carney as a 'curious shamanistic visionary procedure.' In certain societies the shaman uses hallucinogenics.[16] Derdriu is traumatized by the murder of her lover Naíse, and when musicians are brought to her she breaks into poetry in praise of her life in the wilderness.[17] Conall Corc of Munster is exiled to Scotland and he is left in the snow without food for six days before his discovery by Gruibne, who lights a fire around his frozen body until he is revived and he steams.[18]

Prosimetrum

As noted in the Introduction, sagas written in a combination of prose and poetry (prosimetrum) are unusually common in the early literature; prosimetrum was very popular and survived well beyond the pre-Norman period and into the repertoire of the twentieth-century storytellers. By the eleventh and twelfth centuries verse is used more often and distributed regularly throughout the sagas as in *The Cattle Tribute*, *The Interviewing of the Old Men* and *The Madness of Suibne*. The poetry may be essential to the storytelling; this is not an exclusively Irish feature, but the style probably developed in Ireland independently of other traditions.[19]

Verse is ideal for material like genealogy and tribal traditions that need to be transmitted intact, but the metres are not really suitable for telling stories. Therefore there are hardly any full narrative texts entirely in verse with the odd exception such as *The Adventure of Snédgus and mac Riagla* where the metrical version is older than the prose and the poet Cúan ua Lothcháin (†1024), a friend of Mael Sechlainn the second, the last Uí Néill king of Tara, composed a poem on the story of Niall of the Nine Hostages taking the kingship of Tara.[20]

In prose sagas, the verse is often used to mark dramatic responses to situations in the plot, but verse is also used for greetings in *The Story of Mac Da Thó's Pig* and in *The Death of Aífe's Only Son*, and for prophecy at the beginning of *The Exile of the sons of Uisliu*. The first half of *The Kinslaying of Rónán* is all prose, but the second half is nearly all poetry – the most emotional part of the tale. Sometimes it is difficult to tell poetry from prose as in the section at the end of *The Love-Sickness of Cú Chulainn* where the three-way conversation between Cú Chulainn, his wife Emer and his lover Fann has been interpreted by one editor as prose and by others as poetry.[21] This can happen in African narratives where prose may be 'supported by musical feeling' and a tale is never sung the same way twice. A chant may be used in the same places as poetry in early Irish sagas: the meetings of heroes; their departure; and at sad moments. Sometimes the narrative is 'no more than a frame is to a picture', much like the prose in the story of Liadan and Cuirithir.[22]

Poets and Poetry

We do have the names of many poets from the earliest period onwards, and there are individual poems by poets as well as collections by recognized individuals.[23] Most of the verse is used for laws, genealogy, calendars of saints and even history. The lyric poems that survive have a freshness that is still relevant to the present day, but this is a tiny percentage of the overall corpus of early Irish poetry.

From the very beginning, the early poets are composing a mixture of secular and ecclesiastical material. Eochaid Dallán Forgaill is credited with the Irish-language lament for Colm Cille (†597), but there are also a number of poets who appear to have entered the Church at an early stage, such as Colmán mac Lénéni (†604) who founded a monastery at Cloyne; but very little of his poetry survives.[24]

His Christian background is confirmed by his name Colmán (little dove). Another example is Ailill son of Cormac the abbot of Slane, who was commemorated as a legal expert, and Colmán moccu Cluasaig (described as a learned man of Cork c.664) as well as Luccreth moccu Chiara (c.600), who composed the early poem that may have contained the germ of the *Táin – Medb Makes Bad Contracts*.[25]

Much of the earliest poetry and hymns appears in Latin but after the eighth century the use of Latin declines as the poets begin to write in Irish. One of the first Latin poems is *Hearken, All You Lovers of God* and Sechnall's hymn to St Patrick and bilingual hymns appear quite early, for example *Sén Dé* (The blessing of God) composed by Colmán moccu Cluasaig; there are ten stanzas in Irish before it turns to a mixture of Latin and Irish.[26]

There is also the breastplate (*lorica*), a poem of protection, whether in general or for certain parts of the body or behaviour. There is one called the 'Breastplate of St Patrick' although it is an eighth-century composition; it is used as a charm before a journey.

> Today I gird myself
> With great strength,
> The invocation of the Trinity,
> Belief in the threeness,
> Confession of the oneness,
> On my way to meet the Creator.
> ...
> Christ with me, Christ before me, Christ behind me,
> Christ in me, Christ under me,
> ...
> Christi est salus (Salvation is of Christ)
> Salus tua, Domine, sit simper nobiscum. (May your salvation, Lord, always be with us.)[27]

The second has a more pagan flavour. Together, the two poems give a remarkably vivid picture of men's minds in eighth-century Ireland. Here is a section from the second example:

> I call on Senach of the seven lives,
> Whom fairy women suckled on the breasts of good fortune.
> May my seven candles not be quenched.
> I am an invincible fortress,
> I am an unshakable cliff,
> I am a precious stone,
> ...

> May the grace of the Holy Spirit be on me.
> Domini est salus
> Christi est salus
> Super populum tuum, Domine benedictio tua.[28]

One of the largest collections of the early period was composed by Blathmac son of Cú Bretan of the Airgialla (*c.*750).[29] His father died in 740, and his brother, Donn Bó, appears as an entertainer in *The Battle of Allen*. The poet uses the apocryphal, second-century Gospel of Thomas for a description of the youth of Jesus.[30]

One of the longest religious poems of this and any other period is *Saltair na Rann* (The Psalter of Verses). It contains one hundred and fifty verses dealing mainly with Old Testament history, but it also has a lot of traditional material that does not derive from biblical sources – for example the story of Gaedel Glas, who married Scotta daughter of a Pharaoh. The metre produces a stilted style and it is full of chevilles (line-fillers). It is quite repetitive, but it manages to give the Bible an Irish flavour. Not all of it is published, but the section on Adam and Eve is available in print.[31]

It was the responsibility of the poet to compose praise poetry and to lament his patron. Flann file Ó Ronáin is credited with the lament for Mael Sechlainn II, king of Ireland (†1022):

> The house in which the king lies is closed ...

> For the sake of Mael Sechlainn of the road of Bregia I do not avoid in brave Meath my boon companions in the hill yonder in the east, the fair descendants of Colmán though they no longer live ...

> A last stanza from me to my king: my feather-bed was the reward for my first. Many a kingly grace he bestowed in the past; many a defensive structure held by stout hosts has he closed.[32]

Cinaed ua hArtacáin (†973 FM) is the author of several poems, some of which are included in the metrical version of *The Lore of Famous Places*; he is the author of *Fianna bátar i n-Emain* (Heroes who were in Emain), one of the first lists of the deaths of the Irish kings, and many of the references correspond to the death tales. He was associated with Olaf king of Dublin (†980), who spent a lot of time in Meath and was defeated in the battle of Tara in 980.[33]

Flann mac Lonáin (†896 FM or 918 AU) is recognized as the author of a poem on famous Leinster kings, but he gives little concrete information apart from the reign and the names of the kings:

Crimthann the heir of Catháir
Was king of Leinster with numerous septs;
The grandson of Énnae Ceinnselach reigned
Forty years – a long reign.[34]

The same poet composed a strange praise poem for Écnechán son of Dálach (†906 AU) king of Tír Chonaill. He mentions Gartnel son of Cathalán of the Uí Maíl Fábaill, who were a leading family in Inis Eogain until 1199. The poet is particularly concerned with the story of Gartnel's mother, Duiblinn daughter of Écnechán, who was one of three sisters married to three Vikings. Duiblinn married Cathais and they sailed to Inis Eogain. Duiblinn managed to escape from Cathais when he was asleep and took with her a thousand ounces of red gold. Duiblinn went to Carraic Brachaide because she preferred Cathalán son of Mael Fábaill as a husband. The father asks his son-in-law why he left her 'without a hard fetter on her leg?' Cathais replies that he loved her and that she had 'a soft, comfortable bed with pillows, with a fine quilt.' The father says, 'You should not trust a woman till she has been a while in your abode', but he does gives Duiblinn to Cathalán of Tír Chonaill as a wife, and she becomes the mother of Gartnel.[35]

Dallán mac Móre (c.900–20) was an *ollam* and the first recognizable court poet whose poems have survived in any great quantity; he wrote for Cerball king of Leinster, who was killed in the battle of Belach Mugna in 908. Cuan ua Lothcháin, who was murdered in 1024, has five poems attributed to him, including some found in *The Metrical Dinnshenchas* and the story of Niall of the Nine Hostages beginning *Temair Breg, baile na Fian* (Tremair of Breg, Home of Warrior Bands).[36] One of the major poets of the eleventh century is Flann Mainistrech; ten of his poems survive but unfortunately most of them are still unpublished. The list of Christian kings of Ireland is found in *Éri Óg-Inis na Naem* (Ireland, the Virgin Island of Saints), part of *The Book of Invasions*; it is a poem composed by Gilla Mo-Dutu Ó Caiside in 1143 where he gives the names of the kings, the length of their reigns and how they died. He also composed the *Lore of Women* in 1147.[37]

The importance of place names has been noticed on many occasions already, including the metrical text of this material – *The Metrical Dinnshenchas*. It contains the names of dwelling-places, battlefields, mountains, rivers, lakes; and, drawing as it does on mythology, it contains stories that do not exist anywhere else. The Tuatha Dé Danann figure prominently here in contrast with the saga material; there are hardly any saints, and Patrick is only mentioned once.[38] Most of the poems are anonymous, and others are attributed to famous figures of the past such as Finn mac Cumaill and Colm Cille. Others are ascribed to named poets like Cinaed ua hArtacáin, mentioned above – for example, the poem about Achall (hill of Skryne):

Achall over against Temair,
The youths from Emain loved her;
She was mourned when she died,
The white bride of Glan, son of Carbad.
...

Amlaíb of Áth Cliath the hundred-strong,
Who gained the kingship of Benn Étair;
I bore from him as price of my song
A horse of the horses of Achall.[39]

There are a number of poems on Temair at the beginning of the text.

Temair, whence Temair Breg is named,
Rampart of Tea wife of the son of Míled,
Nemnach is east of it, a stream through the glen
On which Cormac set the first mill.
...

Thereupon the grandson of Conn took pity on her,
He brought a mill-wright over the wide sea;
The first mill of Cormac mac Airt
Was a help to Ciarnait.[40]

Early Irish Lyrics

The early lyrics are the best known poetry of this era; these are available in a number of collections but they represent only a tiny percentage of the poetry of the period.[41] They have a modern appeal and resonance that the historical, chronological and synthetic poetry does not possess. There are poems on animals, birds and nature in general. Many are attributed to important figures from the past. All these examples are taken from G. Murphy's *Early Irish Lyrics*.

In the following little gem, the metre reflects the hopping of the bird that is its subject. The metre is intrinsically important so the original Irish poem is included here.

Int én bec	The little bird
Ro léic feit	That has whistled
Do rinn guip	From the end of a bill
glanbuidi:	Bright-yellow.
Fo-ceird faíd	It utters a note
Ós Loch Laíg,	Above Belfast Lough
Lon do chraíb	A blackbird from a branch
charnbuidi.	Yellow-heaped. (pp 6–7)

There are a number of poems on the conditions in which hermits are said to live; some describe an idealized existence, but others give a picture of the reality of the harsh Irish winter. The romantic, idealized picture appears in this hermit lyric as king Guaire asks the ascetic monk Marbán why he does not sleep in a bed and gets the answer:

> I have a hut in the wood;
> Only my Lord knows it;
> An ash-tree closes it on one side, and a hazel,
> Like a great tree by a rath on the other. (pp 10–15)

He describes the 'heather doorposts' and the food that God sends – eggs, honey, apples, red cranberries, whortleberries, beer and herbs, strawberries, haws, yew-berries and nuts.

The lyrics also include prayers, hymns, and many of these contain the repetition that is still a feature of prayers today and facilitates the memorizing of such material. Indeed, some of these have survived the centuries and are used as prayers and hymns today. 'Be thou my vision' survives to the present and it uses repetition throughout:

> Be thou my vision,
> Beloved Lord;
> None other is aught
> But the king of the seven heavens. (p. 42)

Most of these religious lyrics are anonymous but there is a collection of poems from the identifiable eleventh – century Mael Íosa Ua Brolcháin (†1086). He prays directly to the Trinity, to St Michael and to God, using his poetry as a vehicle for religious teaching and personal prayer. His most famous poem, still used as a hymn, is the macaronic (a mixture of two languages) hymn *Deus meus, adiuva me* (My God, help me).

Deus meus, adiuva me,	My God, help me.
Tuc dom do sheirc, a meic mo Dé,	Give me love of thee, o son of my God.
Tuc dam do sheirc, a meic mo Dé.	Give me love of thee, o son of my God.
Deus meus, adiuva me.	My God, help me. (p. 51)

Some of the lyrics that appear in the sagas strike a personal note. The following image comes from *The Kinslaying of Rónán* where king Rónán describes Mael Fhothartaig's dog searching for his dead master:

Doílin
Has served me;
Her head is on everyone's lap,
Searching for one she will not find.[42]

There is a collection of short, generally one-stanza, poems that are often quoted. But some of them are gems of composition and these examples are all taken from the *Golden Treasury*. This includes the verse on a storm that prevents the Vikings from sailing and landing.

Bitter is the wind tonight,
It tosses the sea's white hair;
I do not fear the wild warriors from Norway,
Who course on a quiet sea. (pp 113–14)

There is also the short, pithy and pretty:

Cride é,	He's my heart,
Daire cnó,	A grove of nuts,
Ócán é,	He's my boy,
Pócán dó.	Here's a kiss for him. (pp 112–14)

The last example of these short poems is more earthy:

There is a woman in the country
(I do not mention her name)
Who breaks wind
Like a stone from a sling. (pp 111, 113)

Despite these lyrics, there is a notable absence of personal, emotional poetry, and poets may even make fun of emotions, as happens in a poem addressed to a possible queen of Tara who is mourning the death of her pet goose; the poet lists the deaths of various famous heroes.[43] This may be Mór the wife of Mael Sechlainn I (†985). In a second poem, the same poet (perhaps) addresses another queen of Tara, Derbáil (†1010) daughter of Tadg (†956), the wife of Domnall ua Néill who mourns her son who died as a child. The poet reminds her that 'her treasure was just on loan' but 'let the queen leave her keening now.'[44] In a later example, Giolla Brighde Mac Con Mide, a thirteenth-century poet from Donegal, tells of the inconsolable grief of the parents and foster parents of the young Gormlaith, who died at the age of five. She was the daughter of Domhnall Mór Ó Domhnaill king of Tír Chonaill (modern Donegal) and had been fostered to another Domhnall, possibly king of Tír Eogain (Tyrone). He says: 'For five full years you had grown/Before your dying days/Dimmed the lustrous joy/Of your shining face,/Laid in its resting-place'.[44a]

M. Tymoczko shows that personal poetry existed on the Continent, but in Ireland poets hide behind masks, whether male or female, when expressing emotions. When Celtic poets do speak in their own personal voices, what they say is already determined by training and cultural tradition. By using a mask, the poet had the freedom to make statements that might not be acceptable.[45] She outlines three types of masks: traditional such as Oisín, who is associated with a large body of poetry; mythic as in the Caillech Bérre (the Hag of Bérre); and narrative as in the poetry of Fedelm the female prophet (*banfháith*) from the *Táin*, who composes verse within the context of a specific tale. Figures such as Finn mac Cumaill, Colm Cille, Oisín and Caílte have lyrics attributed to them.

One definition of a lyric is: 'A lyric, like a drama, is a direct presentation, in which a single actor, the poet or his surrogate, sings, or muses, or speaks for us to hear or overhear.'[46] When a second voice is added, this moves to drama; and when the speaker tells a story this is narrative. Dialogue poems are found between Suibne and his wife Eorann; Marbán and Guaire; and Mac Dá Cherda and Cuimine Fota. Three voices are used in *The Love-Sickness of Cú Chulainn* – Cú Chulainn, his wife Emer, and Fann, his otherworldly lover.

There are two poems that M. Tymoczko considers an exception to this rule – the first being the poem on the scribe writing outdoors, and the second, the *Pangur Bán* (White Pangur) poem; both appear in European manuscripts and may have been influenced by Latin poetry. She says that the *Pangur* poem in particular feels modern, individual and self-reflective, and that the 'I' is different here from other uses of the persona. The comparison between the poet applying his skill to the text and the cat catching a mouse is particularly striking:

> I and white Pangur
> Practise each of us his special art:
> His mind is set on hunting,
> My mind on my special craft.
>
> I love (it is better than all fame)
> To be quiet beside my book, diligently
> Pursuing knowledge. White Pangur does not envy me:
> He loves his childish craft ... [47]

Female masks are also used; even if the audience was entirely male, there would still be the need for female masks that allow the the male poet to express emotions that might not be acceptable from a man. Women usually speak about love and lamentation; and famous voices are used such as those of Gráinne and Derdriu. Derborgaill recites a poem before her death, and Créide laments her lover Dínertach son of Gúaire, just as Liadan laments her lover Cuirithir.[48]

Women are seldom mentioned as professional poets; they appear more often as female satirists or prophets such as Fedelm in the *Táin*, who warns Medb of the future and is ignored although she is said to have the *imbas forosna* (knowledge that illuminates).[49] J. Carney comments on the position of the *banfháith* (female prophet) in Irish sagas and says that they are seldom introduced as characters in a casual way and that they warn against courting disaster. They are high-class professional women with specialist training, and they could also be called a *bandraí* (female druid) or a *banfhile* (female poet) and their function would be to 'deliver oracles.'[50]

Other female poets appear in the sagas. Rothniam foretells the birth of Conn and laments him in his death tale. Laitheóc composes a poem for her son Flann Aidne, and it is said that she 'went with poetry.'[51] *Bretha Nemed* (The Judgments of Nemed) uses a story to illustrate a legal point. Eithne daughter of Amalgaid son of Muiredach was the lover of Eochaid Buadach (victorious) son of Fergus Dubdétach (black toothed) who was imprisoned by Cormac mac Airt in Tory Island. Eithne wishes to plead his case to the king at Tara, but no one without a poem could enter Tara, so she goes dressed as a boy to learn poetry from Rirchertne. She arrives at Tara and recites a poem that stirs the men to march to Tory to free her lover.[52] Poetry is put in the mouth of the historical Gormlaith (†946/8) daughter of Flann Sinna (†916) of the Clann Colmáin of Meath, she laments the death of her husbands Niall and Cerball. Women were involved in learning in Europe; in Ireland the monasteries of Ita and Monenna are said to exchange books. Monenna is praised for her learning and Ita teaches her nephew.[53]

The poem *Aithbe damsa bés Mara* (Ebb-tide to me as to the Sea) is attributed to the Caillech Bérre (the old woman/hag of Bérre), who was the wife of Fothad Canainne. The prose introduction mentions four female poets: 'The Old Woman of Beare, whose name was Digde, was of the Corcu Duibne ... Brigit daughter of Iustán belonged to them also, and Liadan wife of Cuirithir, and Uallach daughter of Muimnechán ...'[54] Digde, Uallach, Liadan and Brigit daughter of Iustán are all said to belong to the same group of people; this includes the only female poet in the Annals, Uallach (†934) daughter of Muinechán, called 'female poet of Ireland.' M. Ní Dhonnchadha uses this poem to argue for the existence of female poets and says that Digde composed the poem.[55] Caillech Bérre has been interpreted as the sovereignty goddess; her name is preserved in the Beare peninsula of Co. Cork and she survived into modern folklore. The introduction to the poem also says: 'This is why she was called the Old Woman/Nun of Beare: she had fifty foster children in Beare. She passed into seven periods of youth, so that every husband used to pass from her to death of old age, so that her grandchildren and great-grandchildren were peoples and races. And for a hundred years she wore the veil.' Here is a section of the text that D. Ó hAodha dates to approximately 900:

Ebb-tide to me as to the sea;
Old age causes me to be sallow;
Although I may grieve thereat,
It comes to its food joyfully.

I am the Old Woman of Beare, from Dursey; (*Is mé Caillech Bérre Buí*)
I used to wear a smock that was always new.
Today I am become so thin that I would not
Wear out even a cast-off smock ...

When my arms are seen
All bony and thin! –
In fondest fashion they acted, once;
They used to be around glorious kings ...[56]

T. Clancy says that the speaker is probably human but that the poem may draw on the images of sovereignty and may reflect the ebb and flow of the Corcu Duibne in whose territory the poem is set.[57]

The author did not hesitate to put that poem in the mouth of a woman; and the heroine of *Comrac Liadaine ocus Cuirithir* (The Meeting of Liadan and Cuirithir) is also a female poet (*banéces*), who is torn between the love God and love of a man as in the real-life story of Abelard and Heloise. The setting seems to be the women's monastery at Cill Aiched Conchinn, Killagh, Co Kerry. Liadan the female poet agrees to marry Cuirithir the male poet but postpones the wedding until she finishes her poetic tour.[58] On her return he visits her, and arrives badly dressed and with only one servant. He sees Mac Dá Cherda, 'chief poet and the fool of Ireland', and sends a message to Liadan that is delivered in riddles because she is not alone. Both poets put themselves under the spiritual guidance of a saint who gives them various ordeals; they are put in one bed with a novice between them to ensure that nothing happens. Cuirithir goes to another monastery and, when she follows him, he sails across the sea and she dies on the stone on which he prayed. Some critics have dismissed this as botched text or as a storyteller's notes, but T. Clancy disagrees and describes it as: 'a finely wrought, integrated work, with both poetry and prose employing similar language and ideas, the whole bound together by two dominant themes: that of madness and folly.'[59] Liadan parallels Derdriu, and the verses from the last poem recall Derdriu's wilderness poems. Liadan's death on the praying stone is a passive echo of Derdriu's suicide stone. She is different: her poems carry weight. The following is probably the most striking love poem from this period, and no English translation will do it credit.

Cen áinius	Without pleasure
In gním í do-rigénus:	the deed that I have done;
An ro carus ro cráidius.	The one I loved I have vexed (tormented.)
Bad mire	It were madness
Nád dernad a airersom,	not to do what he wished
Mainbed omun Ríg nime.	Were it not for fear of the King of Heaven.
Níbu amlos	Not profitless
Dosom in dál dúthracair,	to him was that which he desired,
Ascnam sech phéin i Pardos.	To reach past pain to Paradise.
Bec mbríge	A small thing
Ro chráidi frium Cuirithir;	vexed Cuirithir against me,
Frissium ba mór mo míne.	My gentleness to him was great.
Mé Líadan;	I am Liadan;
Ro carussa Cuirithir;	I loved Cuirithir,
Is fírithir ad-fíadar.	It is as true as is said.
Gair bása	A short time I was
I comaitecht Chuirithir;	in Cuirithir's company;
Frissium ba maith mo gnássa.	To him my behaviour was good.
Céol caille	Music of the forest
Fom-chanad la Cuirithir,	used to sing to me beside Cuirithir;
La fogur fairge flainne.	With the sound of the fierce sea.
Do-ménainn	I should have thought
Ní cráidfed frim Cuirithir	that no arrangement I might make
Do dálaib cacha dénainn.	Would have vexed Cuirithir in regard to me.
Ní chela:	Conceal it not;
Ba hésium mo chridesherc,	he was my heart's love,
Cía no charainn cách chena.	Even though I should love all others besides.
Deilm ndega	A roar of fire
Ro thethainn mo chridese;	has split my heart;
Ro-fess, nicon bía cena.	For certain, without him it will not live.[60]

Afterword

It is hardly possible to provide a conclusion for such a book but it seemed necessary to provide some sort of overview or afterword on the content and subject matter. The study of early Irish sagas and related texts as literature is really in its infancy and dates from the late 1940s. Before that the main emphasis was on the linguistic aspect of the texts with very little attention to the content; this is slowly giving way to a more holistic view of the literature and its relationship with history and archaeology in particular. The richness of this material still awaits discovery of the wider world of European and world literature.

Old Irish was 'discovered', as it were, by J.K. Zeuss, and followed by E. O'Curry and J. O'Donovan, in the days of the antiquarian, those who had an interest in all aspects of the tradition and did not draw the strict lines between the linguist, the historian, literary critic and archaeologist. These were followed by scholars like W. Stokes, R. Thurneysen, S.H. O'Grady and E. Windisch who passed the mantle to such people as K. Meyer, D. Binchy, O. Bergin and R.I. Best. But the study of the literature, whether in prose or in poetry, was somewhat stifled by the concentration on the linguistic aspect and its place in the Indo-European family of languages. The Ninth Irish Conference of Medievalists, held at the then St Patrick's College at Maynooth, chose to review the 'state of play in a number of key areas in Medieval Irish Studies'. One day was set aside for lectures on such topics as language, narrative literature, poetry, hagiography, Hiberno-Latin sources, Law, pre-Norman History and archaeology. These lectures were then published, along with others, in K. McCone and K. Simms (eds), *Progress in Medieval Irish Studies* (Department of Old Irish, Saint Patrick's College, Maynooth 1996). In his contribution, T. Ó Cathasaigh said that 'our studies do not have an entirely secure foundation in earlier scholarship' (p. 55) as the work of the earlier centuries that occurred in other literatures had not taken place with early Irish material. He points to what John Kelleher had said some thirty years before: 'the celticists and linguists ... all too seldom have shown sufficient interest in the historical or literary content of what they so skilfully edit.' (p. 55) T.Ó Cathasaigh also said that 'The study of

early Irish literature has never really been established as a university discipline in its own right' and later 'It is something of an embarrassment to have
to say that we have no estimate of the extent or quantity of saga literature
which survives in the manuscripts.' (p. 56)

T. Ó Cathasaigh himself has been to the forefront in the scholarship on
the literature, along with others such as J. Carey and J.F. Nagy. They follow
in the footsteps of such great scholars as J. Carney and P. Mac Cana. The
work of the Navan Research Group, published in *Emania* along with the
publications of H. Tristram on the *Táin* have added greatly to an understanding of this Cycle of stories. There have been a series of debates on
issues such as the pagan versus Christian elements of the literature as well as
the 'nativist' and 'anti-nativist' stance of various leading scholars that have
caused some serious rivalries within the discipline. There is a welcome move
towards a more inter-disciplinary approach as seen in the work, and various
publications, of E. Bhreathnach, J. Fenwick and C. Newman on Tara.

However, there is still a marked reluctance to produce books aimed at
popularizing the topic and making it available to the general public. Very
little of the research carried out has filtered into the education system at first
or second level. Apart from M. Dillon's *Early Irish literature*, J. MacKillop's
Myths and legends of the Celts, M.L. Sjoestedt's *Gods and heroes of the
Celts* and *Celtic mythology* by P. Mac Cana, there are very few general publications and there are hardly any collections of translations for the general
public produced by Irish scholars. There are two main volumes of translations, *Early Irish myths and sagas* by J. Gantz and *Ancient Irish tales* by
Cross and Slover and these were produced outside Ireland; the latter is out
of print. There are the few outstanding exceptions of work published in
Ireland such as T. Kinsella's *The Táin* and M. Heaney's *Beyond Nine Waves*
and Jim Fitzpatrick has also popularized the material through his art and his
books. There are even less publications available in Modern Irish, one that
merits mention is the artistic collection of sagas, *Scéalaíocht na Ríthe*, translated by T. Ó Floinn and P. Mac Cana and illustrated by M. Mac Liammóir
that is unavailable and out of print.

To finish with a quote from T. Ó Cathasaigh from the article mentioned
above: 'But the very considerable shortcomings to which I have alluded at
the beginning must be addressed if the astonishingly rich saga-literature of
early Ireland is to receive the academic treatment which it merits'. (p. 64)

Notes

Introduction

1 Bruford, 'Why an Ulster Cycle?', p. 30 – a timely warning against taking the stories too seriously.

CHAPTER I
The background

1 Carney, 'The deeper level of early Irish literature', 160–71.
2 Dillon, *Early Irish literature*, p. xix. See also Murphy, *Saga and myth in ancient Ireland*, still a useful little book.
3 Meyer, *Aislinge meic Con Glinne*, p. 2.
4 Abrams, *The mirror and the lamp: romantic theory and the critical tradition*, p. 6.
5 Watt, *The rise of the novel*, p. 30.
6 Byrne, '*Senchas*; the nature of the Gaelic historical tradition', 137–59.
7 Mac Cana, *The learned tales of medieval Ireland*, pp 41–9; the number depends on the manuscript.
8 Mac Eoin, 'Orality and literacy in some Middle-Irish king-tales', p. 157.
9 Toner, 'Reconstructing the earliest Irish tale lists', 110 and 114–15.
10 Gwynn, *The Metrical Dindshenchas*, iii, 18–21.
11 Dobbs, 'The *Ban-shenchus*', *Revue Celtique* 47 (1930), 283–339; *Revue Celtique* 48 (1931), 163–234 and *Revue Celtique* 49 (1933), 437–89.
12 Byrne, *Irish kings and high-kings*, p. 52.
13 Delargy, *The Gaelic story-teller*, p. 20.
14 Mac Cana, *The learned tales of medieval Ireland*, p. 25.
15 Ibid., p. 4, referring to Curtain, *Tales of the fairies and the ghost world*, p. 143.
16 Basso, *Wisdom sits in places*, pp 23, 46–50 and 86–7 and Mac Cana, 'Placenames and mythology in Irish tradition: places, pilgrimages, and things', pp 319–41.
17 Booker, *The seven basic plots*, p. 2. Nagy, 'Fenian heroes and their rites of passage', pp 161–3 says that the central subject of heroic stories, if not storytelling in general, is the process of social maturation.

18 Nagy, *Conversing with angels and ancients*, p. x.
19 O'Donovan, *The banquet of Dún na n-Gédh and the battle of Magh Rath*, pp 280–5.
20 Nagy, *Conversing with angels and ancients*, p. 327.
21 Dooley and Roe, *Tales of the elders of Ireland*, pp 111–12. See Nagy, 'Compositional Concerns in the *Acallam na Senórach*', pp 149–50.
22 Mac Cana, *The learned tales of medieval Ireland*, p. 21.
23 Lord, *The singer of tales*, p. 78.
24 Dégh, *Folktales and society*, p. 180.
25 Posidonius was a Stoic philosopher from Apameia (135–51 BC). His writings are compiled in Tierney, 'The Celtic ethnography of Posidonius', 189–275.
26 Piggott, *The druids*.
27 All references from Koch and Carey, *The Celtic heroic age*; see pp 13–14, 18–19, 21–2, 31–2.
28 Breatnach, *Uraicecht na Ríar*, p. 140. See Mercier, *The Irish comic tradition*.
29 Koch and Carey, *The Celtic heroic age*, pp 13–4, 10–11 and 31.
30 Hamilton, ' "Ancient" Irish music', p. 289 says: 'Early Irish literature is so extensive that, had it existed, almost certainly dancing would have been mentioned.'
31 Mac Cana, *The learned tales of medieval Ireland*, pp 122–5 and Gwynn, 'An Old-Irish tract on the privileges and responsibilities of poets', 31.
32 Mac Cana, *The learned tales of medieval Ireland*, pp 41–9.
33 Murphy, *Early Irish lyrics*, pp 90–1.
34 Ford, 'The blind, the dumb, and the ugly: aspects of poets and their craft in early Ireland and Wales', 27–40; Bergin, *Irish bardic poetry*, pp 6–8 quotes from the 1722 publication of the *Memoirs of the Marquis of Clanricarde* and *description of the Western Islands of Scotland* (1703).
35 Ó Dónaill, *Talland Étair*.
36 Bannerman, 'The Convention of Druim Cett', pp 157–70.
37 Koch and Carey, *The Celtic heroic age*, pp 1–4.

38　Ibid., pp 44–5 from *Histories*, 4.61, 66.

39　Richter, *The formation of the medieval West*, p. 190.

40　Byrne, 'Latin poetry in Ireland', p. 34.

41　Carey, *King of mysteries*, p. 22. Apocryphal texts refer to religious material that is not contained in the canon of church teaching and writings. The Gnostics were a group of early Christians who believed that they possessed a secret knowledge and they are credited with such texts as the Gospel of Thomas and the Gospel of Mary as well.

42　de Paor, *St Patrick's world*, p. 96 and Bieler, *Libri Epistolarum Sancti Patricii Episcopi*.

43　The lives by Tírechán and Muirchú in Bieler and Kelly, *The Patrician texts in the Book of Armagh* and Mulchrone, *Bethu Phátraic: the tripartite life of Patrick*.

44　Bieler and Kelly, *The Patrician texts in the Book of Armagh*, pp 84–7, 132–3.

45　Murphy, *Early Irish lyrics*, pp 52–5.

46　Anderson, *Adomnan's life of Columba* and Meyer, *Cáin Adamnáin: an Old-Irish treatise on the Law of Adamnan*.

47　Kelly, *A guide to early Irish law* and Kelly, 'Text and transmissions: the law-texts', pp 230–42.

48　Stokes, *Cóir Anmann*, pp 306–7, §42 = Arbuthnot, *Cóir Anmann* (Part 2), pp 14, 90.

49　Meyer, *Sanas Cormaic*.

50　Dobbs, 'The *Ban-shenchus*', *Revue Celtique* 47 (1930), 283–339; Dobbs, 'The *Ban-shenchus*', *Revue Celtique* 48 (1931), 163–234 and Dobbs, 'The *Ban-shenchus*', *Revue Celtique* 49 (1933), 437–89.

51　Meyer, *The instructions of King Cormac mac Airt*, pp 32–5.

52　Meyer, *The triads of Ireland*, pp 6–7, 12–13.

53　O'Brien, *Corpus Genealogiarum Hiberniae* is the main published collection. There is no translation.

54　Macalister, *Lebor Gabála Érenn*, 5 vols, ii, 35.

55　Ó Cathasaigh, 'Mythology in *Táin Bó Cúailnge*', pp 114–32. Also see Richter, *The formation of the medieval West*, p. 82; Mac Eoin, 'Orality and literacy in some Middle-Irish king-tales', pp 158–9 and Mac Cana, 'Mongán mac Fiachna and *Immram Brain*', 107. A comparison may be made between the oral lecture style and the formal written style of an article – even if the material is the same.

56　Ó Coileáin, 'Oral or literary? Some strands of the argument', 7–35.

57　Carney, *Studies in Irish literature and history*, pp 277–8 and 78 in a footnote.

58　McCone, *Pagan past and Christian present*, p. 24; see Sims-Williams, Review of *Pagan past and Christian present*, in *Éigse* 19 (1996), 180, 196.

59　Thurneysen, *Die irische Helden-und Königsage*, pp 66–7, 72.

60　Carey, *King of mysteries*, p. 10.

61　Ó Cuív, 'The changing face of the Irish language', p. 23; McManus, *A guide to Ogam*, 150 and Harvey, 'Early literacy in Ireland: the evidence of Ogam', 1–16.

62　Cf. Senger, 'Literacy, Western European', pp 597–602.

63　These can be found at http://www.isos.dias.ie where the major manuscripts have now been captured and there are many texts also available on the web at http://www.ucc.ie/ celt.

64　O'Neill, *The Irish hand*, pp xiii, xxvi in the introduction by F.J. Byrne. O'Neill speculates that some scribes may have been chosen for their myopia that would help with some of the very detailed work (oral communication). See Ní Shéaghdha, 'Collectors of Irish manuscripts: motives and methods', 1–28.

65　Meyer, *Selections from ancient Irish poetry*, p. 99.

66　Cf. Bischoff, *Latin palaeography: antiquity and the Middle Ages*, p. 80 translated by D. Ó Cróinín and D. Ganz. M. Tullius Tiro, secretary to Cicero, is credited with inventing the abbreviations.

67　O'Neill, *The Irish hand*, introduction, p. xviii. Druim Snechta was established by Lugaid moccu Óchae (†615) also known as St Mo-Lua of Clonfertmulloe. He was educated at Bangor, established by St Comgall (†601/5) and noted for the strict rules. Tuaim Drecain, where Cenn Faelad was brought, is only twenty miles from Druim Snechta. See Mac Cana, 'Mongán mac Fiachna and *Immram Brain*', 102 and McCone, *Echtra Chonnlai and the beginnings of vernacular narrative writing in Ireland*, p. 119 where they both identify this area as the place where the written literature probably began.

68　O'Neill, *The Irish hand*, p. 2. Herrity and Breen, *The Cathach of Colum Cille: an introduction* that includes a CD-ROM of the manuscript with an English translation.

69　O'Kelleher and Schoepperle, *Betha Colaim Chille: Life of Columcille*, pp 176–84.

70　A diplomatic edition means the texts are reproduced exactly as they are in the manuscript, unedited.

71　Dillon, 'Laud misc. 610 (cont.)', 135–55.

72　Hull, *Longes mac nUislenn*, pp 43, 60.

CHAPTER 2
The Mythological Cycle

1 Mac Cana, *Celtic mythology*, pp 49–50.
2 Macalister, *Lebor Gabála Érenn* 5 vols. and sections in Cross and Slover, *Ancient Irish tales*, pp 3–27. Stokes, 'The prose tales in the Rennes Dinnshenchus', *Revue Celtique* 15 (1894), 272, 336, 418–84; *Revue Celtique* 16 (1895), 31–83, 135–67, 269–312; Stokes 'The Bodleian Dinnshenchas', 467–516; Stokes, 'The Edinburgh Dinnshenchas', 471–97 and Gwynn, *The Metrical Dindshenchas*, 5 vols.
3 The word euhemerization from the Greek Euhemeros (*c*.316 BC) is used for the belief that deities were originally human. He maintained that the Greek myths came from historical events and that they were originally human beings.
4 Baring and Cashford, *The myth of the goddess: evolution of an image*.
5 Meyer, *Sanas Cormaic*, §150, 15.
6 Ó Catháin, *The festival of Brigit: Celtic goddess and holy woman*, p. 56.
7 Carey, 'Time, space, and the Otherworld', 1–27, discussed in the chapter on the Otherworld, below.
8 Borsje, *From chaos to enemy: encounters with monsters in early Irish texts*.
9 Danaher, *The year in Ireland*, pp 200–27.
10 MacNeill, *The festival of Lughnasa*, p. 316, 424 says there are 195 sites still associated with the festival.
11 Danaher, *The year in Ireland*, pp 13–37.
12 Danaher, *The year in Ireland*, pp 86–127.
13 Eliade, *Myth and reality*, p. 5.
14 Sjoestedt, *Gods and heroes of the Celts*, p. 1.
15 Frazer, 'The first Battle of Moytura', 1–63 and Carey, 'Fir Bolg: a native etymology revisited', 77–83. Macalister, *Lebor Gabála Érenn* iv, 228 says that Bres died after he drank 'bog-stuff in the guise of milk'.
16 Gray, *Cath Maige Tuired*. It is situated in the modern day Co. Sligo.
17 Ó Cathasaigh, '*Cath Maige Tuired* as exemplary myth', p. 11.
18 Gray, '*Cath Maige Tuired*: myth and structure', 4 discusses the various relationships between fathers and sons in the text.
19 *Fidchell* (wood knowledge) is generally translated as the game of chess but the rules appear to be slightly different. The word is used in Modern Irish as a translation for chess. According to the law on fosterage a prince must learn to play *fidchell* and another game called *brandub*.

20 Early Irish law allows a woman to divorce her husband if he gets too fat for intercourse, Kelly, *A guide to early Irish Law*, p. 74. Strabo and Ephorus both mention that the Celts on the Continent avoided getting fat and a young man was fined if his waist grew too large.
21 Banks, '*Na tri Mairt*, the three marts and the man with the withy', 131–43; Greene, 'Varia i. The Three Tuesdays', 139–40 and Mac Neill, *The festival of Lughnasa*, pp 4–5.
22 Gantz, *Early Irish myths and sagas*, pp 27–59.
23 Gantz, *Early Irish myths and sagas*, pp 60–106. Another account of how he achieves his kingship in Gwynn, '*De shíl Chonairi Móir*', 130–53.
24 Hull, *De Gabáil in tShída*, pp 53–8 and in Gwynn, 'Cináed ua hArtacáin's Poem on Brugh na Bóinne', 210–38.
25 The place is mentioned in death tales.
26 Charles-Edwards, '*Tochmarc Étaíne*: a literal interpretation', p. 166 says that they story may be about marital/ non-marital relationships and the children that result from them. He concludes that 'Étaín was more goddess than human.' (p. 174). A child conceived upon a married woman is the property of her husband until the biological father buys the child from him according to early Irish law. Here the Dagda helps his son just as in the *Battle of Moytura* Oengus helped his father.
27 Under certain circumstances, early Irish law permitted a man to have two wives at the same time and outlines the ways in which the wives are entitled to mistreat one another for a period of time. Fuamnach is legally entitled to attack Étaín. There is also the question of who should receive the huge bride price that has been paid.
28 Early Irish law warns women not to meet men in bushes and there will be no compensation if they are raped while doing so, Kelly, *A guide to early Irish law*, pp 134–6. Meeting a man three times in the open is also a feature of *The Kinslaying of Rónán* discussed in the Cycles of the Kings.
29 McCone, *Pagan past and Christian present*, p. 34 points to a possible biblical analogy in 2 Sam/Kings 13 where David's son Ammon fakes illness for love of Tamar, the sister of his elder half-brother Absalom and then he rapes her as she looks after him. Charles-Edwards, '*Tochmarc Étaíne*: a literal interpretation', p. 176 says: 'I am not quite sure what is going on here. Why is it that Étaín, who was quite willing to

sleep with Ailill, is so coy when it comes to returning to her first husband?'

30 McCone, *Pagan past and Christian present*, p. 112 mentions an episode in the *M h bh rata* where Nala must choose her husband to be from five men who look exactly the same.

31 Gantz, *Early Irish myths and sagas*, pp 107–12 and Shaw, *The dream of Óengus, Aislinge Óenguso*.

32 Duncan, 'Altram Tige dá Medar', 184–225 and Dobbs, 'Altromh Tighi da Medar', 189–229. *Medar* can mean vessel, measurement and a milk pail.

33 O'Curry, *Oidhe Chloinne Lir*, pp 113–55. On being turned into swans they can still speak and they have unequalled singing ability.

34 Littleton, *The new comparative mythology*, pp 32–40.

35 Frazer, *The golden bough*, pp 264–83.

36 Littleton, *The new comparative mythology*, p. 85.

37 Yalman, 'The raw: the cooked: nature: culture – observations on *Le cru et le Cuit*', p. 75.

38 Kirk, *Myth: its meaning and functions in ancient and other cultures*, 42.

39 Nagy, *The wisdom of the outlaw*, p. 15.

CHAPTER 3
The Heroic Cycle

1 Koch, 'Windows on the Iron Age: 1964–1994', 232.

2 Hillers, 'Heroes of the Ulster Cycle', 99–106 and Mallory and Stockman, *Ulidia*, pp 291–301 give a list of translations.

3 Posidonius of Apameia, a Stoic philosopher (135–51 BC), his writings are compiled in Tierney, 'The Celtic ethnography of Posidonius', 189–275.

4 Jackson, *The oldest Irish tradition: a window on the Iron Age* and Tierney, 'The Celtic ethnography of Posidonius', 169.

5 Sayers, 'Early Irish attitudes toward hair and beards, baldness and tonsure', 158 and 168. A bog body discovered in 2003 in Ireland had his hair stiffened in a high style to give the man additional height as he was only five feet tall.

6 Jackson, *The oldest Irish tradition*, pp 3–4, 55.

7 Koch, 'Windows on the Iron Age: 1964–1994', 229–37.

8 Kinsella, *The Táin*, p. 247 = O'Rahilly, *Táin Bó Cúailnge Recension 1*, pp 121, 234.

9 Diodorus Siculus v.29 from O'Rahilly, *Táin Bó Cúailnge Recension 1*, p. xi and

Kinsella, *The Táin*, p. 243.

10 Kinsella, *The Táin*, pp 88–9, Raftery, *Pagan Celtic Ireland*, pp 104–10 contains some related finds.

11 Tymoczko, *Two deaths from the Ulster Cycle*; p. 61; Koch and Carey, *The Celtic heroic age*, pp 140–1.

12 Meyer, 'Aided Chonchobuir', pp 2–21 and Cross and Slover, *Ancient Irish tales*, pp 343–6.

13 Gantz, *Early Irish myths and sagas*, pp 221–55.

14 Women are associated with words, good and bad, in many texts, Findon, *A women's words: Emer and female speech in the Ulster Cycle*, pp 57–84.

15 Gantz, *Early Irish myths and sagas*, pp 179–87.

16 Meyer, *The Death Tales of the Ulster heroes*, pp 28–9.

17 McCone, *Pagan past and Christian present*, pp 77–9 and McCone, 'Aided Cheltchair Maic Uthechair: hounds, heroes and hospitallers in early Irish myth and story', 1–30. Thurneysen drew attention to the similarity between the wife in this tale and the behaviour of Jezebel and her husband Ahab in the Bible, *Die Irische Helden-und Königsage*, p. 495.

18 O'Leary, 'Contention at feasts in early Irish literature', 116–19.

19 O'Leary, 'Verbal deceit in the Ulster Cycle', 16–26.

20 References are to Kinsella, *The Táin* as it is accessible. Backhaus, 'The structure of the list of *Remscéla Tána Bó Cualngi* in the Book of Leinster', 19–26; Chadwin, 'The *Remscéla Tána Bó Cualngi*', 67–75 and Murray, 'The finding of the *Táin*', 17–23.

21 Kinsella, *The Táin*, pp 6–8; Hull, 'Noínden Ulad: the debility of the Ulidians', 1–42 and the Fedelm story in Koch and Carey, *The Celtic heroic age*, pp 67–8.

22 Sjoestedt, *Gods and heroes of the Celts*, p. 28.

23 O'Broin, 'What is the debility of the Ulstermen?', 386–99 and Ó Cathasaigh, 'Mythology in *Táin Bó Cúailnge*', pp 122–7 where he agrees that the debility is a winter sleep and discusses the *cess* and the waste land theme in the birth of Cú Chulainn. O'Broin, 'The word Cess', 109–14 and O'Broin, 'The word Noínden', 165–76.

24 Kinsella, *The Táin*, p. 101 the poets are killed when the river Cronn rises up against the Connacht army to the height of the treetops. Nagy, 'How the *Táin* was lost', 603–9.

25 Kinsella, *The Táin*, pp 46–50.

26 Cf. also Ford, 'A highly important pig', pp 292–304 and Ní Chatháin, 'Swineherds, seers, and druids', 200–11.

27 Stokes, 'Tidings of Conchobar mac Nessa', 18–38.

28 Windisch, 'Táin Bó Flidáis', 206–23 and MacKinnon, 'Toraigecht Tána Bó Flidaise', 104–21, 202–19.

29 Dobbs, 'On Táin Bó Flidáis', 140–1.

30 Gantz, *Early Irish myths and sagas*, p. 256; Kinsella, *The Táin*, pp 8–20; Herbert, 'Celtic heroine? The archaeology of the Deirdre story', pp 13–22, Tymoczko, 'Animal imagery in *Loinges Mac nUislenn*', 145–66 and Ní Bhrolcháin, '*Re thóin mná*: in pursuit of troublesome women', 115–22. The word *derdriu* appears to mean an unpleasant noise and the name is never used again in the literature. There is a later tale about their children, Aeb Gréine (Beauty of the sun) and their son Gaiar who is said to have been the king of Ulster, Breatnach, '*Tochmarc Luaine ocus Aided Athairne*', 1–31.

31 The reference to grabbing his ears is obscure but her husband asks his wife at the beginning of the text: 'The clamour between your sides ... it crushes him who hears with ears.'

32 Meid, *Táin Bó Fraích* = Carney, *Studies in Irish literature and history*, p. 58, translation 1–14 and 189–214 and Evans, 'The learned borrowings claimed for *Táin Bó Fraích*', pp 182–94 questions this borrowing. Ross, *Pagan Celtic Britain*, pp 196–7 associates Conall Cernach and the god Cernunnos, one statue shows him feeding ram-headed serpents around his waist.

33 Kinsella, *The Táin*, pp 39–45 = Gantz, *Early Irish myths and sagas*, pp 147–52. The plot may be borrowed; there is a similar theme in Indo-European tradition of Sohrab and Rustum in Persia and of Hildebrandslied in Germany. The *gae bolga* was the weapon apparently given to Cú Chulainn in the Otherworld.

34 O'Rahilly, *The Stowe Version of Táin Bó Cúailnge*; *Táin Bó Cúalnge from the Book of Leinster* and *Táin Bó Cúailnge recension 1* and Kinsella, *The Táin*, pp 51–253.

35 They use legal terms and the definition of a 'marriage of equal partnership' where both partners are equal in every way, Kelly, *A guide to early Irish law*, pp 70–3.

36 Hull, 'Two tales about Find', 326 explains his name as 'man of smoke' but see Ó Flaithearta, 'The etymologies of (Fer) Diad', pp 218–25 where he suggests biped.

37 Tristram, 'The Cattle-Raid of Cuailnge in tension and transition', pp 79–80.

38 Tristram, 'What is the purpose of *Táin Bó Cúailnge*?', 11–22.

39 Meyer, 'The Laud genealogies and tribal histories', 305 and Olmsted, 'Luccreth's poem *Conailla Medb Míchuru* and the origins of the *Táin*', 3–72; Henry, '*Verba Scáthaige*', 101–2, the poem is also part of *The Wooing of Emer* and Olmsted, 'The earliest narrative version of the *Táin*: seventh-century poetic references to *Táin Bó Cúailnge*', 5–17. Olmsted, '*Conailla Medb míchuru* and the origins of the *Táin*', 333–42 says that one of the main purposes of the poem is to explain how part of the Clann Fergusa settled at Tara. Also Kelly, 'The Táin as literature', pp 69–102.

40 Tristram, 'The Cattle-Raid of Cuailnge in tension and transition', p. 69; Kelleher, 'The *Táin* and the Annals', 107–27 says the *Táin* was reworked in Louth during the early ninth century and brought to Clonmacnoise where it lay dormant until it was included in the the early twelfth-century *Lebor na hUidre*.

41 Ó hUiginn, 'The background and development of *Táin Bó Cúailnge*', pp 37–8.

42 Abrams *A glossary of literary terms*, p. 49 from Ó Cathasaigh, 'Mythology in *Táin Bó Cúailnge*', 116.

43 Mallory, 'The world of Cú Chulainn: the archaeology of the *Táin Bó Cúailnge*', 153.

44 Thurneysen, *Die irische Helden-und Königsage*, 96–7, 112.

45 Ó hUiginn, 'The background and development of *Táin Bó Cúailnge*', p. 39; Ó Cathasaigh, 'Mythology in *Táin Bó Cúailnge*', 118 disagrees with the classical or biblical influence on the text.

46 Tristram, 'The Cattle-Raid of Cuailnge in tension and transmission', 69.

47 Ó hUiginn, 'The background and development of *Táin Bó Cúailnge*', p. 62 and Ó Cathasaigh, 'Mythology in *Táin Bó Cúailnge*', 120.

48 Lincoln, *Priests, warriors and cattle*, pp 69, 92. Mac Cana, 'Placenames and mythology in Irish tradition: places, pilgrimages, and things', 339 refers to the dismembered corpse of Sati wife of Siva scattered on the landscape that became the shrines of the goddess.

CHAPTER 4
The Fenian Cycle

1 Dooley, *Tales of the elders of Ireland*, p. 6. The word Fenian is an anglicization of the word *fianna* and was also used in Ireland by a group of rebels in the nineteenth century.

2 Finn and his followers are generally known as the Fianna.

3 O'Kearney, *Feis Tige Chonáin* and O'Kearney, *The Battle of Gabhra*, pp 49–51.

4 Meyer, *The instructions of king Cormac mac Airt*, p. 46.

5 Ó Riain, 'Boundary association in early Irish society', 26.

6 van Gennep, *Les rites de passage*.

7 Nagy, 'Liminality and knowledge in Irish tradition', 135.

8 Scowcroft, Review of *The wisdom of the outlaw*, 97–100.

9 Ó Cathasaigh, '*Cath Maige Tuired* as exemplary myth', 12–14.

10 Chadbourne, 'The beagle's cry: dogs in the Finn ballads and tales', 1–14.

11 Ó Briain, 'Oisín's biography, conception and birth', pp 454–86, see Dooley and Roe, *Tales of the elders of Ireland*, 74.

12 Nagy, *The wisdom of the outlaw*, pp 118–20 from *Feis Tige Chonáin* (The feast of Conán's House).

13 Stokes, '*Cóir Anmann*', §215, 377 = Arbuthnot, *Cóir Anmann* (Part 2), pp 58, 131; Carey, 'Werewolves in medieval Ireland', 37–72; McCone, 'Werewolves, cyclopes, *díberga* and *fíanna*: juvenile delinquency in early Ireland', 1–22 and Vielle, 'The oldest narrative attestations of a Celtic mythical and traditional heroic cycle', 223–4. Schrijver, 'On henbane and early European narcotics', 17–45 links the use of henbane with the Fianna. People who took the drug think they turn into animals and that they can fly.

14 Meyer, *The voyage of Bran*, pp 45–8, 49–52 and White, *Compert Mongáin*, pp 73–4, 79–81, discussion 35–70.

15 Meyer, *Sanas Cormaic, orc tréith*, 86 and *rincne*, 97 and Stokes, 'Find and the phantoms', 289–307.

16 Nagy, 'Fenian heroes and their rites of passage', 168. He also says: He 'belongs not so much on either side of the gap as within the gap itself ... He never stands still' (pp 120–1).

17 O'Grady, *Áirem muintire Finn*, SG i, 92–3, SG ii, 99–100.

18 Hennessy, 'Fotha Catha Cnucha', 86–93, Nagy, *The wisdom of the outlaw*, pp 218–21, Cross and Slover, *Ancient Irish tales*, pp 357–9. It says that Cumall and Conn's father had the same mother.

19 Meyer, *Macgníomhartha Finn*, pp 195–204; Meyer, 'The boyish exploits of Finn', pp 180–90 and Nagy, *The wisdom of the outlaw*, pp 209–18. See the chapter on Poets and Poetry.

20 Meyer, 'Finn and the man in the tree', 344–6.

21 Meyer, 'Two tales about Finn', 241–7, *Tucait Fhághbhála in Fesa do Find inso ocus Marbad Cúil Duib*, pp 245–7; Hull, 'Two tales about Find', 322–33, the tale about Cúldub, 329–33.

22 Meyer, 'Two tales about Finn', 241–7; *Bruiden Átha*, pp 242–5, reprinted by Hull, 'Two Tales about Find', 322–33, *Bruiden Átha*, pp 323–8.

23 Meyer, *Fianaigecht*, pp 10–17 and Hull, 'The death of Fothath Cananne', 400–4. *Reicne* is a kind of poetical composition, perhaps a rhapsody, extempore poem. Fothad is said to marry the Caillech Bérre.

24 Meyer, *Sanas Cormaic*, §1018 and Clancy, 'Fools and adultery in some early Irish texts', 110–13.

25 Ní Shéaghdha, *Tóruigheacht Dhiarmada agus Ghráinne* discusses the story and its relationships to similar plots.

26 Pregnant women have the right to forbidden food.

27 Schoepperle, *Tristan and Isolt*, pp 413–17 and Ní Shéaghdha, *Tóruigheacht Dhiarmada agus Ghráinne*, p. xxviii.

28 Carney, *Studies in Irish literature and history*, pp 190 and 193.

29 Kinsella, *The Táin*, pp 8–20 and Gantz, *Early Irish myths and sagas*, pp 256–67. The resumé is given in the chapter on the Heroic Cycle.

30 Binchy, *Scéla Cano meic Gartnáin*. Discussed in the chapter on the Cycles of the Kings.

31 Hull, 'The text of *Baile Binnbérlach mac Buain* from MS 23.N.10 of the Royal Irish Academy', 94–7; Meyer, *Hibernica Minora*, p. 84 and Ní Dhonnchadha, 'Baile the sweet-spoken, son of Búan', 218–19.

32 Meyer, 'The death of Finn mac Cumaill', 462–5 and Meyer, 'The chase of Síd na mBan Finn and the death of Finn' in *Fianaigecht*, pp 52–99.

33 Power, '*Cnucha cnoc os cionn Life*', 44, 51.

34 Nagy, *The wisdom of the outlaw*, p. 60; O'Kearney, *The Battle of Gabhra, gabar* now means goat but in Old Irish it also meant horse, especially a white mare. See Ní Bhrolcháin, 'The TaraSkryne or the Gabhra Valley in early Irish literature', 1–15.

35 Dooley and Roe, *Tales of the elders of Ireland*, p. 7; Stokes, *Acallamh na Senórach*, pp 1–226; O'Grady, *Acallamh na Senórach*, SG i, 94–233, SG ii, 101–265 and Ní Shéaghdha, *Acallam na Senórach*, modern Irish version.

36 Nagy, 'Compositional concerns in the *Acallam na Senórach*', pp 149–50. Mac

Cana, 'Placenames and mythology in Irish tradition: places, pilgrimages, and things', p. 333 say that the *Acallam* is 'a constantly reiterated reminder that toponomy is in fact (sacred) history'.

37 Dooley and Roe, *Tales of the elders of Ireland*, pp 111–12.

38 Cross and Slover, *Ancient Irish tales*, pp 439–56 and Ó Briain, 'Some material on Oisín in the Land of Youth', pp 181–99.

CHAPTER 5
The Cycles of the Kings

1 Mac Eoin, 'Orality and literacy in some Middle-Irish king-tales', p. 151.

2 The term is used by Professor Dan Wiley on his very useful website: http://www.hastings.edu/academic/english/Kings/Home.html.

3 Byrne, *Irish kings and high-kings*, p. 52.

4 Greene, *Orgain Denna Ríg*, pp 16–26; Koch and Carey, *The Celtic heroic age*, pp 54–8 and Ó Cathasaigh, 'The oldest story of the Laigin: observations on *Orgain Denna Ríg*', 1–18.

5 O'Grady, *Boramha*, SG i, 359–90, SG ii, 401–24, see Ó Cuív, '*Comrac na Cloenfherta*', 168–79.

6 Jackson, *Cath Maighe Léna*.

7 O'Kelleher and Schoepperle, *Betha Colaim Chille: Life of Columcille*, pp 176–84.

8 Power, '*Cnucha cnoc os cionn Life*', prose section 39–40 and 45–6, Nagy, *Conversing with angels and ancients*, p. 322 says 'Like the devil, Caílte appears when his name is spoken.'

9 Best, 'The settling of the manor of Tara', 121–72.

10 Meyer, *The voyage of Bran*, pp 56–8 and White, *Compert Mongáin*, pp 75, 83.

11 O'Grady, *Geinemain Aeda Shláine*, SG i, 82–4, SG ii, 88–91 and Ní Dhonnchadha, 'The birth of Aed Sláine', 182–4.

12 Greene, *Fingal Rónáin and other stories*, pp 48–51 and Mac Eoin, 'The death of the boys in the mill', 60–4. A short poem, in Greene and O'Connor, *A golden treasury of Irish verse*, pp 108–9, also mentions the incident.

13 Greene, *Fingal Rónáin and other stories*, pp 51–4 entitles it *Aided Maelodráin* (The death of Maelodrán). Wiley comments on his site that the story is probably a rare piece of folklore from the Dál Messin Corb of south-west Wicklow.

14 Binchy, *Scéla Cano meic Gartnáin*. Diarmait also appears in Bhreathnach, 'A new edition of *Tochmarc Becfhola*', 59–91.

15 Ó Cathasaigh, 'The theme of *ainmne* in *Scéla Cano meic Gartnáin*', 78–87.

16 Ó Cathasaigh, 'The rhetoric of *Scéla Cano meic Gartnáin*', pp 242 and 244.

17 O'Grady, *Betha Chellaig*, SG i, 49–65, SG ii, 50–69 and Mulchrone, *Caithréim Cellaig*.

18 Nagy, 'Otters, salmon and eel in traditional Gaelic narrative', 124–5.

19 Herbert, '*Cathréim Cellaig*, some literary and historical considerations', 325.

20 Cf. Kinsella, *The Táin*, p. 46.

21 Knott, 'Why Mongán was deprived of noble issue', 155–60.

22 Discussed in the chapter on the Otherworld. Meyer, *The voyage of Bran son of Febal*, pp 2–35 and Cross and Slover, *Ancient Irish tales*, pp 588–95.

23 Meyer, *The voyage of Bran*, pp 42–3, 44–5 and White, *Compert Mongáin*, pp 71–2, 78–9.

24 Meyer, *The voyage of Bran*, pp 58–70 and 70–84.

25 Meyer, *The voyage of Bran*, pp 45–8, 49–52 and White, *Compert Mongáin*, pp 73–4, 79–81, discussion 35–70.

26 Fothad Airgtech was the brother of Fothad Canainne, the leader of a *fian*-band as mentioned in the chapter on the Fenian Cycle.

27 White, *Compert Mongáin*, pp 74, 81 and Meyer, *The voyage of Bran*, pp 48, 51. Cinaed ua hArtacáin's (†973) poem on the deaths of Irish heroes mentions Mongán and Finn in the same stanza, Stokes, 'On the deaths of some Irish heroes', 310–11.

28 Meyer, *The voyage of Bran*, pp 52–4, 54–6 and White, *Compert Mongáin*, pp 75–6, 81–2, discussion 35–70.

29 Meyer, *The voyage of Bran*, pp 56–8 and White, *Compert Mongáin*, pp 75, 83.

30 Meyer, 'The Colloquy of Colum Cille and the youth at Carn Eolairg', 313–20, the same as Koch and Carey, *The Celtic heroic age*, pp 221–2.

31 Stokes, *Annals of Tigernach*, *Revue Celtique* 17 (1896), 178.

32 The long one, O'Donovan, *The banquet of Dun na n-Gedh and the battle of Magh Rath* and the shorter text, Marstrander, 'A new version of the Battle of Mag Rath', 226–47. Herbert, 'Fled Dúin na nGéd: a reappraisal', 75–87.

33 O'Keeffe, *Buile Suibhne*.

34 Nagy, 'Otters, salmon and eel in traditional Gaelic narrative', 127–8.

35 Another location, Gleann na nGealt, does not appear in the written sources until 1584 and Gleann Bolcáin is not mentioned after the sixteenth century and they are

most likely two names for the same place probably in the Fionntrá (Ventry) area in Co. Kerry. See Mac Eoin, 'Gleann Bolcáin agus Gleann na nGealt', 105–20.

36 Cross and Slover, *Ancient Irish tales*, pp 538–5.

37 The early Irish law says that a woman who meets men in bushes or a woman committing adultery is not entitled to compensation if she is raped in Kelly, *A guide to early Irish law*, pp 135–6. He quotes Triad 100: 'the three darknesses into which women should not go: the darkness of mist, the darkness of a wood, the darkness of night.'

38 The detailed descriptions of the placing of the characters during the killing scene are so precise that they could be stage directions.

39 Stafford, 'Family politics in the early Middle Ages', p. 81.

40 Poppe, 'Deception and self-deception in *Fingal Rónáin*', 141 and Ó Cathasaigh, 'The rhetoric of *Fingal Rónáin*', 123–44.

41 Keuls, *The reign of the phallus: sexual politics in ancient Athens*, p. 92 says that unnamed women can trigger Greek stories.

42 Clancy, 'Fools and adultery in some early Irish texts', 119.

43 Smyth, 'Kings, saints and sagas', 103–5 also says that Aífe is mentioned in the *Bóroma* as Bun Aífe (the bottom of Aífe) and that the Battle of Dún Bolg was fought nearby. Dún Bolg is the older name for Brusselstown Ring only a mile from Kilranelagh Hill and 'White Cow Hill' is mentioned on the Down Survey map of 1655.

44 Ó Riain, *Cath Almaine*, p. 5.

45 Ó Cathasaigh, 'Sound and sense in *Cath Almhaine*', 41.

CHAPTER 6
The Otherworld

1 Zaleski, *Otherworld journeys*, pp 3–4.

2 Campbell, *The hero with a thousand faces*, pp 30, 193.

3 Carey, 'The Irish "Otherworld": Hiberno-Latin perspectives', 154–9 and Carey, 'The location of the Otherworld in Irish tradition', 36–43. MacKillop, *Myths and legends of the Celts*, pp 107–24 refers to 'Otherworlds'.

4 Sellner, *Wisdom of the Celtic saints*, p. 34 says that the Celts did not see time chronologically; this is why they bring together characters from different periods and dimensions.

5 Carey, 'Time, space, and the Otherworld',

15 and Hicks, 'Using archaeological Reconnaissance data to identify *Oenach* sites' (unpublished lecture sent to this writer by the author), the words used are *theatrum*, *spectaculum* or *circus*. The embankments at henge monuments could have been seating or standing areas for spectators at rituals. He also notes that both horses and dogs may have been associated with the *oenach*. Some are associated with Tara such as the Rath Meidbe. The new national monument found at Lismullin in the Gabhra Valley close to Rath Lugh is also one of these sites. See Ettlinger, 'The association of burials with popular assemblies, fairs and races in ancient Ireland', 30–61.

6 Westropp, 'Brazil and the legendary islands of the North Atlantic', 223–60.

7 Martínez Hernández, *Canarias en la Mitología*, pp 92, 102–3.

8 Mac Cana, *The learned tales of medieval Ireland*, pp 45, 53.

9 Dumville, '*Echtrae* and *Immram* some problems of definition', 72–94. The various attempts at separating them elicited the following comments from McCone, *Pagan past and Christian present*, pp 79–80: 'This attempt to apply a classificatory straitjacket has inevitably led to a sterile debate as to whether the early *Immram Brain*, being allegedly less Christian (at least when rid of certain inconvenient "interpolations") than other extant voyage tales, should not rather be considered an *echtrae*.'

10 Meyer, *The voyage of Bran son of Febal*, pp 2–35; Cross and Slover, *Ancient Irish tales*, pp 588–95 and Mac Mathúna, *Immram Brain: Bran's journey to the Land of Women*.

11 Mac Mathúna, 'The structure and transmission of early Irish voyage literature', p. 343.

12 Oskamp, '*Echtra Condla*', 207–28; Cross and Slover, *Ancient Irish tales*, pp 488–90 and McCone, *Echtra Chonnlai* where the translation is in the notes.

13 Ó Cathasaigh, 'The semantics of *síd*', 137–55; *síd* may be translated as both 'fairy mound' and 'peace'.

14 Carney, *Studies in Irish literature and history*, p. 292 and says: 'I think it not unlikely that *Immram Brain* and *Compert Mongáin* derive ultimately from the same pen.' McCone has two different opinions, *Pagan past and Christian present*, 79–83 sees the Bran story as the oldest and in *Echtrae Chonnlai*, p. 47 he sees that text as the oldest, see also p. 106.

15 Carney, *Studies in Irish literature and history*, pp 280–5 and Carney, 'The earliest Bran material', 174–93, reprint in Wooding, *The Otherworld voyage*, p. 90.

16 Mac Cana, 'The sinless Otherworld of *Immram Brain*', 95–6 and Mac Cana, 'Mongán mac Fiachna and *Immram Brain*', 119, 123.

17 Nagy, 'Close encounters of the traditional kind in medieval Irish literature', pp 147–8.

18 Mac Cana, 'Mongán mac Fiachna and *Immram Brain*', 141.

19 Carey, 'The Lough Foyle colloquy texts: *Immacaldam Choluim Chille 7 ind Óclaig oc Carraic Eolairg and Immacaldam in Druad Brain 7 inna Banfhátho Febuil ós Loch Fhebuil*', 77 where he gives a translation. Schrijver, 'On henbane and early European narcotics', 17–45 says that the taker hallucinates and thinks they can fly or change into animals.

20 Meyer, 'The colloquy of Colum Cille and the youth at Carn Eolairg', 313–20 = Koch and Carey, *The Celtic heroic age*, pp 221–2.

21 Meyer, *The voyage of Bran*, pp 88–90. There is also a longer, more modern version of the story of his conception and how meets his wife Dub Lacha, Meyer, *The voyage of Bran*, pp 58–70 and 70–84, that says Manannán took Mongán to the Otherworld until he was twelve years old.

22 O'Grady, *Aided Echach mheic Mhaireda*, SG i, 233–7, ii, 265–9 = Ní Dhonnchadha, 'from Aided Echach maic Maireda', pp 271–2.

23 Kinsella, *The Táin*, pp 25–39 and Cross and Slover, *Ancient Irish tales*, pp 153–71.

23a Ní Bhrolcháin, '*Serglige Con Culainn*: a possible re-interpretation', pp 288–99.

24 Carney, *Studies in Irish literature and history*, pp 287–93.

25 Ó Cathasaigh, 'Reflections on *Compert Conchobuir* and *Serglige Con Culainn*', 85–9.

26 Jackson, 'The adventure of Laeghaire mac Crimhthainn', 377–89 and O'Grady, *Sidh Fiachna*, SG i, 256–7, SG ii 290–1.

27 Marstrander, 'The deaths of Lugaid and Derbforgaill', 201–18.

28 Cross and Slover, *Ancient Irish tales*, pp 346–54.

29 Stokes, *Echtra Cormaic*, pp 183–229 and Cross and Slover, *Ancient Irish tales*, pp 503–7.

30 Dillon, 'The Hindu act of truth in Celtic tradition', 137–40.

31 The *Dictionary of the Irish language* has *baile baird* referring to the inspiration of the bard or poet.

32 Murray, *Baile in Scáil* = Ní Dhonnchadha, 'from Baile in Scáil', p. 260.

33 Bhreathnach and Murray, '*Baile Chuinn Chétchathaig*: edition', pp 73–94 also in the chapter on sovereignty.

34 This was discussed in chapter 1, The Background, and also mentioned in the chapter on the Cycles of the Kings.

35 Meyer, 'Baile Bricín', 449–57.

36 Best, 'The adventures of Art son of Conn, and the courtship of Delbchaem', 149–93 = Cross and Slover, *Ancient Irish tales*, pp 491–502.

37 O'Grady, '*Echtra Thaidg mheic Chéin*', SG i, 342–59, SG ii, 385–401.

38 Dumville, '*Echtrae* and *Immram* some problems of definition', 72–94.

39 Hughes, 'On an Irish litany of pilgrim saints compiled *c*.800', 305–31.

40 Translation O'Meara, *The Voyage of St Brendan: journey to the Promised Land* and O'Donoghue, *Lives and legends of Saint Brendan* and Stokes, *Lives of the saints from the Book of Lismore*, pp 99–116 (text) and 247–61 (translation).

41 Stokes, 'The voyage of Mael Duin', *Revue Celtique* 9 (1888), 447–95, *Revue Celtique* 10 (1889), 50–95 and Oskamp, *The voyage of Máel Dúin*.

42 Stokes, 'The voyage of the Húi Corra', 22–69. Stokes, 'The voyage of Snédgus and Mac Riagla', 14–25.

43 Zaleski, *Otherworld journeys*, pp 206–9. Kenney, *The sources for the early history of Ireland* i, 501–3 discusses the lives of Fursa, there are references to the journey in Bede's *Ecclesiastical history*, 3.19.

44 Meyer, 'The vision of Laisrén', 113–19 and Kenney, *The sources for the early history of Ireland* i, 382.

45 Picard and de Pontfarcy, *Saint Patrick's Purgatory: a twelfth century tale of a journey to the other world*.

46 Picard and de Pontfarcy, *The vision of Tnugdal* (translation of 1882 text).

47 Windisch, 'Die Vision des Adamnán', 165–96; translations Boswell, *An Irish precursor to Dante*, pp 28–47 and Carey, *King of mysteries*, pp 263–74.

48 According to Boswell, *An Irish precursor to Dante*, p. 183 this is inspired by the Book of Revelations and is also found in the Book of Enoch.

49 Boswell, *An Irish precursor to Dante*, p. 176 and Dumville, 'Towards an interpretation of *Fís Adamnán*', 77.

50 Meyer, *Aislinge Meic Conglinne*, pp 110–13, also Jackson, *Aislinge meic Con Glinne* but there is no translation.

51 Under early Irish law a person could fast

against a king looking for compensation; the king must also fast to show good faith.

52 Meyer, *Aislinge Meic Conglinne*, p. li mentions the Land of Cockayne.

CHAPTER 7
Kings, goddesses and sovereignty

1 Byrne, *Irish kings and high-kings*, p. 56.
2 Dillon, 'The taboos of the kings of Ireland', 1–36.
3 Kelly, *Audacht Morainn*, pp 4–5 and 18–19.
4 Doherty, 'Kingship in early Ireland', p. 31; Carey, 'Tara and the supernatural', pp 32–48 and Binchy, 'Fair of Tailltiu and Feast of Tara', 127 and 133. For later inauguration sites see FitzPatrick, *Royal inauguration in Gaelic Ireland, c.1100–1160: a cultural landscape study*.
5 O'Meara, *The history and topography of Ireland*, pp 109–10.
6 Doherty, 'Kingship in early Ireland', p. 19, reference to Stokes, *The birth and life of St Moling*, also Bhreathnach, ' Appendix 3: Observations on the occurrence of dog and horse bones at Tara', pp 117–22.
7 Meyer, 'Stories and songs from Irish manuscripts. VII King Eochaid has horses's ears', 46–54; Ó Briain, 'The horse-eared kings of Irish tradition and St Brigit', p. 110 and Green, 'The symbolic horse in pagan Celtic Europe: an archaeological perspective', pp 1–22.
8 Gantz, *Early Irish myths and sagas*, p. 65.
9 Stokes, 'Mythological notes', 197–203 also in Dinneen, *Foras Feasa ar Éirinn: History of Ireland*, vol. ii, 172–5.
10 Gray, *Cath Maige Tuired*; Gray, '*Cath Maige Tuired*: myth and structure', *Éigse* 18 (1981), 183–209, *Éigse* 19 (1982), 1–35, 230–62 and K. McCone, 'A tale of two ditties: poet and satirist in *Cath Maige Tuired*', pp 122–43.
11 Dumézil, *The destiny of a king*, pp 110–12 says that the Celts have nothing to correspond with the single sin but Ó Cathasaigh, '*Cath Maige Tuired* as exemplary myth', 3 says that Bres's judgement fulfils this function.
12 *Fidchell*, along with *brandub*, is the game of kings and one of the skills taught to a young prince on fosterage, MacWhite, 'Early Irish board games', 25–35.
13 McCone, 'The cyclops in Celtic, Germanic and Indo-European myth', 89–111.
14 Cf. Gray, '*Cath Maige Tuired*: myth and structure', *Éigse* 19 (1982), ii, 252; Banks, 'Na tri Mairt, the three Marts and the man with the withy', 131–43 and Greene, 'Varia i. The three Tuesdays', 139–40.

15 Gray, '*Cath Maige Tuired*: myth and structure', *Éigse* 19 (1982), ii, 261–2.
16 Ó Cathasaigh, '*Cath Maige Tuired* as exemplary myth', 14.
17 Carey, 'Myth and mythography in *Cath Maige Tuired*', 58, 60.
18 O'Daly, *Cath Maige Muccrama*, pp 38–63; Olc Aiche see Sayers, 'Early Irish attitudes toward hair and beards', 156 and Ó Cathasaigh, *The heroic biography of Cormac mac Airt*, 31–6 for the association of *olc* with a wolf.
19 O'Daly, *Cath Maige Muccrama*, 80 has references to the importance of music. See also Buttimer, '*Longes mac nUislenn* reconsidered', 1–41 and Herbert, 'Ár n-urlaisí ceoil', 21–30.
20 Cf. also Ford, 'A highly important pig', pp 292–304 and Ní Chatháin, 'Swineherds, seers, and druids', 200–11.
21 Kelly, *Early Irish farming*, woad discussed pp 141–2, the appropriate coloured clothes on pp 263–4 and their dyeing pp 266–7.
22 The word *fert* is generally used for the memorial stone for the dead. See the story of the death of the thirty princesses at Claenfherta at Samain in Ó Cuív, '*Comram na Cloenfherta*', pp 168–79.
23 Ó Cathasaigh, 'The theme of *lommrad* in *Cath Maige Muccrama*', 211 and Ó Cathasaigh, 'The semantics of *síd*', 137–55.
24 O'Daly, *Scéla Éogain 7 Cormaic*, pp 64–7 and Ó Cathasaigh, *The heroic biography of Cormac mac Airt*, pp 119–27. Kelly, *A guide to early Irish law*, p. 75. It may be deliberate, to draw attention to the judgement of Solomon on the two women and the baby.
25 Hull, '*Geneamuin Chormaic ua Chuind ann-so*', 79–85 and O'Grady, *Geinemain Cormaic ua Chuinn*, SG i, 253–6, SG ii, 286–9.
26 Marstrander, 'A new version of the Battle of Mag Rath', 226–47.
27 Greene, *Esnada Tige Buchet*, p. 27 prints this section as an appendix and calls it a 'clumsy interpolation.'
28 Gantz, *Early Irish myths and sagas*, pp 60–106 = Cross and Slover, *Ancient Irish tales*, pp 93–126.
29 Ó Cathasaigh, 'The semantics of *síd*', 142.
30 Ó Cathasaigh, '*Gat* and *díberg* in *Togail Bruidne Da Derga*', pp 203–13 and Sjöblom, 'Advice from a birdman: ritual injunctions and royal instructions in TBDD', pp 233–51.
31 Gwynn, *De shíl Chonairi Móir*, pp 138–40 and Newman, 'Procession and symbolism at Tara; analysis of Tech Midchúarta (the

'Banqueting Hall') in the context of the sacral campus', 425.

32 Stokes, 'Tidings of Conchobar mac Nessa', 24–5.

33 Koch, and Carey, *The Celtic heroic age*, p. 63.

34 Cross and Slover, *Ancient Irish tales*, pp 503–9 and poetic version Joynt, '*Echtra mac Echdach Mugmedóin*', 91–111.

35 When Cormac made his slave girl Ciarnait pregnant, he built her the reputed first mill in Ireland in Gwynn, *Metrical Dinnshenchas* i, 22. Niall releases his mother from her bondage as a slave when he gets the ear of the king in Joynt, '*Echtra mac Echdach Mugmedóin*', 98.

36 Binchy, 'The saga of Fergus mac Léti', 40–52; Cross and Slover, *Ancient Irish tales*, pp 471–87 and O'Grady, *Aided Fergusa meic Léide*, SG i, 238–52, SG ii, 269–85. This is where the modern word leprechaun has its origins, from the little underwater men who appear in the story called *lúchoirp* or *lúchorpáin* (little bodies). By metathesis (switching of consonants c and p) this becomes *luprachán* giving leprechaun.

37 Best, 'The adventure of Art son of Conn, and the courtship of Delbchaem', 149–73 and Cross and Slover, *Ancient Irish tales*, pp 491–502.

38 O Hehir, 'The Christian revision of *Eachtra Airt meic Cuind ocus Tochmarc Delbchaime ingine Morgain*', p. 168 says: 'in the almost completely demythologized Fingal Rónáin, it is Rónán's nameless replacement wife who brings about his catastrophe.'

39 Cross and Slover, *Ancient Irish tales*, pp 248–53.

40 Watson, 'A structural analysis of *Echtra Nerai*', 133.

41 Breatnach, 'The lady and the king. A theme of Irish literature', 321–36. Jeffares, *W.B. Yeats: selected plays*, p. 256.

42 Jaski, *Early Irish kingship and succession*, pp 70–1; Trindade, 'Irish Gormlaith as a sovereignty figure', 143–56 and Herbert, 'Goddess and king: the sacred marriage in early Ireland', pp 264–75.

43 Coomaraswamy, 'On the loathly bride', 393.

44 O'Rahilly, 'On the origin of the names Érainn and Ériu', 11–21.

45 Koch and Carey, *The Celtic heroic age*, pp 38–9.

46 Bergin and Best, '*Tochmarc Étaíne*', 186.

47 Murray, *Baile in Scáil*.

48 Bhreathnach and Murray, '*Baile Chuinn Chétchathaig*: edition', pp 73–94 and Ó

Cathasaigh, 'The eponym of Cnogba', 27–38.

49 Dumézil, *The destiny of a king*, pp 85–107 and McCone, *Pagan past and Christian present*, pp 118–20.

50 Ó Máille, 'Medb Chruachna', 129–46; Meyer, '*Ferchuitred Medba*', 18 = O'Neill, '*Cath Boinde*', 174.

51 Carey, 'Tara and the supernatural', pp 46–8. Ó Raithbheartaigh, *Genealogical tracts*, pp 147–8 adds that a man cannot be king of Tara without being her husband.

52 Duncan, *Altram Tige dá Medar*, p. 224. Dagger, 'Eithne ban-dia agus ban-Naomh', 61–78 and Dagger, 'Eithne – the sources', 84–124.

53 Gantz, *Early Irish myths and sagas*, p. 156, see Sayers, 'Early Irish attitudes toward hair and beards, baldness and tonsure', 172–3.

54 Meyer, 'The Laud genealogies and tribal histories', 291–338 and Olmsted, '*Conailla Medb míchuru* and the origins of the *Táin*', 333–42.

55 Newman, 'Procession and symbolism at Tara; analysis of Tech Midchúarta (the 'Banqueting Hall') in the context of the sacral campus', 425 and Byrne, *Irish kings and high-kings*, p. 57.

56 Dobbs, 'On *Táin Bó Flidais*', 140.

57 Ó hUiginn, 'Fergus, Russ and Rudraige, a brief biography of Fergus mac Róich', pp 36, 38 and Sayer, 'Fergus and the cosmogonic sword', 30–56. Reference to the mountains, see O'Rahilly, *Táin Bó Cúailnge Recension 1*, p. 122, 235, l. 4072.

58 Hull, 'The cause of the exile of Fergus Mac Roig', 293–8.

59 Carney, 'Early Irish literature: the state of research', 125.

60 O'Rahilly, 'On the origin of the names Érainn and Ériu', 15. McCone, *Pagan past and Christian present*, p. 148 suggests that they be called 'women' rather than 'goddesses' of sovereignty in order to avoid confusion.

61 O'Rahilly, *Táin Bó Cúalnge from the Book of Leinster*, p. liv says: 'Above all the unity of character is observed throughout in the depiction of Medb in all her pride and arrogance.'

62 Kelly, 'The *Táin* as literature', p. 78.

63 Sessle, 'Misogny and Medb: approaching Medb with feminist criticism', pp 135–38.

64 Kinsella, *The Táin*, p. 251, Dooley, 'The invention of women in the *Táin*', 130 and Bowen, 'Great-bladdered Medb; mythology and invention in the *Táin Bó Cuailnge*', 14–34.

65 Mac Cana, 'Aspects of the theme of king

and goddess in Irish literature', *Études Celtiques* 7 (1956), 77–114, 356–413, 8 (1957), 59–65 and Herbert, 'Transmutations of an Irish goddess', pp 141–51.

66 Stokes, *Cóir Anmann*, pp 316–23, §70 = Arbuthnot, *Cóir Anmann* (Part 1), pp 101–3, 139–40 and Gwynn, *The Metrical Dindshenchas* iv, 138–42.

67 O'Nolan, 'Mór of Munster and the tragic fate of Cuanu', 261–82. Byrne, *Irish kings and high-kings*, p. 165 comments on the otherworldly nature of Munster. Mór usually means large but could also mean the sun; it is a relatively common name for Irish women in the eleventh and twelfth centuries.

68 Mac Eoin, 'Suithchern and Rónán Dícholla', 63–82 and Ó Coileáin, 'The structure of a literary cycle', 116.

69 Mac Cana, *The learned tales of medieval Ireland*, pp 46, 57. It is followed by the title *Aithed R/Suithcherne re Cuana mac Cailchine*, a reference to the previous story. Ó Cuív, 'Mis and Dub Rois', 325 and Greene, *Great Irish short stories*, pp 32–6.

70 *Fulachta* are common in the Irish land-scape and many of those excavated have huts in the vicinity of the cooking-places, see Ó Ríordáin, *Antiquities of the Irish countryside*, pp 84–8.

71 Nagy, 'Fenian heroes and their rites of passage', pp 161–82 and Herbert, 'Ár n-úrlaisí ceoil', 21–30.

72 Stokes, 'Tidings of Conchobar mac Nessa', 22–3.

73 Greene, *Esnada tige Buchet*, pp 27–44 and partial translation Dillon, *The cycles of the kings*, pp 25–7.

74 According to the text on fosterage, the king's daughter was usually taught sewing, cloth-cutting and embroidery in contrast with the daughter of a farmer who learns how to use a quern, kneading-trough and a sieve. Cf. Kelly, *A guide to early Irish law*, p. 87.

75 Under early Irish law this is known as a marriage by abduction (*lánamnas foxail*) Kelly, *A guide to early Irish law*, p. 70.

76 Power, '*Cnucha cnoc os cionn Life*', 48; and Ó Cathasaigh, *The heroic biography of Cormac mac Airt*, p. 76 and Ó Raithbheartaigh, *Genealogical tracts* 1, 147–8. Eithne is also Conn's wife in the story of Art's visit to the Otherworld.

77 Mac Eoin, 'Gleann Bolcáin agus Gleann na nGealt', 105–20 and in the story of Mis, her father went mad in Ventry.

78 This text is still unedited but a section in O'Keeffe, 'Mac Dá Cherda and Cummaine Foda', 18–44. See Mac Eoin, 'The life of

Cuimine Fota', 192–205 and Clancy, 'Fools and adultery in some early Irish texts', 105–24.

79 O'Keeffe, *Buile Suibhne*, full story in the chapter on the Cycles of the Kings.

80 Milk and cheese are found in other death tales in the chapter on the Heroic Biography.

81 Gantz, *Early Irish myths and sagas*, p. 178.

82 Ó Riain, 'A study of the Irish legend of the wild man', 205 and Ó Riain, 'Boundary association in early Irish society', 12–29.

83 Meyer, *Líadain and Cuirithir*, pp 22–3. = Ní Dhonnchadha, 'Comrac Líadaine ocus Cuirithir', pp 115–18.

84 Partridge, 'Wild men and wailing women', 37.

85 Ó Tuama, *Caoineadh Airt Uí Laoghaire*, ll. 69–71.

86 Gantz, *Early Irish myths and sagas*, p. 178.

CHAPTER 8
The Hero and Heroic Biography

1 Campbell, *The hero with a thousand faces*, p. 104.

2 Bray, 'Heroic tradition in the lives of the early Irish saints: a study in hagio-biographical patterning', p. 266 and McCone, *Pagan past and Christian present*, pp 179–202.

3 De Vries, *Heroic song and heroic legend*, 211–26; Ó Cathasaigh, *The heroic biography of Cormac mac Airt*, pp 2–8 mentions the article by Taylor, 'The biographical pattern in traditional narrative', 114–29 that he considers an excellent guide.

4 Van Gennep, *Rites of passage*, introduction, p. ix.

5 Nagy, 'Liminality and knowledge in Irish tradition', 135.

6 Cf. O'Leary, 'Honour-bound: the social context of early Irish heroic *geis*', 85; Sjöblom, 'Before *geis* became magical – a study of the evolution of the early Irish religious concept', 85–94 and Charles-Edwards, 'Geis, prophecy, omen and oath', 38–59.

7 Ó Riain, 'Boundary association in early Irish society', 26.

8 Turner, 'Betwixt and between: the liminal period in *rites of passage*', pp 93–111.

9 Nagy, J.F., *The wisdom of the outlaw*, p. 192; Scowcroft, Review of *The wisdom of the outlaw*, 97–100 says that even the Fianna lived complete lives.

10 Campbell, *The hero with a thousand faces*, p. 104.

11 De Vries, *Heroic song and heroic legend*, p. 180.

12 O'Rahilly, *Táin Bó Cuailnge recension 1*,
    pp 20, 143.
13 Sjoestedt, *Gods and heroes of the Celts*, Cú
    Chulainn, pp 58–80, Finn, pp 81–91;
    Vielle, 'The oldest narrative attestations of
    a Celtic mythical and traditional heroic
    cycle', pp 217–27 and Gray, 'Lug and Cú
    Chulainn: king and warrior, god and man',
    38–52.
14 Hogan, *Cath Ruis na Ríg*, pp 1–107 and
    Dobbs, 'Miscellany from H. 2. 7. (T.C.D.)',
    307–18.
15 O'Rahilly, *Táin Bó Cúalnge from the Book
    of Leinster*, pp 61–2, 201–2 and O'Rahilly,
    Táin Bó Cuailnge recension 1, pp 67–8,
    187–8. Sjoestedt, *Gods and heroes of the
    Celts*, p. 79 shows the parallels in
    Scandinavia and the head of Ogmios on
    coins from Armorica. In Old Irish the word
    for fighting is the same as boiling (*fichid*)
    and the word for strength of the same as
    steam (*gal*) – that is used in personal names
    such as Fergal (manly strength).
16 Lowe, 'Kicking over the traces: the
    instability of Cú Chulainn', 127 maintains
    that Cú Chulainn's sexuality is uncertain.
    See Bruford, 'Cú Chulainn – an ill-made
    hero?', pp 185–215 and Sharpe, 'Hiberno-
    Latin laicus, Irish láech, and the devil's
    men', 75–92.
17 Cf. Ó Cathasaigh, '*Cath Maige Tuired* as
    exemplary myth', pp 13–14.
18 Van Gennep, *Rites of passage*, pp 50–64.
19 McCone, *Pagan past and Christian present*,
    p. 231 says that this may come from a
    biblical ordeal where women are given
    water to drink containing earth from the
    floor of the tabernacle to determine whether
    they have committed adultery or not. If she
    is guilty, her stomach swells and her thighs
    rot but if she is innocent she will survive.
20 Stokes, *Cóir Anmann*, §251 = Arbuthnot,
    Cóir Anmann (Part 1) pp 87, 126 and *Cóir
    Anmann* (Part 2) pp 69–70, 141–42.
21 Ganz, *Early Irish myths and sagas*, pp
    130–3 and Kinsella, *The Táin*, pp 21–5.
    Resumé in the chapter on the Heroic Cycle.
22 The text is obscure. In early Irish law
    abortion is grounds for divorce.
23 Stokes, 'Tidings of Conchobar mac Nessa',
    22–3 and Hull, *Compert Conchobair*, pp
    4–12.
24 Koch and Carey, *The Celtic heroic age*, pp
    59–63.
25 O'Daly, *Cath Maige Muccrama*, pp 64–7
    and also in Stokes, *Cóir Anmann*, pp
    306–7, §42 = Arbuthnot, *Cóir Anmann*
    (Part 2) pp 14, 90.
26 Stokes, *Cóir Anmann*, §273 = Arbuthnot,
    Cóir Anmann (Part 1), pp 117, 151–2,

184, 192. Cumain is said to be Brigit's
mother in other versions.
27 Cf. Ní Dhonnchadha, 'from Vita Prima
    Sanctae Brigitae', pp 64–5.
28 Meyer, *Macgníomhartha Finn*, pp
    195–204; trans. Meyer, 'The boyish
    exploits of Finn', 180–90 and Nagy, *The
    wisdom of the outlaw*, 209–18.
29 Hennessy, '*Fotha Catha Cnucha*', 86–93;
    trans. Nagy, *The wisdom of the outlaw*, pp
    218–21.
30 O'Daly, *Cath Maige Muccrama*, §§44–7.
31 O'Daly, *Cath Maige Muccrama*, pp 64–7.
32 Gantz, *Early Irish myths and sagas*, pp
    27–59.
33 Gantz, *Early Irish myths and sagas*, pp
    60–106.
34 Stokes, *Cóir Anmann*, §§62, 66 =
    Arbuthnot, *Cóir Anmann: a Late Middle
    Irish treatise on personal names* (Part 1),
    pp 88, 93, 127 and 131.
35 O'Neill, '*Cath Boinde*', 174–85 = Meyer,
    Ferchuitred Medba, pp 17–22 and Ni
    Dhonnchadha, '*Ferchuitred Medba*', pp
    259–60.
36 O'Grady, *Echtra mac nEchach*, SG i,
    326–30; SG ii, 368–72 and the metrical
    version in Joynt, '*Echtra mac Echdach
    Mugmedóin*', 91–111.
37 Stokes, *Félire Óengusso Céli Dé*, p. lxxxix
    and Ní Dhonnchadha, 'The conception of
    Saint Bóethíne', p. 127.
38 Wiley, 'Niall Frossach's true judgement',
    19–36 and Ní Dhonnchadha, 'Níall
    Frassach's act of truth', p. 220.
39 Van Gennep, *Rites of passage*, pp 15–25
    and 65–115.
40 Melia, 'The parallel versions of the
    boyhood deeds of Cúchulainn', 211–26
    and Kinsella, *The Táin*, pp 76–92 for all
    the boyhood deeds.
41 This is recognized as being the first
    reference to hurling in early Irish literature.
42 Gray, 'Lug and Cú Chulainn: king and
    warrior, god and man', 43.
43 Sjoestedt, *Gods and heroes of the Celts*, pp
    61–8, 66 and she adds in a footnote that
    Dumézil suggested this to her.
44 Cormier, 'Pagan shame or Christian
    modesty?', 46. Mess Buachalla
    accompanies Conaire to Tara with her
    cloak down to her waist, Gwynn, '*De shíl
    Chonaire móir*', 130–43, 135.
45 Meyer, 'The chase of Síd na mBan Finn and
    the death of Finn', *Fianaigecht*, 82–3.
    Dooley, 'The invention of women in the
    Táin', 133 gives another example.
46 Watson, *Mesca Ulad*, 46–7 and Gantz,
    Early Irish myths and sagas, p. 217.
47 Gal, 'Between speech and silence: the

problematics of research on language and gender', p. 193 mentions that the women protested by marching nude and lying on the ground kicking their legs in the air.

48 Meyer, *Macgníomhartha Finn*, pp 195–204; trans. Meyer, 'The boyish exploits of Finn', 180–90 and Nagy, *The wisdom of the outlaw*, pp 209–18 and Nagy, 'Otters, salmon and eel in traditional Gaelic narrative', 127–9.

49 Nagy, *The wisdom of the outlaw*, p. 169.

50 O'Daly, *Scéla Eogain*, in *Cath Maige Muccrama*, pp 64–7, §11.

51 Binchy, *Scéla Cano meic Gartnáin*. Meek, 'Táin Bó Fraích and other "Fráech" texts: a study in thematic relationships', *Cambrian Medieval Celtic Studies* 8 (Winter 1984), 65–85 (part 2).

52 Schoepperle, *Tristan and Isolt* and Carney, *Studies in Irish literature and history*, pp 190, 193.

53 Gantz, *Early Irish myths and sagas*, pp 153–78 The phantom chariot text in Cross and Slover, *Ancient Irish tales*, pp 346–54.

54 Dooley and Roe, *Tales of the elders of Ireland*, pp 51–5 and Nagy, *The wisdom of the outlaw*, pp 184–92.

55 Meid, *Táin Bó Fraích* = Carney, *Studies in Irish literature and history*, translation, pp 1–14.

56 Binchy, 'The saga of Fergus mac Léti', 33–48.

57 Meyer, *Fianaigecht*, pp 6–9, text 4–17 and Hull, 'The death of Fothath Cananne', 400–4. Borsje, 'The "terror of the night" and the Morrígain: shifting faces of the supernatural', p. 87.

58 Gwynn, *The Metrical Dindshenchas*, iii, 190–3.

59 Joynt, *Tromdám Guaire* and resumé in Dillon, *The cycles of the kings*, pp 90–8.

60 Radner, *Fragmentary annals of Ireland*, p. 721. §177, 60–6.

61 Van Gennep, *Rites of passage*, pp 116–45, 123, 129 and 142.

62 The ceremony known as 'hand-fasting' is not mentioned in the early sources.

63 Kinsella, *The Táin*, 25–39 and Cross and Slover, *Ancient Irish tales*, pp 153–71, they omit some sections.

64 Excellence at embroidery is a characteristic of royal women elsewhere as well. It is also interesting that he insists on having a virgin wife, this is never mentioned in the laws tracts but it is a quality that appears in the Triads, cf. Meyer, *The Triads of Ireland*, p. 17 that says 'the three drops of a *cétmuin-ter*, a drop of blood, a drop of sweat, a tear-drop' (number 126). The term *cétmuinter* here refers to the principal wife in a marriage. Men could have two wives

simultaneously in the early period, cf. Kelly, *A guide to early Irish law*, p. 70.

65 Fedelm Foltchaín wife of Elcmar in Koch and Carey, *The Celtic heroic age*, pp 67–8 and he married Finnchaem daughter of Eochu Ronn in Hollo, *Fled Bricrenn ocus loinges mac nDúil Dermait*, p. 102 and 106.

66 Meyer, 'Anecdota from the Stowe MS. no. 992' (*Aithed Emere la Tuir nGlesta mac ríg Lochlainn*), 184–5.

67 Meyer, *Sanas Cormaic*, pp 86–8 and Clancy, 'Fools and adultery in some early Irish texts', 110–13.

68 Meyer, *Macgníomhartha Finn*, pp 195–204; Meyer; 'The boyish exploits of Finn', 80–90 and Nagy, *The wisdom of the outlaw*, pp 209–18.

69 Meyer, 'Finn and Gráinne', 458–61; Corthals, 'Die Trennung von Finn und Gráinne', 71–91 and Ó Corráin, 'The separation of Finn and Gráinne', pp 36–7.

70 Thurneysen, 'Das Werben um Ailbe', 250–82 = Ní Dhonnchadha, from 'Tochmarc Ailbe', pp 206–10 and a more modern version, Ó Cuív, 'Miscellanea, 2. Agallamh Fhinn agus Ailbhe', 111–15.

71 Ní Dhonnchadha, *Tochmarc Ailbe*, 209.

72 Campbell, *The hero of a thousand faces*, p. 30 and Ó Cathasaigh, *The heroic biography of Cormac mac Airt*, p. 85.

73 Full resumé in chapter on the Otherworld. Stokes, *Echtra Cormaic*, pp 183–229; translation Cross and Slover, *Ancient Irish tales*, pp 503–7.

74 Cross and Slover, *Ancient Irish tales*, pp 346–54.

75 Kinsella, *The Táin*, pp 25–39 but some sections are missing.

76 Gantz, *Early Irish myths and sagas*, pp 153–78 and Cross and Slover, *Ancient Irish tales*, pp 176–98 – there are two different versions of the story in the one text and they are perceptibly woven together.

77 Nagy, *The wisdom of the outlaw*, pp 38–9.

78 Meyer, 'Finn and the man in the tree', 344–6 and Hull, 'Two tales about Find', 329–30.

79 Joynt, *Feis Tighe Chonáin*, lines 1331–76.

80 Dooley and Roe, *Tales of the elders of Ireland*, pp 51–5.

81 O'Grady, *Echtra mac nEchach, SG* i, 326–30, *SG* ii, 368–73 and poetic version Joynt, 'Echtra mac Echdach Mugmedóin', 91–111.

82 Greene, *Esnada Tige Buchet*, p. 27.

83 Carney, 'Nia son of Lugna Fer Trí', 187–97 and Ó Cathasaigh, *The heroic biography of Cormac mac Airt*, pp 87–92.

84 Murray, *Baile in Scáil*, §13, 53–4.

85 O'Grady, *Cath Crinna, SG* i, 324–5 and ii, 366–7.

86 Melia, 'Remarks on the structure and composition of the Ulster death tales', 36–57.
87 Bruford, 'Why an Ulster Cycle?', p. 30.
88 Van Gennep, *Rites of passage*, pp 146–65.
89 Jackson, 'The motif of the threefold death in the story of Suibne Geilt', pp 535–50 and Ó Cuív, 'The motif of the threefold death', 145–50.
90 Bhreathnach, 'Goddess of sovereignty as goddess of death', 243–60 and Scowcroft, 'Abstract narrative in Ireland', 130–7.
91 O'Grady, *Aided Diarmada meic Cherbaill*, SG, i, 72–82, SG ii, 76–88 and Koch and Carey, *The Celtic heroic age*, pp 212–16.
92 MacBeth derives from the Irish surname Mac Bethaidh (son of life/living).
93 Radner, 'The significance of the threefold death in Celtic tradition', pp 184–5; Ó Cathasaigh, 'The threefold death in early Irish sources', 53–76 and Ó Cuív, 'The motif of the threefold death', 145–50. McCone, *Pagan past and Christian present*, pp 146–7 agrees with Radner.
94 Cross and Slover, *Ancient Irish tales*, pp 518–32; Nic Dhonnchadha, *Aided Muirchertaig meic Erca* and Ní Dhonnchadha, 'from: Aided Muirchertaich meic Erca', pp 213–18.
95 This place is also associated with Cormac's death.
96 Radner, 'The significance of the threefold death in Celtic tradition', pp 196–9.
97 Gantz, *Early Irish myths and sagas*, pp 60–106.
98 Byrne, *Irish kings and high-kings*, p. 60 where he mentions that Cernae was an ancient cemetery, one tradition says that Uí Néill kings were buried there. It may be Carnes, Co. Meath, possibly the Neolithic passage-graves at Fourknocks some 6km from Carnes.
99 Meyer, '*Goire Conaill Chernaig i Crúachain ocus Aided Ailella ocus Conaill Chearnaig*', 102–11.
 1 Koch and Carey, *The Celtic heroic age*, pp 134–43 and Tymoczko, *Two death tales from the Ulster Cycle*, pp 37–83. Some taboos seem totemic in nature.
 2 Cf. O'Leary, 'Honour-bound, the social context of early Irish heroic *geis*', 85–107.
 3 In the modern Irish version, he kills an otter, the waterdog of the early literature.
 4 Cf. Nagy, *Conversing with angels and ancients*, pp 223–6.
 5 Gwynn, *The Metrical Dindshenchas* i, *Temair* iii, 16–7 and Bhreathnach, 'A medieval guided tour of the Hill of Tara', 83.
 6 Meyer, '*Aided Chonchobuir*', pp 4–21, 17

= Cross and Slover, *Ancient Irish tales*, pp 333–46.
 7 Meyer, '*Aided Chonchobuir*', p. 7.
 8 Meyer, '*Aided Chonchobuir*', pp 10–11.
 9 Stokes, '*Bruiden Da Choca*', 149–65, 312–27, 388–402 = Toner, *Bruiden Da Choca*.
10 Hull, *Geneamuin Chormaic*, pp 82–5, O'Grady, *Coimpert Cormaic meic Airt*, SG i, 253–6, SG ii, 286–9, see Ó Cathasaigh, *The heroic biography of Cormac mac Airt*, pp 68–72.
11 Power, '*Cnucha cnoc os cionn Life*', 39–55. Bhreathnach and Murray, '*Baile Chuinn Chétchathaig*: Edition', p. 83 says 'He will perish from a morsel of food'.
12 Meyer, 'The expulsion of the Déssi', 101–35.
13 Power, '*Cnucha cnoc os cionn Life*', 44, 51.
14 Meyer, '*Aided Lóegairi Búadaig*', pp 22–3 and Meyer, '*Aided Fergusa maic Róich*', pp 32–5.
15 O'Grady, *Aided Crimthainn meic Fidaig*, SG i, 330–6, SG ii, 373–8.
16 O'Grady, *Aided Echach maic Maireda*, SG i, 233–7, SG ii, 265–9 and Ní Dhonnchadha, 'from Aided Echach maic Maireda', pp 271–2.
17 Hull, '*Aided Meidbe*: the violent death of Medb', 52–61. See Wong, 'Water-births, murder, mystery and Medb Lethderg', pp 233–41.
18 Cross and Slover, *Ancient Irish tales*, pp 328–32; Tymoczko, *Two death tales from the Ulster Cycle* and Best, 'The tragic death of Cúroí Mac Dári', 18–25. Fenian women tie the hero Garaid mac Mórna by his hair and beard to the side of the hostel so that he cannot attack them in Gwynn, 'The burning of Finn's house', 13–37. Green, *Celtic goddesses: warriors, virgins and mothers*, pp 60–1, Blodeuwedd brings about the death of Lleu. She cannot be killed so she is turned into an owl to live in darkness.
19 Marstrander, 'The deaths of Lugaid and Derbforgaill', 201–18 and Ní Dhonnchadha, 'The deaths of Lugaid and Derbforgaill', pp 204–6 (translation by A. Dooley).
20 Meyer, 'The death of Finn mac Cumaill', 462–5. The *geis* in Joynt, *Feis Tighe Chonáin*, §§xxi–xxiii. O'Leary, 'Honour-bound, the social context of early Irish heroic *geis*', 102–3 discusses the *dantmír* (tooth bit).
21 The location of Áth Breá/ó is unclear. Stokes, 'On the deaths of some Irish heroes', 310–11.

22 O'Grady, *Tesmolad Corbmaic uí Chuinn ocus Aided Finn meic Cumhaill sunn*, *SG* i 89–92, *SG* i, 96–9 says that he was killed by Aiclech and the three sons of Urgriu, the Luigne of Tara, at Áth Breá.

23 Meyer, 'The chase of Síd na mBan Finn and the death of Finn', pp 52–99, p. xxxi; Cross and Slover, *Ancient Irish tales*, pp 424–38.

CHAPTER 9
Poets and Poetry

1 Murphy, *Early Irish lyrics*, pp 2–3.

2 Breatnach, *Uraicecht na Ríar* and Reynolds, ' "At sixes and sevens" – and eights and nines: the sacred mathematics of Sacred Orders in the early Middle Ages', 669–84.

3 Breatnach, *Uraicecht na Ríar*, §6. The reference echoes the strictures of the Christian rules on marriage.

4 Breatnach, 'The cauldron of poesy', 45–93.

5 Mac Mathúna, 'On the expression and concept of blindness in Irish', 58.

6 Nagy, 'Liminality and knowledge in Irish tradition', 135–43.

7 Stokes, '*Echtra Cormaic*', 188–90.

8 Greene, *Orgain Denna Ríg*, pp 16–26 and translation Stokes, 'The destruction of Dind Ríg', 1–15.

9 Stokes, 'The prose tales in the Rennes Dindshenchas', 327–8.

10 Meyer, *The triads of Ireland*, p. 10.

11 Meid, *Táin Bó Fraích*, pp 4–5; translation in Carney, *Studies in Irish literature and history*, p. 4, Boann speaks to Uaithne saying: 'Men will die on hearing them being played.' See Radner, ' "Men will die": poets, harpers and women in early Irish literature', pp 172–86 and Hamilton, ' "Ancient" Irish music', pp 283–91, 289 where he refers to the different types of music and some of the instruments.

12 Meyer, 'Finn and the man in the tree', 344–6 and Hull, 'Two tales about Find', 329–30. Nagy, 'Shamanic aspects of the "Bruidhean" tale', 3–22.

13 Nagy, 'Demne Mael', 8–14 and Sayers, 'Early Irish attitudes toward hair and beards, baldness and tonsure', 164–5, 178.

14 Cf. Meyer, *Macgnimartha Finn*, pp 195–204 and Nagy, 'The boyhood deeds of Finn', 209–21. Nagy, 'Liminality and knowledge', 139–43. The Welsh poet Taliesin and the Norse hero Sigurd also acquire knowledge through a burnt finger.

15 The *imbas* is mentioned in Meyer, *Sanas Chormaic*, 64, §756.

16 Carney, 'The earliest Bran material' repr. in Wooding, *The Otherworld voyage*, p. 82; Klass, *Ordered universes*, pp 72–8 and Schrijver, 'On henbane and early European narcotics', 17–45, this drug produces hallucinations and the taker thinks they can fly or that they become animals. See also Melia, 'Law and the shaman saint', pp 113–28.

17 Gantz, *Early Irish myths and sagas*, 263–6.

18 Hull, 'The exile of Conall Corc', 937–50.

19 Mac Cana, 'Notes on the combination of prose and verse in early Irish narrative', pp 125–47 and Mac Cana, 'Prosimetrum in Insular Celtic literature', pp 99–130.

20 Stokes, 'The voyage of Snédgus and Mac Riagla', 14–25. O'Grady, *Echtra mac nEchach*, *SG* i, 326–30, *SG* ii, 368–73; Joynt, '*Echtra mac Echdach Mugmedóin*', 91–111.

21 Dillon, *Serglige Con Culaind*, p. 24 as prose and Greene and O'Connor, *A golden treasury of Irish poetry*, pp 130–3 as poetry.

22 Okpewho, *The epic in Africa*, pp 154, 179 and Finnegan, *Oral literature in Africa*, pp 108–10.

23 Carney, 'The dating of early Irish verse texts 500–1100', 177–216.

24 Thurneysen, 'Colmán mac Léneni und Senchán Torpéist', 193–209. There is the collection of early Leinster poems translated by Koch and Carey, *The Celtic heroic age*, pp 52–8.

25 Printed in Meyer, 'The Laud genealogies and tribal histories', 291–338; Olmsted, '*Conailla Medb míchuru* and the origins of the *Táin*', 333–42.

26 Byrne, 'Latin poetry in Ireland', p. 33.

27 Greene and O'Connor, *A golden treasury of Irish poetry*, pp 27–32.

28 Ibid., pp 33–5.

29 Carney, *The poems of Blathmac son of Cú Brettan* and Carney, 'Poems of Blathmac, son of Cú Brettan', pp 45–57.

30 Carney, 'Two old Irish poems', 1–43.

31 Greene and Kelly, *The Irish Adam and Eve story from Saltair na Rann* and Carey, *King of mysteries*, p. 97.

32 Carney, 'The Ó Cianáin miscellany', 145–6. The poem is said to be have been written on Sunday, 2 September the day that Mael Sechlainn died.

33 Stokes, 'On the deaths of some Irish heroes', 303–48.

34 O'Brien, 'A Middle-Irish poem on the Christian kings of Leinster', 38–9.

35 Dobbs, 'A poem ascribed to Flann mac Lonáin', 18–19. Mac Cana, 'Praise poetry in Ireland before the Normans', 11–40

addresses the dearth of praise poetry in the early period.

36 Joynt, 'Echtra mac Echdach Mugmedóin', 91–111, his death in the Annals of the Four Masters: 'Cuan Ua Lothchain, chief poet of Ireland, and a learned historian, was slain in Teathbha, and the party who killed him became putrid in one hour; and this was a poet's miracle'.

37 Dobbs, 'The Ban-shenchus', 283–339.

38 Gwynn, The Metrical Dindshenchas, 5 vols and O'Daly, 'The Metrical Dindshenchas', pp 59, 60–1.

39 Gwynn, The Metrical Dindshenchas i, 46–53.

40 Ibid., i, 20–3.

41 Murphy, Early Irish lyrics and Greene and O'Conor, A golden treasury are two of the best collections available. Ó Corráin, 'Early Irish hermit poetry?', pp 251–67 takes issue with the authenticity of the hermit poetry. Also Carney, Medieval Irish lyrics.

42 Greene and O'Connor, A golden treasury, pp 95–7.

43 Murphy, Early Irish lyrics, pp 88–91.

44 Ní Dhonnchadha, 'Apair damsa re Der Fáil', pp 305–7 (translation by Moya Cannon).

44a Ní Dhonnchadha, 'Teastá eochair ghlais Ghaoidheal', 308–11 (new translation by Seamus Deane).

45 Tymoczko, 'A poetry of masks: the poet's persona in early Celtic poetry', pp 190, 206.

46 Scholes and Kellogg, The nature of narrative, p. 4.

47 Murphy, Early Irish lyrics, pp 2–3.

48 Marstrander, 'The deaths of Lugaid and Derbforgaill', 201–18; Ní Dhonnchadha, 'The deaths of Lugaid and Derbforgaill', pp 204–6, 204 (translation by Ann Dooley) where she says: 'Her poem places her firmly before us as one of the most appealing figures in the whole repetoire of Irish literary women'. Créd in Murphy, Early

Irish lyrics, pp 86–9.

49 O'Rahilly, Táin Bó Cúailnge Recension 1, p. 2, l. 41 (banfhili), l. 48 (banfháith). O'Rahilly, Táin Bó Cúalnge from the Book of Leinster, ll. 40–50 (banfhili).

50 Carney, 'The earliest Bran material', pp 174–93, repr. in Wooding, The Otherworld voyage, p. 87.

51 Dobbs, 'From the Book of Fermoy', 163 (Rothniam) and Meyer, 'Mittelungen aus Irischen Handshriften', 109–10 (Laitheóc).

52 Gwynn, 'An old-Irish tract on the privileges and responsibilities of poets', 34. There is a story about the abbot of Drimnagh who was temporarily turned into a woman, Meyer, 'Story of the abbot of Druimenaig who was changed into a woman', pp 76–9; Montague, Mounts of Venus, pp 57–8; Ní Dhonnchadha, 'The abbot of Drimnagh who was changed into a woman', pp 131–2 and Hillers, 'The abbot of Druimenaig: gender bending in Gaelic tradition', pp 175–97.

53 Clancy, 'Women poets in early medieval Ireland', 43–72.

54 Ó hAodha, 'The lament of the Old Woman of Beare', p. 308; Ní Dhonnchadha, 'Digde', pp 111–15 (translation by Seamus Deane).

55 Ní Dhonnchadha, 'Reading the so-called Caillech Bérri poem', 15.

56 Ó hAodha, 'The lament of the Old Woman of Beare', p. 309. Caillech usually 'hag, old woman' today, originally came from caille 'veil' and meant 'the veiled one'.

57 Clancy, 'Women poets in early medieval Ireland', pp 43–72.

58 Meyer, Comrac Líadaine ocus Cuirithir.

59 Meyer, Cormac Líadaine ocus Cuirithir, p. 12 and Clancy, 'Women poets in early medieval Ireland', p. 68. Carney, Studies in Irish literature and history, pp 220–1 calls the text 'confused and improbable' and 'utterly unlikely'.

60 Murphy, Early Irish lyrics, pp 82–5.

Bibliography

Abrams, M.H., *A glossary of literary terms* (New York, 1971).

— *The mirror and the lamp: Romantic theory and the critical tradition* (Oxford, 1971).

Anderson, A.O., and M.O. Anderson (eds), *Adomnán's life of Columba* (London, 1961).

Arbuthnot, S. (ed.), *Cóir Anmann: a Late Middle Irish treatise on personal names* (Part 1), Irish Texts Society 59 (London, 2005).

— (ed.), *Cóir Anmann: a Late Middle Irish treatise on personal names* (part 2), Irish Texts Society 60 (London, 2007).

Backhaus, N., 'The structure of the list of *Remscéla Tána Bó Cualngi* in the Book of Leinster', *Cambridge Medieval Celtic Studies* 19 (Summer 1990), 19–26.

Banks, M.M., '*Na tri Mairt*, the three marts and the Man with the withy', *Études Celtiques* 3 (1938), 131–43.

Bannermann, J., 'The Convention of Druim Cett', in J. Bannerman (ed.), *Studies in the history of the Dal Riada* (Edinburgh, 1974), pp 157–70.

Baring A., and J. Cashford, *The myth of the goddess: evolution of an image* (London, 1993).

Basso, K., *Wisdom sits in places: landscape and language among the Western Apache* (Albequerque, NM, 1996).

Bergin, O., and R.I. Best (eds),'*Tochmarc Étaíne*', *Ériu* 12 (1938), 137–96.

Bergin, O. (ed.), *Irish bardic poetry*, edited by David Greene and Fergus Kelly (Dublin, 1970).

Best, R.I. (ed.), 'The tragic death of Cúroí Mac Dári', *Ériu* 2 (1905), 18–25.

— (ed.), 'The adventure of Art son of Conn, and the courtship of Delbchaem', *Ériu* 3 (1907), 149–73.

— (ed.), 'The settling of the manor of Tara', *Ériu* 4 (1908–10), 121–72.

Bhreathnach, E., 'Appendix 3: Observations on the occurrence of dog and horse bones at Tara', *Discovery Programme Reports* 6 (Royal Irish Academy/ Discovery Programme, Dublin 2002), pp 117–22.

— 'A medieval guided tour of the Hill of Tara', in J. Fenwick (ed.), *Lost and found: discovering Ireland's past* (Bray, 2003), pp 77–88.

Bhreathnach, E., and K. Murray (eds), '*Baile Chuinn Chétchathaig*: edition', in E. Bhreathnach (ed.), *The kingship and landscape of Tara* (Dublin, 2005), pp 73–94.

Bhreathnach, M., 'Goddess of sovereignty as goddess of death', *Zeitschrift für celtische Philologie* 39 (1982), 243–60.

— (ed.), 'A new edition of *Tochmarc Becfhola*', *Ériu* 35 (1984), 59–91.

Bieler, L. (ed.), *Libri Epistolarum Sancti Patricii Episcopi* (1952).

Bieler, L., and F. Kelly (eds), *The Patrician texts in the Book of Armagh* (1979).

Binchy, D.A. (ed.), 'The saga of Fergus mac Léti', *Ériu* 16 (1952), 33–48.

— 'Fair of Tailltiu and Feast of Tara', *Ériu* 18 (1958), 113–38.

— (ed.), *Scéla Cano meic Gartnáin*, Medieval and Modern Irish Series 18 (DIAS, 1975).

Bischoff, B., *Latin palaeography: antiquity and the Middle Ages* (Cambridge, 1986), trans. by D. Ó Cróinín and D. Ganz.

Booker, C., *The seven basic plots: why we tell stories* (London, 2004).

Borsje, J., *From chaos to enemy: encounters with monsters in early Irish texts. An investigation related to the process of Christianisation and the concept of evil*. Instrumenta Patristica 29 (Turnhout, 1996).

Borsje, J., 'The "terror of the night" and the Morrígain: shifting faces of the supernatural', in M. Ó Flaithearta (ed.), *Proceeding of the Seventh Symposium of Societas Celtologica Nordica*. Studia Celtica Upsaliensia 6 (Stockholm, 2007), pp 71–98.

Boswell, C.S., *An Irish precursor to Dante: a study on the vision of Heaven and Hell ascribed to the eighth-century Irish Saint Adamnán, with translation of the Irish text* (London, 1908).

Bourke, A., S. Kilfeather, M. Luddy, M. Mac Curtain, G. Meaney, M. Ní Dhonnchadha, M. O'Dowd and C. Wills (eds), *The Field Day Anthology of Irish Writing; iv, Irish women's writing and traditions* (Cork, 2002).

Bowen, C., 'Great-bladdered Medb; mythology and invention in the *Táin Bó Cuailnge*', *Éire-Ireland* 10 (1975), 14–34.

Bray, D., 'Heroic tradition in the lives of the early Irish saints: a study in hagio-biographical patterning', in G. MacLennan (ed.), *Proceedings of the First North American Congress of Celtic Studies* (Ottawa, 1988), pp 261–71.

Breatnach, L. (ed.), '*Tochmarc Luaine ocus Aided Athairne*', *Celtica* 13 (1980), 1–31.

— (ed.), 'The cauldron of poesy', *Ériu* 32 (1981), 45–93.

— (ed.), *Uraicecht na Ríar – the poetic grades in early Irish law* (Early Irish Law 12 Series, DIAS, 1987).

Breatnach, R.A., 'The lady and the king. A theme of Irish literature', *Studies* 62: 167 (1953), 321–36.

Bruford, A., 'Why an Ulster Cycle?', in J.P. Mallory and G. Stockman (eds), *Ulidia* (Belfast, 1994) pp 23–30.

— 'Cú Chulainn – an ill-made hero?', in H.L.C. Tristram (ed.), *Text und Zeittiefe*, ScriptOralia 58 (Tübingen, 1994), pp 185–215.

Buttimer, C., '*Longes mac nUislenn* reconsidered', *Éigse* 28 (1994–5), 1–41.

Byrne, F.J., 'Latin poetry in Ireland', in J. Carney (ed.), *Early Irish poetry* (Cork, 1965), pp 29–44.

— *Irish kings and high-kings* (London, 1973, repr. Dublin, 2001).

— '*Senchas*; the nature of the Gaelic historical tradition', *Historical Studies* 9 (Belfast, 1974), 137–59.

Caerwyn Williams, J.E. and M. Ní Muiríosa, *Traidisiún Liteartha na nGael* (BÁC, 1979).

Campbell, J., *The hero with a thousand faces* (2nd ed., Princeton, 1968).

Carey, J., 'The location of the Otherworld in Irish tradition', *Éigse* 19 (1982), 36–43.

— 'Fir Bolg: a native etymology revisited', *Cambrian Medieval Celtic Studies* 16 (Winter, 1988), 77–83.

— 'Time, space, and the Otherworld', *Proceedings of the Harvard Celtic Colloquium* 7 (1987), pp 1–27.

— 'Myth and mythography in *Cath Maige Tuired*', *Studia Celtica* 24/25 (1989/90), 53–69.

— 'The Irish "Otherworld": Hiberno-Latin perspectives', *Éigse* 25 (1991), 154–9.

— *King of mysteries: early Irish religious writings* (Dublin, 1998).

— 'The Lough Foyle colloquy texts: *Immacaldam Choluim Chille 7 ind Óclaig oc Carraic Eolairg* and *Immacaldam in Druad Brain 7 inna Banfhátho Febuil ós Loch Fhebuil*', *Ériu* 52 (2002), 53–87.

— 'Werewolves in medieval Ireland', *Cambrian Medieval Celtic Studies* 44 (2002), 37–72.

— 'Tara and the supernatural', in E. Bhreathnach (ed.), *The kingship and landscape of Tara* (Dublin, 2005), pp 32–48.

Carney, J., 'Nia son of Lugna Fer Trí', *Éigse* 2 (1940), 187–97.

— *Studies in Irish literature and history* (Dublin 1955, repr. 1979).

— (ed.), 'Two old Irish poems', *Ériu* 18 (1958), 1–43.

— (ed.), *The Poems of Blathmac son of Cú Brettan together with the Gospel of Thomas and a Poem on the Virgin Mary*, Irish Texts Society 47 (1964).

— 'Poems of Blathmac, son of Cú Brettan', in J. Carney (ed.), *Early Irish poetry* (Cork, 1965), pp 45–57.

— (ed.), *Medieval Irish lyrics* (Dublin 1967).

— 'The deeper level of early Irish literature', *Capuchin Annual* (1969), 160–71.

— 'The Ó Cianáin miscellany', *Ériu* 21 (1969), 122–47.

— 'The earliest Bran material', in J.J. O'Meara and B. Naumann (eds), *Latin script and letters, AD 400–900* (Leiden, 1976) pp 174–93, repr. in J.M. Wooding, *The Otherworld voyage in early Irish literature: an anthology of criticism* (Dublin, 2000), pp 73–90.

— 'Early Irish literature, the state of research', in G. Mac Eoin, A. Ahlqvist and D. Ó hAodha (eds), *Proceedings of the Sixth International Congress for Celtic Studies* (Dublin, 1983), pp 113–30.

— 'The dating of early Irish verse texts, 500–1100', *Éigse* 19, ii (1983), 177–216.

Chadbourne, K., 'The beagle's cry: dogs in the Finn ballads and tales', *Proceedings of the Harvard Celtic Colloquium* 16/17 (1996/7), 1–14.

Chadwick, N.K., *The Celts* (1970, repr. 1972).

Chadwin, T., 'The *Remscéla Tána Bó Cualngi*', *Cambrian Medieval Celtic Studies* 34 (Winter 1997), 67–75.

Charles-Edwards, T., 'Geis, prophecy, omen and oath', *Celtica* 23 (1999), 38–59.

— '*Tochmarc Étaíne*: a literal interpretation', in M. Richter and J-M. Picard (eds), *Ogma: essays in Celtic studies in honour of Próinséas Ní Chatháin* (Dublin, 2002), pp 165–81.

Clancy, T.O., 'Fools and adultery in some early Irish texts', *Ériu* 44 (1993), 105–24.

— 'Women poets in early medieval Ireland', in C. Meek and K. Simms (eds), *'The fragility of her sex'? Medieval Irish women in their European context* (Dublin, 1996), pp 43–72.

Condren, M., *The serpent and the goddess: women, religion, and power in Celtic Ireland* (San Francisco, 1989).

Coomaraswamy, A.K., 'On the loathly bride', *Speculum* 20 (1945), 391–404.

Cormier, R.J., 'Pagan shame or Christian modesty?', *Celtica* 14 (1981), 43–6.

Corthals, J., 'Die Trennung von Finn und Gráinne', *Zeitschrift für Celtische Philologie* 49–50 (1997), 71–91.

Cross, T.P. and C.H. Slover, *Ancient Irish tales* (New York, 1936, repr. 1996).

Cunliffe, B., *The ancient Celts* (London, 1997).

Curtain, J., *Tales of the fairies and the ghost world* (London, 1895).

Dagger, C., 'Eithne ban-dia agus ban-Naomh', *Ár Naomhsheanchas, Léachtaí Cholm Cille* 15 (1985), 61–78.

Dagger, C., 'Eithne – the sources', *Zeitschrift für Celtische Philologie* 43 (1989), 84–124.

Danaher, K., *The year in Ireland: Irish calendar customs* (Cork, 1972).

de Paor, Liam, *St Patrick's world: the Christian culture of Ireland's apostolic age* (Dublin, 1993).

De Vries, J., *Heroic song and heroic legend* (1959, English translation, London, 1963).

Dégh, L., *Folktales and society* (Bloomington, IN, 1969).

Delargy, J., *The Gaelic story-teller*, Sir John Rhŷs Memorial Lecture (British Academy 1945). *Proceedings of the British Academy* 31 (1945).

Dillon, M., 'The Hindu act of truth in Celtic tradition', *Modern Philology* 44 (1947), 137–40.

— *The cycles of the kings* (Oxford, 1946, repr. Dublin, 1995).

— *Early Irish literature* (London, 1948, repr. Dublin, 1995).

— 'The taboos of the kings of Ireland', *Proceedings of the Royal Irish Academy* 54, C (1951), 1–36.

— (ed.), *Serglige Con Culaind*, Medieval and Modern Irish Series 14 (Dublin 1953, repr. 1975).

— 'Laud misc. 610 (cont.)', *Celtica* 6 (1963), 135–55.

— (ed.), *Irish sagas*, Thomas Davis Lectures (Cork, 1968, 1970).

Dillon, M., and N. Chadwick, *The Celtic realms* (London, 1967, 1973).

Dinneen, P.S. (ed.), *Foras Feasa ar Éirinn: History of Ireland*, vol. ii, Irish Texts Society 8 (London, 1908), vol. iii, Irish Texts Society 9 (London 1908), vol. iv, Irish Texts Society 15 (London, 1914).

Dobbs, M. (ed.), 'Altromh Tighi da Medar', *Zeitschrift für Celtische Philologie* 18 (1930), 189–229.

— (ed.), 'The Ban-shenchus', *Revue Celtique* 47 (1930), 283–339; *Revue Celtique* 48 (1931), 163–234 and *Revue Celtique* 49 (1933), 437–89.

— (ed.), 'From the Book of Fermoy', *Zeitschrift für Celtische Philologie* 20 (1936), 161–84.

— 'Miscellany from H. 2. 7. (TCD)', *Zeitschrift für Celtische Philologie* 21 (1940), 307–18.

— (ed.), 'A poem ascribed to Flann mac Lonáin', *Ériu* 17 (1955), 16–34.

— 'On *Táin Bó Flidais*', *Ériu* 8 (1916/17), 133–49.

Doherty, C., 'Kingship in early Ireland', in E. Bhreathnach (ed.), *The kingship and landscape of Tara*, pp 3–31.

Dooley, A., 'The invention of women in the *Táin*', in J.P. Mallory and G. Stockman (eds), *Ulidia*, pp 123–33.

— and H. Roe, *Tales of the elders of Ireland* (Oxford, 1999).

— *Playing the hero: reading the Táin Bó Cuailnge* (Toronto, 2005).

Dumézil, G., *The destiny of a king* (Chicago, 1973) trans. by Alf Hiltebeitel.

Dumville, D., '*Echtrae* and *Immram* some problems of definition', *Ériu* 27 (1976), 72–94.

— 'Towards an interpretation of *Fís Adamnán*', *Studia Celtica* 12/13 (1977/8), 62–77.

Duncan, L. (ed.), '*Altram Tige dá Medar*', *Ériu* 11 (1932), 184–225.

Eliade, M., *Myth and reality* (London, 1963).

Ettlinger, E., 'The association of burials with popular assemblies, fairs and races in ancient Ireland', *Études Celtiques* 6 (1952), 30–61.

Evans, D.W., 'The learned borrowings claimed for *Táin Bó Fraích*', in M. Richter and J-M. Picard (eds), *Ogma: essays in Celtic studies in honour of Próinséas Ní Chatháin* (Dublin, 2002) pp 182–94.

Findon, J., *A women's words: Emer and female speech in the Ulster Cycle* (Toronto, 1997).

Finnegan, R., *Oral literature in Africa* (Oxford, 1970).

FitzPatrick, E., *Royal inauguration in Gaelic Ireland, c.1100–1160: a cultural landscape study*, Studies in Celtic History 22 (Woodbridge, Suffolk, 2004).

Ford, P.K., 'The blind, the dumb, and the ugly: aspects of poets and their craft in early Ireland and Wales', *Cambrian Medieval Celtic Studies* 19 (Summer, 1990), 27–40.

— 'A highly important pig', in A.T.E. Matonis and D.F. Melia (eds), *Celtic language, Celtic culture: a festschrift for Eric P. Hamp* (Van Nuys, CA, 1990), pp 292–304.

Frazer, J. (ed.), 'The first Battle of Moytura', *Ériu* 8 (1916), 1–63 (CMT 1).

Frazer, J.G., *The golden bough: a study in magic and religion* (New York, 1922; New York, Bartleby.com, 2000).

Gal, S., 'Between speech and silence: the problematics of research on language and gender', in M. di Leonardo (ed.), *Gender at the crossroads of knowledge: feminist anthropology in the postmodern era* (California, 1991), pp 175–203.

Gantz, J., *Early Irish myths and sagas* (London, 1981).

Georgi, D., 'A stunning blow to the head: literacy and the anxiety of memory in the legend of Cenn Faelad's brain of forgetting', *Proceedings of the Harvard Celtic Colloquium* 16/17 (1996/7), pp 195–205.

Gray, E., '*Cath Maige Tuired*: myth and structure', *Éigse* 18, ii (1981), 183–209: *Éigse* 19 (1982), 1–35, 230–62.

— (ed.), *Cath Maige Tuired*, Irish Texts Society 52 (London, 1983).

— 'Lug and Cú Chulainn: king and warrior, god and man', *Studia Celtica* 24/5 (1989/90), 38–52.

Green, M.A., 'The symbolic horse in pagan Celtic Europe: an archaeological perspective', in S. Davies and N.A. Jones (eds), *The horse in Celtic culture. Medieval Welsh perspectives* (Cardiff, 1997), pp 1–22.

— *Celtic goddesses: warriors, virgins and mothers* (London, 1995).

— *Exploring the world of the druids* (London, 1997).

Greene, D., 'The Romance of Mis and Dubh Rois', in V. Mercier (ed.), *Great Irish short stories* (New York, 1964; repr. London, 1991) 32–6.

— (ed.), *Fingal Rónáin and other stories*, Medieval and Modern Irish Series 16 (DIAS, 1955).

— (ed.), *Esnada Tige Buchet*, in Greene (ed.), *Fingal Rónáin*, pp 27–44.

— (ed.), *Fingal Rónáin*, in Greene (ed.), *Fingal Rónáin*, pp 1–15.

— (ed.), *Orgain Denna Ríg*, in Greene (ed.), *Fingal Rónáin*, pp 16–26.

— (ed.), *Orgguin trí mac Diarmata mic Cerbaill la Maelodrán i Fothauch Muilinn mic Dímmae*, in Greene (ed.), *Fingal Rónáin*, pp 48–51.

— (ed.), *Aided Maelodráin*, in Greene (ed.), *Fingal Rónáin*, pp 51–4.

— 'Varia i. The three Tuesdays', *Ériu* 42 (1991), 139–40.

— and F. O'Connor (eds), *A golden treasury of Irish poetry*, AD 600 to 1200 (London, 1967).

— and F. Kelly (eds), *The Irish Adam and Eve Story from Saltair na Rann* (DIAS, 1976).

Gwynn, A., 'Some notes on the history of the Book of Leinster', *Celtica* 5 (1960), 8–13.

Gwynn, E.J. (ed.), 'The burning of Finn's house', *Ériu* 1 (1904), 13–37.

— 'An Old-Irish tract on the privileges and responsibilities of poets', *Ériu* 13 (1940), 1–60, 220–36.

— (ed.), *The Metrical Dindshenchas* i, Todd Lecture Series 8 (1903); ii Todd Lecture Series 9 (1906); iii Todd Lecture Series 10 (1913); iv Todd Lecture Series 11 (1924); v Todd Lecture Series 12 Todd Lecture Series (1935) (all repr. Dublin, 1991).

Gwynn, L. (ed.), '*De shíl Chonairi Móir*', *Ériu* 6 (1912), 130–53.

Gwynn, L. (ed.), 'Cináed uá hArtacáin's Poem on Brugh na Bóinne', *Ériu* 7 (1914), 210–38.

Hamilton, N., ' "Ancient" Irish music', in G. MacLennan (ed.), *Proceedings of the First North American Congress of Celtic Studies* (Ottawa, 1988), pp 283–91.

Harvey, A., 'Early literacy in Ireland: the evidence of Ogam', *Cambrian Medieval Celtic Studies* 14 (Winter 1987), 1–16.

Henderson, G. (ed.), *Fled Bricrenn*, Irish Texts Society 2 (London, 1899).

Hennessy, W.H. (ed.), 'Fotha Catha Cnucha', *Revue Celtique* 2 (1873–5), 86–93.

Henry, P.L., *Saoithiúlacht na Sean-Ghaeilge* (Dublin, 1976).

— (ed.), '*Verba Scáthaige*', *Celtica* 21 (1990), 101–2.

Herbert, M., 'Ár n-úrlaisí ceoil', *Léachtaí Cholm Cille* 7 (An Sagart, 1976), 21–30.

— 'Fled Dúin na nGéd: a reappraisal', *Cambridge Medieval Celtic Studies* 18 (1989), 75–87.

— 'Celtic heroine? The archaeology of the Deirdre story', in T. O'Brien Johnson and D. Cairns (eds), *Gender in Irish writing* (Milton Keynes, 1991), pp 13–22.

— 'Goddess and king: the sacred marriage in early Ireland', in L.O. Fradenburg (ed.), *Women and sovereignty* (Edinburgh, 1992), pp 264–75.

— 'Transmutations of an Irish goddess', in S. Billington and M. Green (eds), *The concept of the goddess* (London and New York, 1996), pp 141–51.

— '*Cathréim Cellaig*: some literary and historical considerations', *Zeitschrift für Celtische Philologie* 49/50 (1997), 320–32.

Herrity, M., and A. Breen, *The Cathach of Colm Cille, An introduction* (Dublin, Royal Irish Academy, 2002) This is accompanied by a DVD.

Hicks, R., 'Using archaeological reconnaissance date to identify *Oenach* sites' (paper from 39th International Congress of Medieval Studies, Kalamazoo, MI, May 2004). Received from the author.

Hillers, B., 'Heroes of the Ulster Cycle', in J.P. Mallory and G. Stockman (eds), *Ulidia*, pp 99–106.

— 'The abbot of Druimenaig: gender bending in Gaelic tradition', *Proceedings of the Harvard Celtic Colloquium* 15 (1995), 175–97.

Hogan, E. (ed.), *Cath Ruis na Ríg for Bóinn*, Todd Lecture Series 4 (1892), pp 1–107.

Hollo, K. (ed.), *Fled Bricrenn ocus loinges mac nDúil Dermait and its place in the Irish literary and oral narrative traditions: a critical edition with introduction, notes, translation, bibliography and vocabulary*, Maynooth Medieval Irish Texts 2 (Maynooth, 2005).

Hughes, K., 'On an Irish litany of pilgrim saints compiled *c*.800', *Analecta Bollandiana* 77 (1959), 305–31.

Hull, V. (ed.), 'The cause of the exile of Fergus mac Roig', *Zeitschrift für Celtische Philologie* 18 (1930), 293–98.

— (ed.), '*De Gabáil in tShída*', *Zeitschrift für Celtische Philologie* 19 (1931), 53–8.

— (ed.), *Compert Conchobair*, Irish Texts iv (London, 1934), 4–12.

— (ed.), 'The death of Fothath Cananne', *Zeitschrift für Celtische Philologie* 20 (1936), 400–4.

— (ed.), '*Aided Meidbe*: the violent death of Medb', *Speculum* 13 (1938), 42–61.

— 'The exile of Conall Corc', *Proceedings of the Modern Language Association* 56 (1941), 937–50.

— (ed.), 'Two tales about Find', *Speculum* 16 (1941), 322–33.

— (ed.), *Loinges mac nUislenn* (New York, 1946).

— (ed.), 'The text of *Baile Binnbérlach mac Buain* from MS 23.N.10 of the Royal Irish Academy', *Journal of Celtic Studies* 1 (1950), 94–7.

— (ed.), '*Geneamuin Chormaic ua Chuind ann-so*', *Ériu* 16 (1952), 79–85.

— (ed.), '*Noínden Ulad*: the debility of the Ulidians', *Celtica* 8 (1968), 1–42.

Jackson, K. (ed.), *Cath Maighe Léna* (Dublin, 1938, repr. with corrigenda as Medieval and Modern Irish Series 9, 1990).

— *The oldest Irish tradition: a window on the Iron Age* (Cambridge, 1964).

— 'The motive of the threefold death in the story of Suibne Geilt', in J. Ryan (ed.), *Féilsgríbhinn Eóin mhic Néill* (Dublin, 1940), pp 535–50.

— (ed.), 'The adventure of Laeghaire mac Crimhthainn', *Speculum* 17 (1942), 377–89.

— (ed.), *Aislinge meic Con Glinne* (Dublin, DIAS, 1990).

Jaski, B., *Early Irish kingship and succession* (Dublin, 2000).

Jeffares, A.N., *W.B. Yeats selected plays* (London, 1964).

Joynt, M. (ed.), '*Echtra mac Echdach Mugmedóin*', *Ériu* 4 (1908–10), 91–111.

— (ed.), *Feis Tighe Chonáin*. Medieval and Modern Irish Series 7 (Dublin, 1936).

— (ed.), *Tromdámh Guaire*, Medieval and Modern Irish Series 2 (Dublin, 1931, repr. 1941).

Kelleher, J., 'The *Táin* and the annals', *Ériu* 22 (1971), 107–27.

Kelly, F. (ed.), *Audacht Morainn* (Dublin, 1976).

— *A guide to early Irish law* (Dublin, DIAS, 1988).

— *Early Irish farming* (Dublin, DIAS, 2000).

— 'Text and transmissions: the law-texts', in P. Ní Chatháin and M. Richter (eds), *Ireland and Europe in the early Middle Ages: texts and transmission* (Dublin, 2002), pp 230–42.

Kelly, P., 'The *Táin* as literature', in J. Mallory (ed.), *Aspects of the Táin* (1992), pp 69–102.

Kenney, J.K., *The sources for the early history of Ireland: Ecclesiastical* (New York, 1929, repr. Dublin, 1993).

Keuls, E.C., *The reign of the phallus: sexual politics in ancient Athens* (California, 1985, repr. 1993).

Kimpton, B., *The death of Cú Chulainn: a critical edition of the earliest version of Brislech Mór Maige Muirthemni with introduction, translation, notes, bibliography and vocabulary* (Maynooth Medieval Irish Texts vi, Maynooth 2009).

Kinsella, T., *The Táin* (Oxford, 1969).

Kirk, G.S., *Myth: its meaning and functions in ancient and other cultures* (Cambridge/Berkeley, CA, 1970).

Knott, E., 'Why Mongán was deprived of noble issue', *Ériu* 8 (1916), 155–60.

— (ed.), *Togail Bruidne Da Derga*. Medieval and Modern Irish Series 8 (Dublin, 1963).

Koch, J., 'Windows on the Iron Age: 1964–1994', in Mallory and Stockman (eds), *Ulidia*, pp 229–38.

— *Celtic culture: a historical encyclopedia* (Santa Barbara, CA, 2005).

— and J. Carey, *The Celtic heroic age, third edition* (Andover, MA, 2000).

Kolbenschlag, M., *Goodbye Sleeping Beauty* (Dublin, 1983).

Lincoln, B., *Priests, warriors and cattle* (Berkeley, CA, 1981).

Littleton, C.S., *The new comparative mythology: an anthropological assessment of the theories of Georges Dumézil* (Berkeley, CA, 1966).

Lord, A.B., *The singer of tales* (New York, 1965).

Lowe, J., 'Kicking over the traces: the instability of Cú Chulainn', *Studia Celtica* 34 (2000), 119–29.

Macalister, R.A.S. (ed.), *Lebor Gabála Érenn* i, Irish Texts Society 34 (1932/38); ii, Irish Texts Society 34 (1939); iii, Irish Texts Society 39 (1940); iv, Irish Texts Society 41 (1941) and v, Irish Texts Society 44 (1956).

Mac Cana, P., 'Aspects of the theme of king and goddess in Irish literature', *Études Celtiques* 7 (1956), 77–114, 356–413 and *Études Celtiques* 8 (1957), 59–65.

— *Celtic mythology* (London, 1970).

— 'Mongán mac Fiachna and *Immram Brain*', *Ériu* 23 (1972), 102–42.

— 'On the "prehistory" of *Immram Brain*', *Ériu* 26 (1975), 33–52.

— 'The Sinless Otherworld of *Immram Brain*', *Ériu* 27 (1976), 95–115.

— *The learned tales of medieval Ireland* (Dublin, DIAS, 1980).

— 'Placenames and mythology in Irish tradition: places, pilgrimages, and things', in G. MacLennan (ed.), *Proceedings of the First North American Congress of Celtic Studies* (Ottawa, 1988), pp 319–41.

— 'Notes on the combination of prose and verse in early Irish narrative', in S.N. Tranter and H.L.C. Tristram (eds), *Early Irish literature – media and communication: mündlichkeit und Schriftlichkeit in der Frühen Irischen Literatur* (Tübingen, 1989), pp 125–47.

— 'Prosimetrum in Insular Celtic literature', in J. Harris and K. Reichl (eds), *Prosimetrum: crosscultural perspectives on narrative in prose and verse* (1997), pp 99–130.

— 'Praise poetry in Ireland before the Normans', *Ériu* 54 (2004), 11–40.

Mac Eoin, G., 'Gleann Bolcáin agus Gleann na nGealt', *Béaloideas* 30 (1962) [1964], 105–20.

— 'The life of Cuimine Fota', *Béaloideas* 39/40 (1971/3), 192–205.

— (ed.), 'Suithchern and Rónán Dícholla', *Zeitschrift für Celtische Philologie* 36 (1977), 63–82.

— 'The death of the boys in the mill', *Celtica* 15 (1983), 60–4.

— 'Orality and literacy in some Middle-Irish king-tales', in S.N. Tranter and H.L.C. Tristram (eds), *Early Irish literature – media and communication* (Tübingen, 1989), pp 149–83.

MacKillop, J., *Myths and legends of the Celts* (London, 2005).

MacKinnon, D. (ed.), '*Toraigecht Tána Bó Flidaise*', *Celtic Review* 4 (1907–8), 104–21, 202–19.

MacManus, D., *A guide to Ogam*, Maynooth Monographs 4 (An Sagart, 1991).

Mac Mathúna, L., 'On the expression and concept of blindness in Irish', *Studia Hibernica* 19 (1979), 26–62.

Mac Mathúna, S. (ed.), *Immram Brain: Bran's journey to the Land of Women* (Tübingen, 1985).

— 'The structure and transmission of early Irish voyage literature', in H.L.C. Tristram (ed.), *Text und Zeittiefe,* ScriptOralia 58 (Tübingen, 1994), 313–57.

Mac Néill, M., *The festival of Lughnasa* (Oxford, 1962).

MacWhite, E., 'Early Irish board games', *Éigse* 5 (1948), 25–35.

McCone, K., 'Aided Cheltchair Maic Uthechair: hounds, heroes and hospitallers in early Irish myth and story', *Ériu* 35 (1984), 1–30.

— 'Werewolves, cyclopes, *díberga* and *fíanna*: juvenile delinquency in Early Ireland', *Cambridge Medieval Celtic Studies* 12 (1986), 1–22.

— 'A tale of two ditties: poet and satirist in *Cath Maige Tuired*' in Ó Corráin et al. (eds), *Sages, saints and storytellers*, pp 122–43.

— 'The cyclops in Celtic, Germanic and Indo-European myth', *Studia Celtica* 30 (1996), 89–111.

— *Pagan past and Christian present* (Maynooth, 1990).

— (ed.), *Echtra Chonnlai and the beginnings of vernacular narrative writing in Ireland: a critical edition with introduction, notes, bibliography and vocabulary*, Maynooth Medieval Irish Texts v (Maynooth, 2000).

Mallory, J.P. (ed.), *Aspects of the Táin* (Belfast, 1992).

— and G. Stockman (eds), *Ulidia: Proceedings of the First International Conference on the Ulster Cycle of Tales* (Belfast, 1994).

— 'The world of Cú Chulainn: the archaeology of the *Táin Bó Cúailnge*', in Mallory and Stockman (eds), *Ulidia* (Belfast, 1994).

Marstrander, C. (ed.), 'The deaths of Lugaid and Derbforgaill', *Ériu* 5 (1911), 201–18.

— (ed.), 'A new version of the Battle of Mag Rath', *Ériu* 5 (1911), 226–47.

Martínez Hernández, M., *Canarias en la Mitología: Historia Mítica del Archipiélago* (Tenerife, 1992).

Meek, D., '*Táin Bó Fraích* and other "Fráech" texts: a study in thematic relationships', *Cambrian Medieval Celtic Studies* 7 (Summer, 1984), 1–37; 8 (Winter, 1984), 65–86.

Meid, W. (ed.), *Táin Bó Fraích*, Medieval and Modern Irish Series 22 (Dublin, DIAS, 1967); translation in J. Carney, *Studies in Irish literature and history* (Dublin, DIAS, 1955, repr. 1979), pp 1–14.

Melia, D., 'The parallel versions of the boyhood deeds of Cúchulainn', *Forum for Modern Language Studies* 10 (1974), 211–26.

— 'Remarks on the structure and composition of the Ulster death tales', *Studia Hibernica* 17/18 (1978), 36–57.

— 'Law and the shaman saint', in P. Ford (ed.), *Celtic folklore and christianity: studies in Memory of Willian W. Heist* (California, 1983), pp 113–28.

Mercier, V., *The Irish comic tradition* (Oxford, 1992).

Meyer, K., 'Mitteilungen aus Irischen Handschriften', *Zeitschrift für Celtische Philologie* 5 (1905) 500–4. (*Feis Tige Becfholtaig*).

— (ed.), '*Macgníomhartha Finn*', *Revue Celtique* 5 (1881–3), 195–204.

— (ed.), 'Anecdota from the Stowe MS. no. 992', *Revue Celtique* 6 (1883–5), 184–5. (*Aithed Emere la Tuir nGlesta mac ríg Lochlainn*).

— (ed.), *Aislinge meic Conglinne* (London, 1892; facs. repr. Somerset, 1999).

— (ed.), 'Two tales about Finn', *Revue Celtique* 14 (1893), 245–7. (*Tucait Fhághbhála in Fesa do Find inso ocus Marbad Cúil Duib*).

— (ed.), '*Scél Baili Binnbérlaig*', in *Hibernica Minora* (Oxford, 1894), p. 84.

— (ed.), *The voyage of Bran son of Febal to the Land of the Living*, 2 vols (London, 1895–97, repr. vol. i, Somerset, 1994).

— (ed.), '*Compert Mongáin*', in K. Meyer (ed.), *The voyage of Bran* i, pp 42–3, 44–5.

— (ed.), '*Tucaid Baile Mongáin inso*', in K. Meyer (ed.), *The voyage of Bran* i, pp 56–7 and 57–8.

— (ed.), '*Scél asa mberar co mbad hé Find mac Cumaill Mongán*', in K. Meyer (ed.), *The voyage of Bran* i, pp 45–8 and 49–52.

— (ed.), *Compert Mongáin ocus Serc Duibe Lacha do Mongán*, in K. Meyer (ed.), *The voyage of Bran* i, pp 58–70 and 70–84.

— (ed.), *Scél Mongáin inso*, in K. Meyer (ed.), *The voyage of Bran* i, pp 52–4 and 54–6.

— (ed.), '*Goire Conaill Chernaig i Crúachain ocus Aided Ailella ocus Conaill Chearnaig*', *Zeitschrift für Celtische Philologie* 1 (1897), 102–11.

— (ed.), 'The colloquy of Colum Cille and the youth at Carn Eolairg', *Zeitschrift für Celtische Philologie* 2 (1899), 313–20.

— (ed.), 'The death of Finn mac Cumaill', *Zeitschrift für Celtische Philologie* 1 (1897), 462–5.

— (ed.), 'Finn and Gráinne', *Zeitschrift für Celtische Philologie* 1 (1897), 458–61.

— (ed.), 'The vision of Laisrén', *Otia Merseiana* 1 (Liverpool, 1899), 113–19.

— (ed.), 'Stories and songs from Irish Manuscripts: III. Cormac and Ciarnat', *Otia Merseiana* 2 (Liverpool, 1900), 75–6.

— (ed.), 'The expulsion of the Déssi', *Y Cymmrodor* 14 (London, 1901), 101–35.

— (ed.), *Comrac Líadaine ocus Cuirithir: The meeting of Líadain and Cuirithir* (London, 1902).

— (ed.), 'Stories and songs from Irish manuscripts. VII. King Eochaid has horses's ears', *Otia Merseiana* 3 (Liverpool, 1903) 46–54.

— 'The boyish exploits of Finn', *Ériu* 1 (1904), 180–90.

— (ed.), 'Finn and the man in the tree', *Revue Celtique* 25 (1904), 344–6.

— (ed.), *Cáin Adamnáin: an Old-Irish treatise on the Law of Adamnan*, Anecdota Oxoniensia, Medieval and Modern Series 12 (Oxford, 1905).

— (ed.), *The triads of Ireland*, Todd Lecture Series 13 (Dublin, 1906).

— (ed.), '*Aided Cheltchair meic Uithechair*', in K. Meyer (ed.), *The Death Tales of the Ulster Heroes*, Todd Lecture Series 14 (Dublin, 1906, repr., Dublin, DIAS, 1993), pp 28–9.

— (ed.), '*Aided Chonchobuir*', in K. Meyer (ed.), *The Death Tales of the Ulster Heroes*, Todd Lecture Series 14 (Dublin, 1906, repr. Dublin, DIAS, 1993), pp 2–21.

— (ed.), '*Aided Fergusa maic Róich*', in K. Meyer (ed.), *The Death Tales of the Ulster Heroes*, Todd Lecture Series 14 (Dublin, 1906, repr. Dublin, DIAS, 1993), pp 32–5.

— (ed.), '*Aided Lóegairi Búadaig*', in K. Meyer (ed.), *The Death Tales of the Ulster Heroes*, Todd Lecture Series 14 (Dublin, 1906, repr. Dublin, DIAS, 1993), pp 22–3.

— (ed.), 'Story of the abbot of Druimenaig who was changed into a woman', in O.J. Bergin, R.I. Best, K. Meyer, and J.G. O'Keeffe (eds), *Anecdota from Irish manuscripts* 1 (Halle, 1907), pp 76–9.

— (ed.), *The instructions of King Cormac mac Airt*, Todd Lecture Series 15 (Dublin, 1909).

— (ed.), *Fianaigecht: being a collection of hitherto unedited Irish poems and tales relating to Finn and his Fiana with an English translation*, Todd Lecture Series 16 (Dublin, 1910, repr. Dublin, 1993).

— (ed.), 'The chase of Síd na mBan Finn and the death of Finn', in *Fianaigecht: being a collection of hitherto unedited Irish poems and tales relating to Finn and his Fiana with an English translation*, Todd Lecture Series 16 (Dublin, 1910, repr. Dublin 1993), pp 52–99.

— (ed.), 'The death of Fothath Cananne', in *Fianaigecht: being a collection of hitherto unedited Irish poems and tales relating to Finn and his Fiana with an English translation*, Todd Lecture Series 16 (Dublin, 1910, repr. Dublin, 1993), 400–4.

— (ed.), 'The Laud genealogies and tribal histories', *Zeitschrift für Celtische Philologie* 8 (1912), 291–338.

— (ed.), '*Sanas Cormaic*', in O.J. Bergin, R.I. Best, K. Meyer, and J.G. O'Keeffe (eds), *Anecdota from Irish Manuscripts* 5 (Halle and Dublin, 1913, repr. Somerset, 1994).

— (ed.), 'Immacallam in Druad Brain ocus inna Banfháitho Febuil', *Zeitschrift für Celtische Philologie* 9 (1913), 339–40.

— (ed.), '*Ferchuitred Medba*', in O.J. Bergin, R.I. Best, K. Meyer, and J.G. O'Keeffe (eds), *Anecdota from Irish Manuscripts* 5 (Dublin 1913, repr. Somerset, 1994), 17–22.

— (ed.), 'Baile Bricín', *Zeitschrift für Celtische Philologie* 9 (1913), 449–57.

— (ed.), *Selections from ancient Irish poetry* (London, 1913).

— 'Mittelungen aus Irischen Handshriften', *Zeitschrift für Celtische Philologie* 8 (1912), 109–10.

Montague, J., *Mounts of Venus: the Picador book of erotic prose* (London, 1980), 57–8. (Story of the abbot changed into a woman).

Mulchrone, K. (ed.), *Bethu Phátraic: the tripartite life of Patrick* 1 (Dublin, 1939).

— (ed.), *Cathréim Cellaig*, Medieval and Modern Irish Series 24 (Dublin, 1933).

Murphy, G. (ed.), *Early Irish lyrics* (London, 1956, 1962, repr. Dublin, 1998).

— *Saga and myth in ancient Ireland* (Dublin, 1961).

Murray, K. 'The finding of the *Táin*', *Cambrian Medieval Celtic Studies* 41 (2001), 17–23.

— (ed.), *Baile in Scáil*, Irish Texts Society 58 (Dublin, 2004).

Nagy, J.F., 'Shamanic aspects of the "Bruidhean" tale', *History of Religions* (1981), 3–22.

— 'Demne Mael', *Celtica* 14 (1981), 8–14.

— 'Liminality and knowledge in Irish tradition', *Studia Celtica* 16/17 (1981–2), 135–43.

— 'The wisdom of the Geilt', *Éigse* 19 (1982), 44–60.

— 'Close encounters of the traditional kind in medieval Irish literature', in P.K. Ford (ed.), *Celtic folklore and Christianity: studies in memory of Willian W. Heist* (California, 1983), pp 129–49.

— 'Heroic destinies in the Macgnímrada of Finn and Cú Chulainn', *Zeitschrift für Celtische Philologie* 40 (1984), 23–39.

— *The wisdom of the outlaw: the boyhood deeds of Finn in Gaelic narrative tradition* (California, 1985).

— 'Otters, salmon and eel in traditional Gaelic narrative', *Studia Celtica* 20–1 (1985–6), 123–44.

— 'The boyhood deeds of Finn', *The wisdom of the outlaw: the boyhood deeds of Finn in Gaelic narrative tradition* (California, 1985), pp 209–21.

— 'Fenian heroes and their rites of passage', in B. Almqvist, S. Ó Catháin and P. Ó hÉalaí (eds), *The heroic process: form, function and fantasy in folk epic*. The Proceedings of the International Folk Epic Conference, University College Dublin, 2–6 September 1985 (Dublin 1987), pp 161–82.

— 'Compositional concerns in the *Acallam na Senórach*', in D. Ó Corráin, L. Breatnach and K. McCone (eds), *Sages, saints and storytellers, Celtic studies in honour of Professor James Carney* (Maynooth, 1989), pp 149–58.

— 'The herons of Druim Cet, revisiting, and revisited', *Celtica* 21 (1990), 368–76.

— *Conversing with angels and ancients: literary myths of medieval Ireland* (Dublin, 1997).

— 'How the *Táin* was lost', *Zeitschrift für Celtische Philologie* 49–50 (1997), 603–9.

Newman, C., 'Procession and symbolism at Tara; analysis of Tech Midchúarta (the 'Banqueting Hall') in the context of the sacral campus', *Oxford Journal of Archaeology* 26:4 (2007), 415–38.

Ní Bhrolcháin, M., '*Re thóin mná*: in pursuit of troublesome women', in Mallory and Stockman (eds), *Ulidia*, pp 115–22.

— 'The TaraSkryne or the Gabhra Valley in early Irish literature', *Ríocht na Midhe, the Journal of the Meath Archaeologial and Historical Society* 17 (2006), 1–15.

— '*Serglige Con Culainn*: a possible re-interpretation', in Ó hUiginn and Ó Catháin (eds), *Ulidia* 2, pp 288–99.

Ní Chatháin, P., 'Swineherds, seers, and druids', *Studia Celtica* 14/15 (1979/80), 200–11.

Ní Dhonnchadha, M., 'Reading the so-called *Cailech Bérri* poem', *School of Celtic Studies Newsletter* 6 (1993), 15 (from Tionól Lecture 1992).

— 'from Vita Prima Sanctae Brigitae', in A. Bourke et al. (eds), *Field Day anthology of Irish writing; iv, Irish women's writing and traditions*, pp 63–9.

— 'Digde', *Field Day anthology; iv, Irish women's writing*, pp 111–15.

— 'Comrac Líadaine ocus Cuirithir', *Field Day anthology; iv, Irish women's writing*, pp 115–18.

— 'The conception of Saint Bóethíne', *Field Day anthology; iv, Irish women's writing*, p. 127.

— 'The abbot of Drimnagh who was changed into a woman', *Field Day anthology; iv, Irish women's writing*, pp 131–2.

— 'The birth of Aed Sláine', *Field Day anthology; iv, Irish women's writing*, pp 182–4.

— 'The deaths of Lugaid and Derbforgaill', *Field Day anthology; iv, Irish women's writing*, pp 204–6.

— 'from Tochmarc Ailbe', *Field Day anthology; iv, Irish women's writing*, pp 206–10.

— 'from: Aided Muirchertaich meic Erca', *Field Day anthology; iv, Irish women's writing*, pp 213–18.

— 'Baile the sweet-spoken son of Búan', *Field Day anthology; iv, Irish women's writing*, pp 218–19.

— 'Níall Frassach's act of truth', *Field Day anthology; iv, Irish women's writing*, p 220.

— 'Ferchuitred Medba', *Field Day anthology; iv, Irish women's writing*, pp 259–60.

— 'from Baile in Scáil', *Field Day anthology; iv, Irish women's writing*, p 260.

— 'from Aided Echach maic Maireda', *Field Day anthology; iv, Irish women's writing*, pp 271–2.

— 'Apair damsa re Der Fáil', *Field Day anthology; iv, Irish women's writing*, pp 305–7.

— 'Teastá eochair ghlais ghaoidheal', *Field Day anthology; iv, Irish women's writing*, pp 271–2.

Ní Shéaghdha, N. (ed.), *Acallam na Senórach*, 3 vols (Dublin, 1942) Modern Irish version.

— (ed.), *Tóruigheacht Dhiarmada agus Ghráinne*, Irish Texts Society 48 (Dublin, 1967).

— 'Collectors of Irish manuscripts: motives and methods', *Celtica* 17 (1985), 1–28.

Nic Dhonnchadha, L. (ed.), *Aided Muirchertaig meic Erca*. Medieval and Modern Irish Series 19 (Dublin, 1964).

Nic Eoin, M., *B'ait leo Bean: gnéithe den ide-éolaíocht inscne i dtraidisiún liteartha na Gaeilge* (Leabhar Taighde 83, An Clóchomhar Tta, Baile Átha Cliath, 1998).

Ó hAodha, D. (ed.), 'The lament of the Old Woman of Beare', in D. Ó Corráin et al. (eds), *Sages, saints and storytellers*, pp 308–22.

O'Beirne Crowe, J. (ed.), 'Siabur-charpat Con Culaind', *Journal of the Royal Historical and Archaeological Association of Ireland*, 4:1 (1870), 371–401.

Ó Briain, M., 'Some material on Oisín in the Land of Youth', in D. Ó Corráin et al. (eds), *Sages, saints and storytellers*, pp 181–99.

— 'The horse-eared kings of Irish tradition and St Brigit', in B.T. Hudson and V. Ziegler (eds), *Crossed paths: methodological approaches to the Celtic aspect of the European Middle Ages* (London and New York, 1991), pp 83–114.

— 'Oisín's biography: conception and birth', in H.L.C. Tristram (ed.), *Text und Zeittiefe*, ScriptOralia 58 (Tübingen, 1994), pp 455–86.

O'Brien, M.A. (ed.), 'A Middle-Irish poem on the Christian kings of Leinster', *Ériu* 17 (1955), 35–51.

— (ed.), *Corpus Genealogiarum Hiberniae* (Dublin, DIAS, 1966).

O'Broin, T., 'What is the debility of the Ulstermen?', *Éigse* 10 (1963), 386–99.

— 'The word cess', *Éigse* 12 (1967–8), 109–14.

— 'The word noínden', *Éigse* 13 (1970), 165–76.

Ó Catháin, S., *The festival of Brigit: Celtic goddess and holy woman* (Dublin, 1995).

Ó Cathasaigh, T., *The heroic biography of Cormac mac Airt* (Dublin, 1977).

— 'The semantics of *síd*', *Éigse* 17 (1977/8), 137–55.

— 'The theme of *lommrad* in *Cath Maige Muccrama*', *Éigse* 18 (1981), 211–24.

— 'The theme of *ainmne* in *Scéla Cano meic Gartnáin*', *Celtica* 15 (1983), 78–87.

— '*Cath Maige Tuired* as exemplary myth', in P. de Brún, S. Ó Coileáin and P. Ó Riain (eds), *Folia Gadelica: essays presented to R.A. Breathnach* (Cork, 1983), pp 1–19.

— 'Pagan survivals; the evidence of early Irish narrative', in P. Ní Chatháin and M. Richter (eds), *Ireland and Europe: the early Church* (Stuttgart, 1984), pp 291–307.

— 'The concept of the hero in Irish mythology', in R. Kearney (ed.), *The Irish mind* (Dublin, 1985), pp 79–90.

— 'The Trial of Mael Fothartaig', *Ériu* 36 (1985), 177–80.

— 'The rhetoric of *Fingal Rónáin*' *Celtica* 17 (1985), 123–44.

— 'The rhetoric of *Scéla Cano meic Gartnáin*', in D. Ó Corráin et al. (eds), *Sages, saints and storytellers*, pp 233–50.

— 'The eponym of Cnogba', *Éigse* 23 (1989), 27–38.

— 'Mythology in *Táin Bó Cúailnge*', in H.L.C. Tristram (ed.), *Studien zur Táin Bó Cuailnge* (Tübingen, 1993), pp 114–32.

— 'Reflections on *Compert Chonchobuir* and *Serglige Con Culainn*', in Mallory and Stockman (eds), *Ulidia*, pp 85–90.

— 'The threefold death in early Irish sources', *Studia Celtica Japonica* 6 (1994), 53–76.

— '*Gat* and *díberg* in *Togail Bruidne Da Derga*', in A. Alqvist, G.W. Banks, R. Latvio, H. Nyberg and T. Sjoblom (eds), *Celtica Helsingiensia: Proceedings from a Symposium on Celtic Studies* (Commentationes Humanarum Litterarum 107) (Helsinki, 1996), pp 203–13.

— 'Knowledge and power in *Aislinge Óenguso*', in A. Ahlqvist and V. Čapková (eds), *Dán don Oide, essays in Memory of Conn R. Ó Cléirigh* (Institiúid Teangeolaíochta Éireann, 1997), pp 431–38.

— 'The oldest story of the Laigin: observations on *Orgain Denna Ríg*', *Éigse* 33 (2002), 1–18.

— 'Sound and sense in *Cath Almhaine*', *Ériu* 54 (2004), 41–7.

Ó Coileáin, S., 'The structure of a literary cycle', *Ériu* 25 (1974), 88–125.

— 'Oral or literary? Some strands of the argument', *Studia Hibernica* 17–18 (1978), 7–35.

Ó Concheanainn, T., 'The Death of Muirchertach mac Erca', *Éigse* 15, ii (1973), 141–4.

O'Connor, F., *The backward look* (London, 1967).

Ó Corráin, D., L. Breatnach and K. McCone (eds), *Sages, saints and storytellers: Celtic studies in honour of Professor James Carney* (Maynooth, 1989).

Ó Corráin, D., 'Early Irish hermit poetry?', in Ó Corráin et al. (eds), *Sages, saints and storytellers*, pp 251–69.

— 'The separation of Finn and Gráinne', in A. Bourke et al. (eds), *Field Day anthology of Irish writing; iv, Irish women's writing*, pp 36–7.

— 'Prehistoric and early Christian Ireland', in R.F. Foster (ed.), *Oxford illustrated history of Ireland* (Oxford, 1989).

Ó Cróinín, D. (ed.), *A new history of Ireland; i, Prehistoric and early Ireland* (Oxford, 2005).

Ó Cuív, B., 'The changing face of the Irish language', in B. Ó Cuív (ed.), *A view of the Irish language* (Dublin, 1969), pp 22–34.

— (ed.), 'Mis and Dub Rois', *Celtica* 2, ii (1954), 325–33.

— 'The motif of the threefold death', *Éigse* 15, ii (1973), 145–50.

— (ed.), '*Comrac na Cloenfherta*', *Celtica* 11 (1976), 168–79.

— 'Miscellanea, 2. Agallamh Fhinn agus Ailbhe', *Celtica* 18 (1986), 111–15.

O'Curry, E. (ed.), *Oidhe Chloinne Lir*, *The Atlantis* 4 (1863), 113–55.

O'Daly, M., 'The Metrical *Dindshenchas*', in J. Carney (ed.), *Early Irish poetry* (Cork, 1965), pp 59–72.

— (ed.), *Cath Maige Muccrama*, Irish Texts Society 50 (Dublin, 1975).

— *Cath Maige Muccrama*, in M. O'Daly (ed.), *Cath Maige Muccrama*, pp 38–63.

— (ed.), *Scéla Éogain 7 Cormaic*, in M. O'Daly (ed.), *Cath Maige Muccrama*, pp 64–73.

— (ed.), *Scéla Moshauluim*, in M. O'Daly (ed.), *Cath Maige Muccrama*, pp 76–87.

O'Donoghue, D., *Lives and legends of Saint Brendan the voyager* (Dublin, 1893, repr. Felinfach, Llanerch, 1994).

Ó Dónaill, C. (ed.), *Talland Étair, a critical edition with introduction, translation, textual notes, bibliography and vocabulary*, Maynooth Medieval Irish Texts iv (Maynooth, 2005).

O'Donovan, J. (ed.), *The banquet of Dun na n-Gedh and the battle of Magh Rath* (Dublin, Irish Archaeological Society, 1842, repr. 1995).

Ó Floinn, T. and P. Mac Cana, *Scéalaíocht na Ríthe* (Baile Átha Cliath, 1956).

Ó Flaithearta, 'The etymologies of (Fer) Diad', in Ó hUiginn and Ó Catháin (eds), *Ulidia* 2, pp 218–25.

O'Grady, S.H. (ed.), *Silva Gadelica. A collection of tales in Irish with extracts illustrating persons and places*. 2 vols (London, 1892).

— (ed.), *Acallamh na Senórach*, in *Silva Gadelica*, i, 94–233; ii, 101–265.

— (ed.), *Aided Crimthainn meic Fidaig*, in *Silva Gadelica* i, 330–6; ii, 373–8.

— (ed.), *Aided Diarmada meic Cherbaill*, in *Silva Gadelica* i, 72–82; ii, 76–88.

— (ed.), *Aided Echach maic Maireda*, in *Silva Gadelica* i, 233–7; ii, 265–9.

— (ed.), *Aided Fergus meic Léide*, in *Silva Gadelica* i, 238–52; ii, 269–85.

— (ed.), *Áirem muintire Finn*, in *Silva Gadelica* i, 92–3; ii, 99–100.

— (ed.), *Betha Chellaig*, in *Silva Gadelica* i, 49–65; ii, 50–69.

— (ed.), *Boramha*, in *Silva Gadelica* i, 359–90; ii, 401–24.

— (ed.), *Cath Crinna*, in *Silva Gadelica* i, 319–26; ii, 359–68.

— (ed.), *Echtra mac nEchach*, in *Silva Gadelica* i, 326–30; ii, 368–73.

— (ed.), *Coimpert Cormaic meic Airt*, in *Silva Gadelica* i, 253–6; ii, 286–9.

— (ed.), *Echtra Thaidg mheic Chéin* i, 342–59; ii, 385–401.

— (ed.), *Geinemain Cormaic ua Chuinn*, in *Silva Gadelica* i, 253–6; ii 286–9.

— (ed.), *Sidh Fiachna*, in *Silva Gadelica* i, 256–7; ii 290–1.

— (ed.), *Geinemain Aeda Shláine*, in *Silva Gadelica* i, 82–4; ii, 88–91.

— (ed.), *Tesmolad Corbmaic uí Chuinn ocus Aided Finn meic Cumhaill sunn*, in *Silva Gadelica* i, 89–92; ii, 96–9.

— (ed.), *Tochmarc Becfhola*, in *Silva Gadelica* i, 85–7; ii, 91–93.

O Hehir, B., 'The Christian revision of *Eachtra Airt meic Cuind ocus Tochmarc Delbchaime ingine Morgain*', in P.K. Ford (ed.), *Celtic folklore and Christianity: studies in memory of William W. Heist* (Santa Barbara, CA, 1983), pp 159–79.

O'Kearney, N. (ed.), *The Battle of Gabhra: Garristown in the County of Dublin Fought A.D. 283*, Transaction of the Ossianic Society 1 (Dublin, 1853).

— (ed.), *Feis Tige Chonain Chinn-Shleibhe: or the Festivities at the House of Conan of Ceann-Sleibhe, in the County of Clare*, Transactions of Ossianic Society 2 (Dublin, 1855).

O'Keeffe, J.G. (ed.), 'Mac Dá Cherda and Cummaine Foda', *Ériu* 5 (1911), 18–44.

— (ed.), *Buile Suibhne*, Irish Texts Society 12 (London, 1913).

O'Kelleher, A. and G. Schoepperle (eds), *Betha Colaim Cille: Life of Columcille compiled by Manus O'Donnell in 1532* (Urbana, IL, 1918).

O'Leary, P., 'Contention at feasts in early Irish literature', *Éigse* 20 (1984), 115–27.

— 'Verbal Deceit in the Ulster Cycle', *Éigse* 21 (1986) 16–26.

— 'Honour-bound: the social context of early Irish heroic *geis*', *Celtica* 20 (1988), 85–107.

— 'Jeers and judgments: laughter in early Irish literature', *Cambridge Medieval Celtic Studies* 22 (Winter, 1991), 15–30.

Ó Máille, T., 'Medb Chruachna', *Zeitschrift für Celtische Philologie* 17 (1927), 129–46.

O'Meara, J.J. (ed.), *The history and topography of Ireland*, Dolmen Texts, 4 (Portlaoise, 1982).

— (ed.), *The voyage of St Brendan: journey to the Promised Land* (Dublin, 1976; repr. Dublin, 1994 special edition).

O'Neill, J. (ed.), '*Cath Boinde*', *Ériu* 2 (1911), 173–85.

O'Neill, T., *The Irish hand* (Dublin, 1984).

O'Nolan, T.P. (ed.), 'Mór of Munster and the tragic fate of Cuanu son of Cailchin', *Proceedings of the Royal Irish Academy* 30 C (1912–13), 261–82.

Ó hÓgáin, D., *Fionn mac Cumhaill: images of the Gaelic hero* (Dublin, 1988).

Ó Raithbheartaigh, T. (ed.), *Genealogical tracts 1*, Irish Manuscripts Commission (Dublin, 1932).

O'Rahilly, C. (ed.), *The Stowe version of Táin Bó Cúailnge* (Dublin, 1960).

— (ed.), *Táin Bó Cúalnge from the Book of Leinster* (Dublin, 1970).

— (ed.), *Táin Bó Cuailnge: recension 1* (Dublin, 1976).

O'Rahilly, T.F., *Early Irish history and mythology* (Dublin, 1946, repr. Dublin 1976).

— 'On the origin of the names Érainn and Ériu', *Ériu* 14 (1946), 7–28.

Ó Riain, P., 'A study of the Irish legend of the wild man', *Éigse* 14 (1971–2), 179–206.

— 'Boundary association in early Irish society', *Studia Celtica* 7 (1972), 12–29.

— (ed.), *Cath Almaine*, Medieval and Modern Irish Series 25 (Dublin, 1978).

— 'The Táin: a clue to its origins', in Mallory and Stockman (eds), *Ulidia*, pp 31–7.

Ó Ríordáin, S.P., *Antiquities of the Irish countryside* (Cork, 1942, repr. London, 1991).

Ó Tuama, S. (ed.), *Caoineadh Airt Uí Laoghaire* (Baile Átha Cliath, 1961).

Ó hUiginn, R., 'The background and development of *Táin Bó Cúailnge*', in J.P. Mallory (ed.), *Aspects of the Táin* (Belfast, 1992), pp 29–67.

— 'Fergus, Russ and Rudraige, a brief biography of Fergus mac Róich', *Emania* 11 (1993), 31–40.

— and B. Ó Catháin (eds), *Ulidia 2: Proceedings of the second international conference on the Ulster Cycle of tales* (An sagart, 2009)

Okpewho, I., *The epic in Africa* (New York, 1979).

Olmsted, G., 'Luccreth's poem *Conailla Medb Míchuru* and the origins of the *Táin*', *Mankind Quarterly* 29 (1988), 3–72.

— (ed.), '*Conailla Medb míchuru* and the origins of the *Táin*', *Études Celtiques* 29 (1992), 333–42.

— 'The earliest narrative version of the *Táin*: seventh-century poetic references to *Táin Bó Cúailnge*', *Emania* 10 (1992) 5–17.

Oskamp, H.P.A. (ed.), *The Voyage of Máel Dúin. A study in early Irish voyage literature* (Groningen, 1970).

— (ed.), '*Echtra Condla*', *Études Celtiques* 14 (1974/5), 207–28.

— 'Mael Muire: compiler or revisor?' *Éigse* 16, iii (1976), 177–82.

Partridge, A., 'Wild men and wailing women', *Éigse* 19, i (1980), 25–37.

Picard, J-M. and Y. de Pontfarcy, *The vision of Tnugdal* (Dublin, 1989).

— *Saint Patrick's Purgatory: a twelfth century tale of a journey to the other world* (Dublin, 1985).

Piggott, S., *The druids* (London, 1968).

Poppe, E., 'Deception and self-deception in *Fingal Rónáin*', *Ériu* 47 (1996), 137–51.

Power, M. (ed.), '*Cnucha cnoc os cionn Life*', *Zeitschrift für Celtische Philologie* 11 (1917), 39–55.

Radner, J., *Fragmentary Annals of Ireland* (Dublin, 1978).

— 'The significance of the threefold death in Celtic tradition', in P.K. Ford (ed.), *Celtic folklore and Christianity. Studies in Memory William W. Heist* (Berkeley, CA, 1983), pp 180–99.

— ' "Men will die": poets, harpers and women in early Irish literature', in A.T.E. Matonis and D.F. Melia (eds), *Celtic language, Celtic culture: a festschrift for Eric P. Hamp* (Van Nuys, CA, 1990), pp 172–86.

Raftery, B., *Pagan Celtic Ireland: the enigma of the Irish Iron Age* (London, 1994).

Rees, A., and B. Rees, *Celtic heritage* (London, 1961, revised, 1989).

Reynolds, R.E., ' "At sixes and sevens" – and eights and nines: the sacred mathematics of sacred Orders in the early Middle Ages', *Speculum* 54 (1979), 669–84.

Richter, M., *The formation of the medieval West: studies in the oral culture of the barbarians* (Dublin, 1994).

Ross, A., *Pagan Celtic Britain* (London, 1967).

Sayers, W., 'Fergus and the cosmogonic sword', *History of Religions* 25 (1985), 30–56.

— 'Early Irish attitudes toward hair and beards, baldness and tonsure', *Zeitschrift für Celtische Philologie* 44 (1991), 154–89.

Schoepperle, G., *Tristan and Isolt: a study in the sources of romance* (London, 1913).

Scholes, R. and R. Kellogg, *The nature of narrative* (London, 1966).

Schrijver, P, 'On henbane and early European narcotics', *Zeitschrift für celtische Philologie* 51 (1999), 17–45.

Scowcroft, R.M., Review of *The wisdom of the outlaw*, *Cambridge Medieval Celtic Studies* 13 (Summer, 1987), 97–100.

—, 'Abstract narrative in Ireland', *Ériu* 46 (1995), 121–58.

Sellner, E.C., *Wisdom of the Celtic saints, revised and expanded edition* (Saint Paul, MN, 2006).

Senger, P., 'Literacy, Western European', in J.L. Strayer (ed.), *Dictionary of the Middle Ages*, vol. 7 (1986), 597–602.

Sessle, E., 'Misogny and Medb: approaching Medb with feminist criticism', in Mallory and Stockman (eds), *Ulidia*, pp 135–8.

Sharpe, R., 'Hiberno-Latin Laicus, Irish láech, and the devil's men', *Ériu* 30 (1979), 75–92.

Shaw, F. (ed.), *The dream of Óengus, Aislinge Óenguso* (Dublin, 1934, repr. Galway, 1976).

Sims-Williams, P., Review of *Pagan past and Christian present*, *Éigse* 19 (1996), 179–96.

Sjoestedt, M.L., *Gods and heroes of the Celts* (trans. M. Dillon 1949 from the original French *Dieux et héros des Celtes*, London, repr. Dublin, 1995).

Sjöblom, T., 'Advice from a birdman: ritual injunctions and royal instructions in TBDD', in A. Alqvist, G.W. Banks, R. Latvio, H. Nyberg and T. Sjoblom (eds), *Celtica Helsingiensia: Proceedings from a Symposium on Celtic Studies* (Helsinki, 1996), pp 233–51.

—, 'Before *geis* became magical – a study of the evolution of the early Irish religious concept', *Studia Celtica* 32 (1998), 85–94.

Smyth, A.P., 'Kings, saints and sagas', in K. Hannigan and W. Nolan (eds), *Wicklow – history and society* (Dublin, 1994), pp 41–111.

Stafford, P., 'Family politics in the early Middle Ages', in D. Baker (ed.), *Medieval women: essays dedicated and presented to Professor Rosalind M.T. Hill* (Oxford, 1978), pp 79–100.

Stokes, W. (ed.), 'Mythological notes', *Revue Celtique* 2 (1873–5), 197–203. (The Story of Labraid's Ears 197–9; Conception of Boethine on Créd 199–200).

— (ed.), 'Find and the phantoms', *Revue Celtique* 7 (1886), 289–307.

— (ed.), 'The voyage of Mael Duin', *Revue Celtique* 9 (1888), 447–95, *Revue Celtique* 10 (1889), 50–95.

— (ed.), 'The voyage of Snédgus and Mac Riagla', *Revue Celtique* 9 (1888), 14–25.

— *Lives of the saints from the Book of Lismore* (Oxford, 1890).

— (ed.), 'The voyage of the Húi Corra', *Revue Celtique* 14 (1893), 22–69.

— (ed.), '*Echtra Chormaic*: the Irish Ordeals, Cormac's Adventure in the Land of Promise, and the Decision as to Cormac's Sword', *Irische Texte* 3, i (Leipzig, 1891) 183–229.

— (ed.), 'The Bodleian Dinnshenchas', *Folklore* 3 (1892), 467–516.

— (ed.), 'The Edinburgh Dinnshenchas', *Folklore* 4 (1893), 471–97.

— (ed.), 'The prose tales in the Rennes Dinnshenchus', *Revue Celtique* 15 (1894), 272–336, 418–84; *Revue Celtique* 16 (1895), 31–83, 135–67, 269–312.

— (ed.), 'Annals of Tigernach', *Revue Celtique* 16 (1895), 374–419; *Revue Celtique* 17 (1896), 6–33, 119–263, 337–420; *Revue Celtique* 18 (1897), 9–59, 150–97, 267–303.

(repr. in 2 vols Somerset, 1993) page numbers refer to the reprint.

— (ed.), '*Cóir Anmann*', *Irische Texte* 3, 2 (1897), 285–444.

— (ed.), 'Tidings of Conchobar mac Nessa', *Ériu* 4 (1906–10), 18–38 (called *Scéla Conchobair maic Nessa*).

— (ed.), *Acallamh na Senórach*, *Irische Texte* 4, i (Leipzig 1900), 1–226.

— (ed.), '*Bruiden Da Choca*', *Revue Celtique* 21 (1900), 149–65, 312–27, 388–402.

— (ed.), 'The destruction of Dind Ríg', *Zeitschrift für celtische Philologie* 3 (1901), 1–14, 225.

— (ed.), 'On the deaths of some Irish heroes', *Revue Celtique* 23 (1902), 303–48.

— (ed.), 'The adventure of St Columba's Clerics', *Revue Celtique* 26 (1905), 130–70.

— (ed.), *Félire Óengusso Céli Dé: the Martryology of Oengus the Culdee* (London, 1905, repr. Dublin, 1984).

— (ed.), *The Birth and life of St Moling, edited from a manuscript in the Royal Library, Brussels with a translation and glossary, specimens of middle-Irish literature No. 1* (London, 1907).

Taylor, A., 'The biographical pattern in traditional narrative', *Journal of the Folklore Institute* 1 (1964), 114–29.

Thurneysen, R., *Die Irische Helden-und Königsage bis zum Siebzehnten Jahrhundert* (Halle, 1921).

— (ed.), 'Das Werben um Ailbe', *Zeitschrift für Celtische Philologie* 13 (1921), 251–82.

— 'Colmán mac Lénéni und Senchán Torpéist', *Zeitschrift für Celtische Philologie* 19 (1933), 193–209.

Tierney, J.J., 'The Celtic ethnography of Posidonius', *Proceedings of the Royal Irish Academy* 60 C, 5 (1960), 189–275.

Toner, G., *Bruiden Da Choca*, Irish Texts Society 61 (London, 2007).

— 'Reconstructing the earliest Irish tale lists', *Éigse* 32 (2000), 88–120.

Trindade, A., 'Irish Gormlaith as a sovereignty figure', *Études Celtiques* 23 (1986), 143–56.

Tristram, H.L.C., 'What is the purpose of *Táin Bó Cúailnge?*', in Mallory and Stockman (eds), *Ulidia*, pp 11–22.

— 'The Cattle–Raid of Cuailnge in tension and transition: between the oral and the written, classical subtexts and narrative heritage', in D. Edel (ed.), *Cultural identity and cultural intergration: Ireland and Europe in the early Middle Ages* (Dublin, 1995), pp 61–81.

Turner, V.W., 'Betwixt and between: the liminal period in *rites of passage*' in V.W. Turner, *The forest of symbols* (Ithaca, NY, 1967), pp 93–111.

Tymoczko, M., *Two death tales from the Ulster Cycle: the death of Cú Roi and the death of Cú Chulainn* (Dublin, 1981)

— 'Animal imagery in *Loinges Mac nUislenn*', *Studia Celtica* 20/1 (1985/6), 145–66.

— 'A poetry of masks: the poet's persona in early Celtic poetry', in P.K. Ford (ed.), *A Celtic florilegium: studies in memory of Brendan O Hehir* (Lawrence, MA, 1996), pp 187–209.

Van Gennep, A., *Les rites de passage* (Paris, 1909, trans. by M.B. Vizedom and G.L. Caffee, 1960).

Van Hamel, A.G. (ed.), *Aided Oenfhir Aífe*, pp 9–15; *Compert Con Culainn*, pp 1–10; *Tochmarc Emere*, pp 20–68; *Aided Con Culainn* pp 72–133 all in A.G. van Hamel (ed.), *Compert Con Culainn and other stories*, Medieval and Modern Irish Series 3 (Dublin, 1933).

— (ed.), *Immrama*, Medieval and Modern Irish Series 10 (Dublin, 1941).

Vielle, C., 'The oldest narrative attestations of a Celtic mythical and traditional heroic cycle', in Mallory and Stockman (eds), *Ulidia*, pp 217–27.

Watson, A., 'A structural analysis of *Echtra Nerai*', *Études Celtiques* 23 (1986), 129–42.

Watson, J. (ed.), *Mesca Ulad*, Medieval and Modern Irish Series 13 (Dublin, 1941).

Watt, I., *The rise of the novel: studies in Defoe, Richardson and Fielding* (London, 1967).

Westropp, T.J., 'Brazil and the legendary islands of the North Atlantic', *Proceedings of the Royal Irish Academy* 30 (1912), 223–60.

White, N. (ed.), *Compert Mongáin and three other early Mongán tales: a critical edition with introduction, translation, textual notes, bibliography and vocabulary*, Maynooth Medieval Irish Texts v (Maynooth, 2006).

Wiley, D., 'Stories about Díarmait mac Cerbaill from the Book of Lismore', *Emania* 19 (2002), 53–59.

— 'Niall Frossach's true judgement', *Ériu* 55 (2005), 19–36.

— (ed.), *Essays on the early Irish king tales* (Dublin, 2008)

Windisch, E. (ed.), 'Die Vision des Adamnán', *Irische Texte* 1 (Leipzig, 1880), 165–96.

— (ed.), '*Táin Bó Flidais*', *Irische Texte* 2, 2 (Leipzig, 1887), 206–23.

— (ed.), '*Táin Bó Regamna*', *Irische Texte* 2, 2 (Leipzig, 1887), 239–54.

— (ed.), '*Táin Bó Regamain*', *Irische Texte* 2, 2 (Leipzig, 1887), 224–38.

— (ed.), '*Tochmarc Ferbe*', *Irische Texte* 3, 2 (Leipzig, 1897), 445–556.

Wong, D., 'Water-births, murder, mystery and Medb Lethderg', *Études Celtiques* 32 (1996), 233–41.

Wooding, J.M., *The Otherworld voyage in early Irish literature: an anthology of criticism* (Dublin, 2000).

Yalman, N., 'The raw: the cooked: nature: culture – observations on *Le cru et le Cuit*', in E. Leach (ed.), *The structural story of myth and totemism* (London, 1967), pp 71–89.

Zaleski, C., *Otherworld journeys: accounts of near-death experience in medieval and modern times* (Oxford, 1987).

Useful bibliographical sites online

www.ucc.ie/celt/MS-OMIT/index.htm
www.hastings.edu/academic/english/Kings/Home.html
www.ucc.ie/academic/smg/CDI/textarchive.html
www.ucd.ie/tlh/published.html
www.hell-on-line.org/BibJC2.html
www.isos.dias.ie
www.ucc.ie/celt.
www.dil.ie/

Index